THE BEST THINGS IN LIFE

ENDPAPERS: *The Cornfield* by Raoul Dufy

FRONTISPIECE: *The Garden of Delights* by Hieronymus Bosch

JOSEPH WECHSBERG

The Best
Things in Life

LITTLE BROWN AND COMPANY
BOSTON   TORONTO

LIBRARY OF CONGRESS CATALOG CARD NO. 64-17574

FIRST EDITION

818
W

PRINTED IN GERMANY

BY JOSEPH WECHSBERG

LOOKING FOR A BLUEBIRD

HOMECOMING

SWEET AND SOUR

THE CONTINENTAL TOUCH

BLUE TROUT AND BLACK TRUFFLES

THE SELF-BETRAYED

AVALANCHE!

RED PLUSH AND BLACK VELVET

DINING AT THE PAVILLON

JOURNEY THROUGH THE LAND OF ELOQUENT SILENCE

THE BEST THINGS IN LIFE

Contents

List of Illustrations

The author and publishers would like to thank the above-mentioned museums and collections for their kind permission to reproduce the photographs.

The following works are © SPADEM Paris, 1964: Dufy, *The Cornfield*; Renoir, *Le Déjeuner*

The picture-research for this book was undertaken by P. N. Furbank

Carousal in a garden, a French engraving dating from the
time of Louis XVI. 'The Best Things in Life are often elusive'

The Best Things in Life

TO WRITE a book called *The Best Things in Life* is, I frankly admit, presumptuous. How can The Best Things be exactly defined? They are elusive phenomena; one's man pleasure is another man's poison. 'The Best Things in Life' are inevitably the things that I love and value — a compendium of my personal enthusiasms.

Therefore you may not find some of the things *you* like in this book. And you may not agree with some I've mentioned. Personally I wouldn't want to miss the joy of music though I know people who can take music or leave it, and others who don't like it at all. One of my friends, a brilliant man, perceives all music as 'noise'. I myself hear certain kinds of music — electronic music, for instance — as noise.

But what is noise, anyway? The noisy explosions of a motorcycle engine that wake up light sleepers in the entire vicinity are sweet music to the owner of the infernal vehicle. Pilots speak poetically of the exhilarating sounds of their jet engines — until they are grounded, whereupon they hate the awful whining as much as everyone else. Hot-rodders seem to listen as happily to the nerve-wrecking racket of their souped-up engines as I listen to a Mozart string quintet.

The excitement of speed, so widespread these days, is completely lost on me. When I have to take a plane, I am more concerned with survival than velocity. Instead of getting elated at the thought of flying through space at nine hundred miles an hour I notice an almost imperceptible crescendo whine in one of the right-side engines, and I have a premonition of trouble. I'm beginning to wonder whether the men in the cockpit have noticed it too; at any rate, nothing is done about it. I'm not exhilarated.

My only excursion into the mystic regions of automotive speed was an utter failure. An old, trusted friend invited me for a ride in his Ferrari

$2+2$, and like a damn fool I accepted. My friend said he didn't want to frighten me; instead, he wanted to convert me to his religion — speed — and so we plodded along at a mere 165 miles an hour. Actually I wasn't frightened; I soon realized that the way we were going, we wouldn't know what hit us, or what we hit. I didn't see the landscape, if there was any; I was too busy staring at the oscillations of the speedometer needle. I didn't become converted.

Gambling is another thrill I can do without, and it's not in this book. My short career as assistant croupier at the Casino Municipal in Nice may have stifled my early enthusiasm for the game. I had been hired to sit at the other end of the roulette or boule table, across from the croupier — the Casino Municipal was a poor man's Monte Carlo with only one croupier behind the wheel — and to discourage the players from trying to claim other people's winnings. I was told 'to observe the players' faces, never their hands'. The faces were greedy and often distorted, and the players' excitement was not infectious but had a lasting deterrent effect. I was only twenty years old.

I've never become involved in the pursuit of hunting, shooting and fishing. I love the settings of these activities — mountains and woods, lakes and the sea — but not the final, unavoidable, lethal action. I like to shoot for shooting's sake though. I was a crack shot in my first military life, in the Czechoslovak infantry, when I won several first prizes in pistol, gun- and heavy machine gun-shooting. The first prize was nearly always a cigarette case, in silver or goldplate, and once even in gold. I don't smoke and gave the prizes away, but that didn't make me popular. (In Washington they're just beginning to learn this.) I gave up shooting until I had to start all over again, during my second military life with the American infantry in the Second World War. In time of war the prizes were medals, not cigarette cases; but I never got any medal.

As an old infantry man, I've marched under military orders for so many years that I no longer enjoy the simple pleasure of walking. (Even in the modern, motorized army there comes a moment when the infantry soldier has to get off his vehicle to crawl through mud and wet grass, through the impenetrable darkness of fear and fog.) Nowadays I like only a certain kind of walk — on a summer night along the beach to the obbligato sounds of the incoming tide, when the air has the fresh tang of algae and seaweed; or through the woods, late in autumn, when the leaves turn and you feel enveloped by beautiful colours and a velvety cloak of tranquillity. Unlike most poets who sing the praises of spring, I believe that the mature serenity of autumn is the most beautiful season of all. But it is short and sometimes one misses it altogether, as so many of the best things in life.

that opens up new worlds at the turn of the page. 'Give me books, fruit, French wine and fine weather, and a little music out of doors . . .', Keats wrote.

And above all, the joy of love. What can be said about love in sober prose? Love is for the poets. When it becomes prosaic it has already turned into sorrow, as love so often does, and perhaps into hatred, which is the exclusive domain of novelists and dramatists. Mere tracts about love are rarely successful because they tell very little about the subject. In love everybody is autodidactic and some people — most, in fact — never learn the first thing about it. They make all the mistakes and some more, and they enjoy making them. Love will always be like that.

Specialists on the subject have treated love as an art since Ovid wrote his *Ars Amatoria*. No one has as yet written a compendium on *Ars Vivendi*, the art of living, though there would be a more urgent need for it. Life often outlasts love although the poets refuse to admit it. The poets claim that love not only outlasts life but survives death as well, and they quote many outstanding case histories since Orpheus and Eurydice started the trend.

Schools don't teach their students how to live though the subject seems far more important than, say, trigonometry or economics. In fact, the schools teach their students almost anything except how to live sensibly. How to enjoy life not because it's so wonderful but although it often isn't. Professors talk at great length about the great achievements of civilization but rarely about the little good things in life, available to all who have learned to enjoy them. A sunset in the country. An early morning in the mountains when the air has the taste of dry champagne, with a sharp edge to it. An unexpected meeting with an old friend or with an old book. The pleasant thought of an almost forgotten memory.

A wise man in France, the country that gave us the art of *savoir vivre* and the omelette, once told me his test for people who claim to know the art of getting the most out of life: 'A simple experiment,' he said. 'You hand them two fresh eggs and a little milk and tell them to make the best use of these ingredients. The pessimist drinks the cold milk, has the eggs hard-boiled and keeps them for later; one never knows when one will need them. The optimist eats the eggs soft-boiled and drinks a glass of hot milk, which gives him a sense of being healthy and happy. The poor fool who suffers from delusions of grandeur, a species that is far more common than one would think, tries to make an omelette and fails because he never tried to learn how to make one. The man who really gets the most out of life knows that it pays to do a thing well. He treats life as a work of art; he is an artist-at-living. He carefully separates the yokes from the whites of the eggs, and then he makes a soufflé out of the eggs and the milk, adding

L'heureux Quatuor by Henri Rousseau (Le Douanier)

'Give me books, fruit, French wine and fine weather, and a little music out of doors...'
The Garden of Paradise, a 15th century painting from Cologne

I have a little trouble identifying the subtle shades of the autumnal landscape. I am not certain whether the leaves are still green or already turning orange and brown or red. Dichromatism, a partial inability to distinguish these colours. It didn't prevent me from spending contented hours of meditation in front of some paintings I love. One doesn't have to define the nuances of the spectrum to enjoy beauty.

There are people who never really enjoy life, and never really suffer. Life goes on for them like music played *con sordino*, with a mute, without the extreme tone colours. They don't know the ability of enjoyment; they haven't really lived. They miss The Very Best Things in Life — the things that are so important that it would be absurd to treat them within the confines of a single chapter. These very best things are taken for granted. There can be no real happiness without them.

The joy of health: does anything else really matter? The enjoyment of beauty: a man who doesn't see beauty (and many don't) is beyond hope — the magic glasses he needs have not yet been invented. The joy of reading

This 12th century monk proudly signed his name, Eadwine, by his
self-portrait, and added that his work would ensure him lasting fame

secretly a little butter and sugar. People won't mind that he broke the rules when they taste the excellent soufflé.'

To enjoy one's work is one of the best things in life. 'I am happy when I work hard and love someone', Hemingway once said. I would put it the other way around – but the ideal is seldom attained. It's rare to enjoy one's work; and how many people have the good fortune to love someone *and* to be loved? So many of them dislike their work or, worse even, are resigned to it. At the slightest chance they run away from it. Having had to do a few things in life which I didn't particularly enjoy – being a soldier, for instance, or being told to defend a man in court who failed to convince me, his lawyer, of his innocence – I now enjoy the super-pleasure of doing what I really want to do. I write.

On mediaeval miniatures, showing self-portraits of writing monks who were the earliest 'writers' in our part of the world, the pious men are often painted in profile, sitting at a low writing desk under a low, vaulted roof. They are bent forward, as under the burden of their effort, and they firmly clasp the pen and erasing knife, staring gravely at the parchment in front of them. The typical predicament of the writer in search of an idea, facing a blank. No window opens into the outside world. No ray of hope brightens the dimness of the confined space.

The eyes of the pious monk are looking inward. Introspection was expected of him even as he wrote his psalter. He called himself *servus servorum Dei*, 'the servant of the servants of God'. He was cheered up by the words of the Apostle Paul, 'For whatever was written in former days was written for our instruction . . .' (Romans XV, 4), and 'All scripture is inspired by God, and profitable for teaching, for reproof, for correction, for training in righteousness . . .' (2 Tim. III, 16). In the beginning was the Word, not the picture.

Writing was worshipping, an act of faith. It was also hard work. Horace, in *De Arte Poetica*, praises the writing of poetry for its sweat-producing effects, which can also be said of a Turkish steambath. In 408 AD Hieronymus advised Rusticus 'to graft wildings, make baskets, knit fishing nets, copy books'. To copy a book was considered a slave's job. (It still is.) To get hold of the right parchment alone was a major undertaking. The papal curia accepted liturgical works only when they were written on 'virginal parchment', made of the skins of unborn lambs. It took time and knowledge to give writing its deeper meaning of an intellectual pursuit. Gaufridus, a Carolingian abbot, called the library of his convent, St Barbara, 'our armory'. Waldo, the abbot of Reichenau and founder of its famous library, when ordered to bow and submit to the Bishop of Constance, said proudly,

it out on paper. A laborious sweat-producing procedure, as Horace so aptly pointed out.

There isn't a single drawer in the entire cell. Everything is open to immediate inspection which doesn't mean that I find things easily. No indexes or cross-indexes, encyclopaedias, catalogues, atlases. Only Roget's *International Thesaurus*, *Le Larousse Elementaire*, *Der Neue Duden*. A small clock. A thermometer showing the temperature both in degrees Fahrenheit and centigrade, a necessity when you live and write and think in more than one language. A telephone which is frequently pulled out of the socket.

There is only one chair besides my own chair. It is often covered with books and papers: sensitive visitors deduce that generally the presence of strangers in the cell is not encouraged. They are absolutely right. Writers may complain about the loneliness of their work, but loneliness is the cross we cannot do without. We must keep out the idle chatter that breaks up the fragile structure of the sentences and stops the tortuous flow of thought.

There are exceptions to the non-admission rule. Somebody one loves may always come in. But the very few who love you, know better than to come in without being asked. A close friend is always welcome but there are not many of them, and the friends one longs to see most are always too far away. Which is perhaps not bad. Routine is the deadly enemy of love, and distance waters the precious flower of friendship.

And once in a while Poppy may come in to show me a new drawing. Watching a child grow up is one of the Very Best Things in Life, although for some people the wonderful experience consists mostly in collecting snapshots or making home-movies, while others specialize in cute sayings and unanswerable questions of their children. ('What does the wind do when it doesn't blow?') The earliest age, that the French call *bébé* and the Germans call *Wurm* (who else would refer to a baby as a worm?), is followed by the age of loveliness when one wishes that time should stand still: the age when they look like little angels that have just stepped out from under a Christmas tree. Alas, it doesn't last, and there follow the ages of measles and bad manners, of the first worries in school, and a faint, uneasy feeling that maybe life is not always as it is in the fairy tales.

I guess everybody has his own timetable of a child's growing up. Mine was always marked by Poppy's drawings and paintings. The earliest go back to the time when she was three years old, and began to draw vague outlines of flowers. Even then she seemed mysteriously drawn toward a piece of paper, the way a writer is drawn toward his writing table. Poppy would have her dolls, her toys, her marbles and her mysterious games played on

'As long as I can move three (writing) fingers of my right hand, I shall refuse to bow to the hands of a person of lower origin.' We could learn a thing or two from the proud servants of the servants of God of the Middle Ages.

'I did the best I could and if there's something I could say, I'd have said it in my book' — Faulkner once said — 'I think if I would do it over I would do it better.' The writer's eternal cross — he is never able to match his dreams of perfection.

Virginal parchment is no longer required, and the name of the Lord does not have to be painted in golden letters on a purple background, but the filling of page after page with words is still hard work, an exacting, responsible job that can be bitterly frustrating or superbly rewarding, an act of faith and an exercise in self discipline. We writers still sit bent forward, although the vaulted roof above us is no longer as low as in the monk's cell. We write often with anguish and pain, and sometimes with delight and happiness. We are unhappy when we write but we are more unhappy when we don't write, and so we go on writing.

My cell has a high ceiling and a large window leading out to a lovely garden with beautiful old trees. Sitting at my table I probably look exactly as the writing monk on the mediaeval miniature — bent forward, staring gravely at the paper in front of me. The trees outside are comforting; I like their shapes and colours, the sense of peacefulness and orderliness. The old walnut tree has already shed its leaves and stands majestically bare but the fir trees farther behind add colour to the white winter landscape and its dark-green contours are reassuring proof that life goes on, notwithstanding the gloomy prognoses of scientists and statesmen, fortune-tellers and editorial writers.

Behind my chair the book shelves form a protective wall. The trees and my books, my Stradivari and an old wooden statue of St Sebastian with the arrows still sticking in his arms and chest. A useful reminder that the arrows may soon start flying again.

It's easier to describe my writer's cell — some people call it a 'study', on the assumption that a writer needs a study as a car needs a garage — by the things that are *not* in it. No radio, no television set, no tape recorder, no copying machine, no filing cabinets, no writing desk. I write on an old Biedermeier table which doesn't remind me of a desk. There is no secretarial desk, and no secretary. The only concession to the mechanical age is the typewriter, but there is a profusion of soft pencils, and the typewritten page is only a sort of blueprint. I've always envied writers who think out every word in their mind and write down the final version. I have to think

17

the pavement in front of the house that was marked all over with cabalist chalk signs, but after the games she would always come in asking for paper and a pencil. The pencil she used was sometimes as short and chewed as a cold cigarette dangling from a Frenchman's mouth. The paper might be the back of a yellow manuscript page that I'd thrown away. So at least something good came out of the waste paper-basket, the garbage can of many high-flying ideas. Children and geniuses are not fussy about their equipment. The back of an old envelope will do. Schubert wrote some immortal songs on the back of a menu. Beethoven used his cuffs, or his landlady's window frames. Naturally the landlady got mad and threw him out; besides, he also liked to bang away on the piano at two in the morning. Poor Beethoven had to move sixty-nine times in his life.

I remember the day – Poppy was about six then – when we happened to be at the Palace Hotel on Bürgenstock, our favourite mountain resort in central Switzerland. It was a rainy afternoon, and we sat in the hall, talking. Poppy had escaped from the dull world of adult conversation into the exciting wonder-world of her own, and was drawing angels and flowers and ice-skaters, oblivious to what was going on around her. A grey-haired man came by, watched and smiled. Poppy didn't look up. At the age of innocence one isn't embarrassed by being watched at the moment of creation. Certain not-so-innocent painters love to be watched and put

Poppy Wechsberg's painting of a group of dark trees – cypresses or poplars

down their easels in a conspicuous place where they are sure to be admired by passers-by. I'm afraid most of them are bad painters.

The grey-haired man nodded as though he'd been reminded of something that happened to him a long time ago. He asked me how long the little girl had been painting. I said she'd never stopped since she was three. He nodded again. 'And she'll always go on painting and drawing. Be sure that she always has something to paint with — paper, pencils, some colours. And don't send her to a painting school.' He left, and I never saw him again. Later, I was told I had been talking to Marc Chagall.

Paper, pencils and colours are always available, and with short interruptions Poppy has always gone back to her drawings and paintings. Her pictures are her diary. What she doesn't confide to us is in her pictures. She finds it easier to draw something than to describe it. Parties, games, vacations, school events are usually reported by way of small paintings. Much easier than to explain or write letters.

The pictures go in cycles. The earlier cycles of flowers, animals and little houses were followed by angel-flowers (or flower-angels), by lilies-of-the-valley skating on pink ice cream and wild flowers sailing through the air. On the whole, her flowers seemed to improve on nature. The houses sometimes had wrong perspectives but they seemed pleasant and lived in, unlike some of the new houses one now sees everywhere. The roads leading up the mountains were too steep for any car from Detroit but not for Poppy's small fantasy-cars that went up a fifty-per-cent gradient in high gear. And the mountains had castles on top, and happy, peaceful villages were nestling at their foot. Gradually the houses became more elaborate and were surrounded by lovely gardens, and there was always the sun, and sometimes the moon and the stars. That was the age of the fairy tales.

Later there were pictures of groups of happy girls; school had started, and with it the age of togetherness. Experts in child psychology who came by professed delight but really took a gloomy view of these paintings. 'No wonder', they would say after they had left, 'She is an only child. Lonely.' The lonely child went on drawing merry dancing girls (that was the time of her early ballet-dancing lessons) that jumped as high as the moon, long before Project Gemini had made the headlines. The girls — it was always girls, never boys — wore more elaborate clothes now. After a while I noticed that the clothes became more important than the girls wearing them, just as in the fashion journals. Poppy had reached the early dress-designer stage. Some of her designs made more sense to me than the latest creations from Paris and Rome, but I'm probably somewhat prejudiced in the matter.

Sometimes the cycles were reversed — proving, as I'd suspected all along,

Marc Chagall in his studio

Fantasies of the writer's imaginative mind.
A French book illustration of the 1840s

that the experts didn't know what they were talking about. Poppy would go back to angels that were motorized or she drew ultra-modern houses that had no hedges around them. There is probably a meaning in this somewhere but I wouldn't worry about it. There were idyllic landscapes, Tyrolean villages with children sledging, and small towns, somewhat in the style of Grandma Moses. Big cities began to appear too: New York's skyline in brilliant colours, the wastelands of Southern California, dotted with swimming pools and oil derricks, and there were hazy, impressionistic images of the Riviera.

Nowadays the designs have taken on strict forms — cubes and prisms and octagons. Everything cool and clear. This is the age of discipline and *modernisme*. There are deeply coloured church-windows with the light filtering through, and geometric designs where every line has its purpose. A large, searching eye looking out from behind a coloured shower of rain. Some people are satisfied that these are true reflections of our time. Personally, I prefer Poppy's excursions into the realm of pure fantasy. I have two hanging in my cell. One is a dream village — a tiny group of houses around the church and the square in front of it, surrounded by fields and woods and mountains; a quiet brook goes through this idyllic landscape which shows the unspoiled charm of childhood. And the other, a group of dark trees — cypresses or poplars — is very quiet and peaceful, with a touch of sadness. Poppy has learned that life isn't only angels skating on pink ice-cream.

22

Visitors entering my cell often look around and seem vaguely disappointed as though they'd expected to see something which isn't there. Perhaps nudes reclining on a staircase like the ones who keep some painters in business; a well-stocked bar — on the current theory that most writers are almost continuously intoxicated; or some instrument of torture such as the drill in a dentist's office. I can reassure the visitors. The images of nudes are often in the writer's imaginative mind; most of us don't mind a drink or two even before the sun goes down; and there are lots of instruments of torture in my cell — but they are invisible to the visitors' untrained eyes. A writer's chair knows more pain than a dentist's chair.

Some visitors step in cautiously as though they were walking on egg-shells. Others come in slowly inhaling the air, sniffing as if this were the boudoir of a popular-fiction heroine. Do they expect a writer's study to have a certain fragrance, exuding a perfume called Inspiration? The truth is that inspiration is like good water — tasteless, colourless, odourless, although it has a strange and wonderful effect on the quickening of one's heart-beat and gets the writer momentarily into the euphoric stratosphere of happiness. Did you ever go down on skis through a cloud of powdery smoke on a lovely day late in spring when the sky is deep blue and the air is soft and warm? Then you'll know what I mean. Except that the writer goes always uphill in such moments, never down.

But these moments are rare. Most of our skiing is a long, hard, cross-country race, with minor ups and downs, through fogs and snowdrifts, on and on and on. Noel Coward once said he had no regard for writers who write only when it's raining. A real writer writes in bad weather and good, under pressure of deadlines and of his conscience, and if he is lucky he is comforted by the rare moments of uphill racing and by a sense of independence.

No man is completely independent, but some men are more independent than others. The writer who cherishes freedoms — freedom from a boss, from the ubiquitous organization, from regular business hours, from daily routine, from deadly dullness, from certain conventions, from un-pleasant social duties, from bores — must pay a high price for it. I don't mind. If I should be reborn I hope to do again exactly what I am doing now.

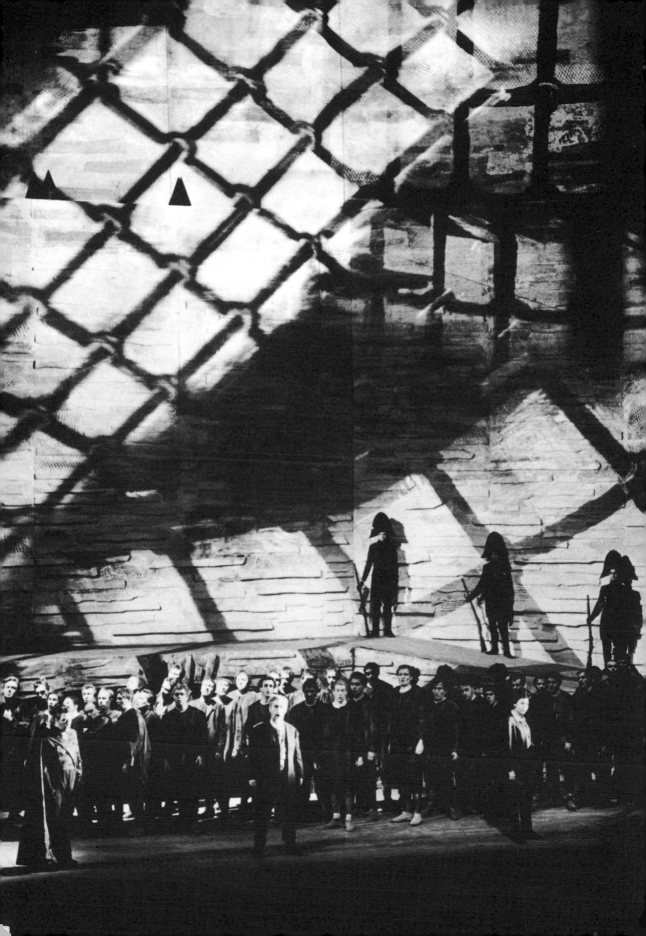

The Art of Listening

I'VE ALWAYS loved music, but it took me a good many years — years of hard work — to learn how to listen to music. I'm still learning. The rewards have been immense. Making music has given me some of the best hours of my life. Mere listening has brought me comfort on bad days and added enchantment to the good ones.

I was a delicate child — no one would believe it now — who suffered from frequent colds. Dr Himmelblau, our family physician, prescribed two tablespoonfuls of cod-liver oil every evening, and said, 'Send him to the mountains and let him fill his lungs with fresh air.' Much later, when I was less delicate but needed treatment of a different sort, I filled my soul with heavenly music.

This is not as easy as it would seem. Most people can hear, but not too many have learned to listen. The song of the nightingale means little to them, and the *Andante cantabile* from Mozart's *Jupiter* Symphony means even less. How many people on earth have ever heard a Schubert *lied*, a Johann Strauss waltz, a Christmas carol? How many Chinese, Indians, Africans have heard *Carmen*? Palestrina's *Missa Papae Marcelli*? How many white people, for that matter? No, the pleasure of listening is not as widespread as we like to think.

And while most people on earth rarely have a chance of hearing good music, a few — some of them music critics and professional musicians — must hear so much of it that they no longer enjoy it. Admittedly the critic's job is not to enjoy the music but to find a way of feeling and thinking that enables him to pronounce clear, intelligible judgements, and to evaluate the music and the performance. That means listening to a great deal of music — good, bad and indifferent. Good critics are painfully aware of the imperfections of the music and often consider listening an un-

25

pleasant task that has to be got over with. Bad critics conceal their uncertainty behind a thin façade of ironical *aperçus*, sometimes at the expense of composer and performers, which is a thoroughly objectionable practice.

The critic's lot is an ungrateful one. Ernest Newman, the great English critic, wrote (in his introduction to Chorley's *Thirty Years of Musical Recollections*), 'It is difficult for the musical critic to achieve any immortality except one of opprobrium. He is remembered solely by his few misses; his many hits are not counted to him. The reason is obvious. If he talks sense, his views become the commonplaces of musical opinion, and no one thinks of crediting him in particular with them. If he talks nonsense, this is regarded as particularly his own and surely to be brought up against him by some musical biographer . . .' And in the introduction to his edition of Berlioz's *Memoirs*, Newman writes, 'Thousands of people who have not the least idea how much good sense Chorley and Hanslick talked remember them for one or two mistakes they made about Wagner.'

It is true that most critics instinctively tend to criticize, not to praise. It is even more true that their criticism rarely exceeds the bounds of convention. The critic criticizes the performance of Beethoven's Ninth Symphony by a celebrated conductor, but even if he believes that the Ninth is not Beethoven's greatest music – in my opinion, it isn't – he would hardly admit it. He might ridicule Wieland Wagner for his latest production of *Tannhäuser*, but to imply that there are stretches of occasional boredom and second-rate music in Richard Wagner's work – and there are – would be heresy. Hemmed in by convention and depressed by his lack of *Zivilcourage*, forced to praise artists whom he personally dislikes, and to criticize artists who are his friends, the critic's pleasure of listening is indeed often nil.

Prominent musicians, too, are often deprived of this pleasure. They have to listen to a lot of music. They must study their own recordings and those of their competitors. They must know the music they perform so well that joy becomes hard labour. One rarely sees them among the *aficionados* in the opera house or in the concert hall. They are afraid of being seen applauding a competitor or, worse even, of being seen *not* applauding. Familiarity with music often breeds antagonism. A friend, one of this era's great performers of the title role in *Boris Godunov*, admitted to me after a number of performances that he felt the music 'coming out of his ears'.

The life of the professional musician is hard and insecure. The men who make up the world's great orchestras – all of them noted instrumentalists who have reached considerable eminence in their chosen calling – go through daily drudgery of practising, rehearsing, instructing, recording,

travelling, performing, more rehearsing and practising, performing concerts, playing at the opera. The lowly second violinist of a great orchestra
has dreams of becoming another Heifetz, just as the lowlier fiddler has
dreams of playing the second violin in that famous orchestra. All of them
want to be somewhere else. And even the Heifetzes of this world are
harassed by competition and have to fight to stay on top. Survival is rare
even among the fittest in today's international music business. Under such
conditions the pleasure of listening becomes a luxury that many cannot
afford.

There are people who don't like music, but perhaps there are even kids
who don't like ice-cream. While I know many people who didn't grow up
with music and are bored by *Götterdämmerung*, I haven't met anybody
yet who doesn't like a simple folk-song, but maybe there are such people.

Then there are those who 'don't mind music' — as long as it doesn't
interfere with whatever else they are doing at the moment — doing the
housework, solving crossword puzzles or trying to make that blonde in a
dim bar. They think of music as a pleasant background sound, like the
proverbial bubbling brook or the rustling trees. I doubt whether they are
aware of it; they don't listen. But what about millions of potential music-
lovers who have become music-haters under the omnipresent anarchy of
piped music and transistor radios, of music from parked cars and through
open windows, in buses and railway stations and elevators? I'm afraid these
frustrated members of the worldwide captive audience will never learn the
pleasure of listening.

Getting the most out of listening means work, patience, good will. I
remember the time when I didn't want to listen to Bach. I thought Bach
was ponderous and repetitious. I had to force myself to listen to Bach time
and again. Gradually I was able to penetrate the magnificent architecture
of Bach's Gothic. To think I might have missed it!

This may not exactly be 'relaxed' listening. It demands concentration,
but you get so much more out of it than when you just lean back and listen
casually. I don't regret it; now Bach is always a pillar of strength to me.
Beethoven sometimes depresses people, Bruckner overwhelms them, and
Wagner infuriates them. Bach is inspiring. Statesmen in times of dire
crisis, leaders before a crucial decision, will be aided by Bach's granitic
greatness and magnificent architecture.

In my melancholy moments I listen to Mozart. To me he is not only the
greatest creative genius of all but a heavenly tranquillizer. I find Mozart
neither sleep-inducing nor habit-forming. After taking him for almost
forty years I have yet to feel a bad after-effect. Doctors don't prescribe

Mozart but he has helped me more than the forced cod-liver oil treatment of my childhood. Mozart is the perfect super-ethical drug for the soul.

The therapeutic value of Mozart's music is as old as his music. In 1787, he wrote from Prague, 'The people are flying about with such delight as to the music of my *Figaro*, transformed into waltzes and quadrilles.' Richard Strauss said, 'The most perfect melodic shapes are found in Mozart; he has the lightness of touch which is the true objective.' It is that sparkling lightness that is so exhilarating. Bruno Walter told me after an exasperating rehearsal that he was going home to listen to a recording of Mozart's G minor String Quartet, 'which will restore my equilibrium'. Mozart wrote it shortly after the death of his beloved father, with earthly sorrow in his soul and an unearthly smile in his heart.

Mozart is not the happiest of all composers; there is always an undertone of sadness in his music, but he takes you through sorrow to heaven. He is the perfect musical antidote to this age of anxiety. His genius has resolved human folly — as in *Figaro* — into pure enchantment.

Provided you will listen with devotion, music is always alive; listening can never be a mere hobby. The romantic moods of Chopin; the impressionistic dreams of Debussy and Ravel — controlled emotions, distilled into sheer beauty; the elegiac moments of Brahms and the bittersweet melodies of Schubert songs; the nostalgia in the music of Dvorák, Albeniz and Bartók; Mahler and Bruckner who carry on humble conversations with God and will give you a sense of tranquillity — like a long, quiet walk through the woods.

The pleasure of listening is greatly enhanced by a moderate knowledge of the music, and of the instrumental and vocal techniques. It helps to know a little about style and phrasing, tempo and intonation, vocalization and falsetto, to be able to distinguish an oboe from a clarinet and an Italian-trained tenor from one who never studied *bel canto*. Repeated hearing gives you a chance of discovering new nuances and hidden gems of the score. You will become catholic in your tastes and tolerant in your prejudices. You will enjoy recitals as well as symphony concerts, jam sessions and oratorios, opera and chamber music; you'll like Bach and Gershwin, Claudio Monteverdi and Giuseppe Verdi, Johann Strauss and Richard Strauss, chorals and swing.

Listening should be both an emotional and intellectual experience. Purely intellectual listening is unrewarding and leaves you with a curious let-down. This must be the reason why so much modern music, conceived with the brain but not inspired by the heart, fails to affect so many listeners.

'Modern music is not modern and is rarely music', writes Henry

28

'Human folly resolved into pure enchantment.'
An early print of Mozart's *Marriage of Figaro*

Pleasants in *The Agony of Modern Music*. 'New music which cannot excite the enthusiastic participation of the listener has no claim to his sympathy and indulgence. Contrary to popular belief, all the music which survives in the standard repertoire has met this condition in its own time . . . Few people like modern music. Even fewer like much of it. Most people do not like it at all.'

There are people who pretend to get an immense pleasure out of listening to festivals of modern music. They will listen to anything as long as it is considered sensational, and is talked about. They speak derisively about all eighteenth- or nineteenth-century music, though they may have some favourites among the sixteenth- or seventeenth-century composers. ('Buxtehude was a Baroque giant.' 'Buxtehude?' 'Yes, 1637–1707.') They distrust composers who were loved in their own time. But the plain matter of fact is

29

that all great composers were admired and listened to by their own contemporaries.

There are modern composers who pretend they don't care about their audiences; whether or not the audience enjoys their music doesn't interest them at all. In *Music and Imagination*, Aaron Copland writes, 'The thought that my music might or might not give pleasure to a considerable number of music-lovers has never particularly stirred me.' Neither has Copland's music stirred a considerable number of music-lovers.

Joseph Haydn, who was the first great protagonist of symphonic music and who single-handed invented the string quartet, that glorious achievement of western civilization, did care about the pleasure that his music gave to people all over Europe. ('While he worked in the solitude of Eszterháza, his name travelled far beyond the borders of his own country, and there was hardly a music-lover in Europe who did not know and admire the works of Haydn,' writes his biographer, Karl Geiringer.) Haydn himself explained the secret of his music and his artistic creed one day in 1802, after the members of the *Musikverein* in Bergen, on the Baltic island of Rügen, had sent him a flattering letter. Haydn wrote back, 'You give me the pleasant conviction . . . that I am often the enviable means by which you, and so many other families sensible to heartfelt emotion, derive, in their homely circle, their pleasure — their enjoyment. How reassuring is this thought to me! Often . . . a secret voice whispered to me: "There are so few happy and contented people here below; grief and sorrow are always their lot; perhaps your labours will once be a source from which the care-worn, or the man burdened with affairs, can derive a few moments' rest and refreshment."'

To derive a few moments' rest and refreshment is not always easy in today's hectic music business. Much has been said about an artist's difficulties of performing when he is not 'in the mood', but nothing about the listener's problem of doing justice to a performance when *he* is not in the mood. The listener has arrived at the concert hall or the opera house after a hard day at the office, a fight with his wife, a couple of urgent, last-minute phone calls, and a desperate struggle to make his way through the jammed streets of the big city. He got there just in time. He is exhausted as he sinks into his seat. How can he immerse himself in the opening theme of Bruckner's Eighth Symphony or Wagner's *Parsifal*?

Richard Wagner, a genius with a down-to-earth approach to the appreciation of art, was aware of the psychological stumbling block between the music and the audience. In Bayreuth he sought to remove the difficulties by producing his works under near-ideal conditions, and by setting down a strict routine for the obedient festival visitor which is still

followed by ardent admirers of the *Meister*. In Bayreuth listening is a full-time occupation, occasionally exhausting but frequently rewarding. The well-trained, well-tempered Wagnerian in Bayreuth starts the day with a leisurely breakfast and spends a quiet morning in pleasant anticipation and immersion in the work he's going to hear, preparing himself emotionally and intellectually for his task. After a light lunch (serious music does not go well with rich food) he gets dressed — I'm told there are people who actually enjoy getting into full-evening dress at three o'clock on a muggy summer afternoon — and slowly walks up the Green Hill toward the *Festspielhaus*. The prescribed festival diet permits no telephone calls, cablegrams, direct contact with district attorneys, dentists or divorced wives. By the time the auditorium gets dark (which is quite a relief because it's so ugly) and the proper Wagnerian hears the beautiful sounds that come out of the covered orchestra pit, he will be superbly rewarded. There is real magic in Bayreuth.

I usually go there before the pomp and circumstance of the annual Festival's opening, during the final week of rehearsals, when the Green Hill throbs with subdued excitement and everybody, from the anonymous third trumpeter to the famous first *Heldentenor*, is gripped by the enthusiasm which is Bayreuth's trademark.

That may surprise you because summer festivals have become commercial enterprises, rather than artistic events. Last year there were eighty-six festivals all over Europe — many of them organized by promoters with little love of music but considerable aptitude for extracting cash out of the pockets of eager listeners. Most opera houses are run by artistically minded people; many festivals are run by Chamber of Commerce types who care more about profits than about quality. A dead and defenceless composer whose image appears on ashtrays and candyboxes is the star attraction. Prominent artists are hired and exploited; a beautiful idea deteriorates into Big Business.

Bayreuth is still different. It has to be heard and seen to be believed. Bayreuth today is the most exciting experience in the contemporary musical theatre. The air is hot and humid but the artistic climate is healthy and invigorating. There are no stars; there is astonishingly little intrigue; the first thing the Wagner brothers do is to make their stars forget that they were primadonnas and *Kammersänger* before they came to Bayreuth. There is a happy tension about the Green Hill and a complete absence of routine. Everybody seems to be operating a little above himself, which makes all the difference between a mediocre performance and an outstanding one. Bayreuth's intensity and enthusiasm are contagious. It's the only place on earth where orchestra musicians don't grumble when the

'Total theatre' at Bayreuth. Wieland Wagner's productions of two of his grandfather's operas, *Tannhäuser* and *Tristan und Isolde*

final rehearsals of *Meistersinger* or *Tristan* start on successive nights at seven and last until two in the morning.

'It could only happen here', a dead-tired violist once told me. 'It's what they call the miracle of Bayreuth. Perhaps the reason is that we spend only two months here. You couldn't keep up this pace any longer than that.'

But there are other reasons.

'Elsewhere I'm fed up with a rehearsal before it starts,' a prominent, hard-bitten *Kammersänger* says. 'Here I enjoy it right down to the end. It's Wieland Wagner, of course. He's inspiring. He listens to your ideas. And he's a perfectionist. He's never improvising. I've learned more in eight weeks here than during the rest of the year everywhere else.'

The Wagner brothers have not only achieved Grandfather Richard's ideal of the 'total theatre', a blending of all components — music, drama, lights, sounds, voices, staging and action — into a magnificent entity. They have also been able to inject genuine enthusiasm into hard, painstaking

labour. And the inspiration reaches over all the way from the back of the stage to the back of the cheerless auditorium with its uncomfortable seats and magnificent acoustics.

Listening in Bayreuth is always an excitement because the music sounds so beautiful there. An opera house is judged by its acoustics. Richard Wagner, who designed his *Festspielhaus*, must have known a lot about the mysterious science. He made the auditorium funnel-shaped (ordinary parallel walls often create dangerous reflections) and he built no boxes along the sides (which have a way of absorbing sound instead of reflecting it.) You can hear every word in Bayreuth – small voices seem to grow, and singers never have to strain. And the orchestra in the covered pit produces a perfectly integrated sound, yet the single instrumental groups and instruments can always be clearly discerned.

Acoustics are still a big mystery. Scientists in many fields can foretell with unvarying accuracy what will result from a combination of known factors, but scientists specializing in acoustics seem to be on no surer footing in making their forecasts than meteorologists are in making theirs. No one can say what the acoustical qualities of an auditorium will be until it is finished, furnished, heated, and filled with musicians, listeners, and music. In the past, the designers of opera houses perhaps knew little or nothing about the science of acoustics but a few of them, aided by instinct or plain good luck, produced auditoriums with fine acoustics – notably, Milan's La Scala, Venice's *Teatro Fenice*, Vienna's Court Opera, London's Covent Garden, New York's Metropolitan, Barcelona's *Liceo*. But more recently several auditoriums, built in Europe and America under the guidance of consultants who applied certain laws of physics and used certain testing devices, turned out to have acoustics that were either disappointing or dreadful.

The glorious exception is the world's most daring, almost revolutionary hall – the new West Berlin *Philharmonie*. Designed by Professor Hans Scharoun, the famous architect and president of the German Academy of Arts, the *Philharmonie* from outside looks like a strange, naked, tentlike structure that challenges one's sense of proportion. No geometric form fits its description. Balconies, platforms, funnels, pits and promontories appear in the unlikeliest places. For no obvious reason baywindows are next to portholes, and casement windows next to rosettes. The hall is surrounded by ruins and empty fields, and the Berlin Wall, not exactly an uplifting structure, is a hundred and fifty yards away.

But at night the hall looks different under the glare of floodlights, a challenge in asymmetry, an adventure in modern baroque. The lobby is a modern world of warmth and togetherness. Slim, graceful stairways go

Berlin's new *Philharmonie* concert-hall, designed by Professor Hans Scharoun, which was inaugurated with a performance of Beethoven's Ninth Symphony

up everywhere, and as you look for 'your' stairway, you see people everywhere walking up, like fellow-hikers climbing up the wide slopes of a hill. And then I walked through a door and gasped: I saw a large, irregular, octagonal structure which Scharoun later described to me as 'an excavated valley whose bottom is a flat trough and whose sides are climbing vineyards'. Cheerful voices came from the vineyards which were full of human grapes — mostly dark grapes that night but there will be many white ones next summer. The walls were wooded slopes, covered with dark wood. The floors were meadows — made of bright, natural wood. And the seats were covered with autumn-coloured upholstery.

Twenty-two hundred people, most of whom I could see from my seat, had gathered around the bottom of the valley where the orchestra was tuning up for its musical campfire. Even before they started to play, I

understood Scharoun's magnificent vision. In the beginning there was the
music; then the people around the music; and finally the landscape around
the people. The trinity 'music-man-room' appeared as a triple pentagram
on a wall in the hall. This hall had been created from inside out — around
the music, and nothing else mattered, and the miracle of belonging, of
warmth and intimacy, was intensified by the miracle of acoustics that need
just a few adjustments to be flawless.

Acoustics are subject to the change of popular taste. High-frequency
recordings made people's hearing more sensitive than it used to be. When
we first heard these new recordings, they sounded too sharp — perhaps a
quartertone high in pitch — but now we've accepted them because they reproduce actual sounds more exactly than ever before. They taught us to hear
more of the overtones of music. You have to listen to an old Caruso recording to realize how far we've progressed. Modern acoustics must meet this
new challenge.

It's the acoustics of a place that gives the listener a sense of warmth and
intimacy. The dimensions of the auditorium have nothing to do with it.
Milan's La Scala, a large house, seems more intimate than many smaller
ones. Carnegie Hall has great warmth, and so has Boston's Symphony Hall
and Amsterdam's *Concertgebouw*. One of the finest halls is the large
auditorium of Vienna's *Gesellschaft der Musikfreunde*, whose warm,
luscious, sweet 'Viennese' sound is attributed to the aged wood of its fixtures. You feel like sitting in a large, private music-room, with two thousand
other people, where music is made for your enjoyment. In such a hall it is
easy to get into the right mood for the pleasure of listening.

A mysterious, mutual relationship exists between performers and
listeners whose elements have never been completely explained. Why is
it that a performance comes off beautifully one night and fails the next
one? Same programme, same performers, same conductors — but not the
same audience. Could it be that the audience radiates a divine sparkle one
night and produces earthbound dullness the next? Or is the climate to
blame, the performers' fatigue, the mood of the conductor?

The conductor exerts his musical, intellectual and emotional leadership
through beat, movements, gestures. A great orchestra whose men have
played together for years and know the repertory, are unanimous in attack
and release, faultless phrasing and intonation, and pay little attention to
the conductor's beat — that's the kindergarten approach. But they read the
meaning behind the gestures. When Wilhelm Furtwängler brought down
both arms in a powerful if erratic movement at the beginning of Beethoven's Fifth Symphony, some listeners wondered exactly at what moment

the orchestra would attack the 'tatata-tah'. When the conductor's fists had reached the uppermost button of his waistcoat? Or when the eighth double-bass player finally lost his patience and started to play? But attack they did, like one man, all at the same moment, exactly and powerfully. It was not an orchestra playing 'tatata-tah' but Fate Knocking at the Door.

The listeners didn't know that the orchestra had learned to read Furt-wängler's beat during rehearsals as a secretary learns to decipher her boss's almost illegible handwriting. A great conductor leads without command-ing; there is such a deep understanding between him and the orchestra that he merely suggests; he doesn't perform but makes beautiful music with the orchestra.

At this point the subtle, unfathomable interplay between the conductor and his artists creates a miraculous reciprocity. The players feel secure under their leader; they rise above mere technicalities to the spiritual task of bringing the music alive. The transformed orchestra in turn stimulates the conductor who feels happy with his pliable, sensitive super-instrument. He conveys his feelings with greater clarity than before. His gestures become almost transparent; his innermost emotions are telegraphed. There is now complete synchronization between his feelings and those of the players. He has moulded one hundred men into a finer, more expressive instrument than man will ever build with his hands.

The audience does not know exactly what happened but feels the glorious fusion of all elements — for now the exaltation of conductor and orchestra has reached over into the auditorium. Abruptly, a spell is cast over thousands of people. No one coughs, no one turns around on his chair, the people sit as in a trance. The big hall is filled with an almost physical sense of elation that affects everybody even the reluctant listener who had to be dragged here by his wife, the 'man burdened with affairs' who came 'to derive a few moments' rest and refreshment', the society woman who doesn't care about this concert but 'cannot afford not to be seen', the old lady suffering from a terrible headache. The excitement of listening — a heightened awareness of the beauty of the music — has gripped them all.

What happens next has never been explained with scientific accuracy. Is it possible that the subtle psychological harmony between performers and listeners creates a further, mysterious chain reaction — inspiring the con-ductor who in turn inspires his players to illuminate and express the com-poser's innermost intentions, the music that is between and behind the written notes?

We don't know. But we do know the result. The performers and the audience agree that it was a memorable evening.

Wilhelm Furtwängler conducting Beethoven's
Fifth Symphony, a drawing by Wilhelm Heiner

Letter from a young girl in England:

. . . I am twenty-three, and have been absolutely mad about opera ever since I was taken to see a performance of *La Bohème* by an Italian touring company when I was twelve. Living as I do in a city where we depend on a visit once a year by Sadler's Wells for our opera, I find it in my heart to envy you so very, very much. I have a burning ambition to go to the Vienna State Opera, La Scala, the Met, and to hear such divine singers as Birgit Nilsson (my idol), Tebaldi, Gobbi etc. I have spent nearly a week's salary to hear Birgit Nilsson at Covent Garden in September. It will be the first time I hear and see her in person, and I can't tell you how much I'm longing for it . . . I shall look forward to your reviews from Vienna, in particular on Karajan who transforms all music into something really wonderful . . .

Opera, the most exciting musical art form and the most difficult to perform, has been declared dead and buried, but is more alive and popular than ever before. This is all the more surprising since grand opera is handicapped by absurd libretti and implausible acting, harassed by financial difficulties and production problems. No opera house on earth ever breaks even, and none gets all the singers, producers, conductors it needs. So many divergent experts and artists — poets, dramatists, composers, producers, conductors, designers, coaches, musicians, singers, dancers, painters, technicians, extras, members of the administrative staff — are involved in a single operatic production that the standards are often precarious and the cost is always staggering. Opera has often been ridiculed — Dr Samuel Johnson called it 'an exotic and irrational entertainment' — but it continues to conquer the souls of its detractors and gladdens the hearts of its addicts.

Producing an opera is like making a very fine watch in which every part is represented by a highly skilled human being. Sometimes a tiny cog falls out of the works and the watch stops running. All opera managers have a recurrent nightmare: a performance has to be cancelled at the last moment and the audience sent home because someone hasn't shown up. It did happen last year at the Vienna State Opera. Twenty minutes *after* a performance of *Meistersinger* was scheduled to begin, the audience was informed by a palefaced member of the management that Wolfgang Windgassen who was to sing the part of Walther von Stolzing was 'suddenly indisposed'. 'We have to ask you to get your money back at the box office, there will be no performance tonight,' said the pale-faced man and fled from public ire behind the curtain. Later it became known that Windgassen hadn't been indisposed, but sitting peacefully in his house in Bavaria when it was discovered in Vienna, one hour before the performance, that owing to a 'misunderstanding' they'd failed to notify him properly. For a frantic hour the management looked all over the big city for a replacement. But *Heldentenors* don't grow on trees nowadays and they found none.

Opera, that 'exotic and irrational entertainment' is more alive now than ever before.
A scene from *Die Meistersinger*

Vienna's newspapers considered the event a national disaster. Actually it
was bound to happen sooner or later. It is a miracle that any operatic performance goes on as scheduled.

At the well-run Metropolitan, which prides itself of having at least two
performers available for every major part, a performance of *Walküre* had
to be interrupted when Wotan suddenly lost his voice. He was replaced by
a second singer who promptly lost *his* voice. By that time the first Wotan
had regained enough of his voice to go through with it. And there was
that ill-fated performance of *Tristan und Isolde* which consumed three
different Tristans before the third was permitted to die a merciful stage
death.

Pompous aesthetes have called opera a fraud, and cold fish call it a
bore. But anyone dead to the divine beauty of Mozart's *Le Nozze di Figaro*
or Verdi's *Falstaff* misses perhaps as much in life as the man who doesn't
enjoy the first touch of spring in the air, the colours of a Rembrandt, the
sight of a lovely woman, the aftertaste of a fine wine, the afterthought of
a good book. Opera remains a phenomenon that seems to rejuvenate itself
as time goes on. Opera hasn't changed its character to become accepted,
yet there are more opera lovers today than ever before.

Perhaps our era has at last caught up with the improbable phenomenon. People don't mind the absurd happenings in *Il Trovatore* which the operatic genius of Giuseppe Verdi transformed into a masterpiece of dramatic intensity. Being driven by *azione per musica* from one musical climax to the next, the listener accepts the unfathomable nonsense of the libretto. He doesn't mind that the protagonists are not lifelike, and dramatically implausible. 'People just don't behave that way', the rationalists say. But they forget that music gives a deeper truth to emotions, sublimates drama into the essentials of love and hatred and cruelty and passion and death, and more love in the end. Love and opera conquer all.

Grand opera is now performed in over a hundred opera houses and theatres all over the world. Some have a season of a few weeks and others play ten months. Germany and Italy lead with thirty-nine and eighteen opera houses respectively. In Western Europe and the countries behind the Iron Curtain even medium-sized cities have permanent opera companies. There are indifferent houses, and good houses, and great houses.

Toscanini once said to a friend, 'In Vienna they claim that their *Staatsoper* is the first house on earth. And in Milan they say, "La Scala? Unquestionably the first house in the world." In New York everybody tells you, "Finest opera on earth? Why, the Met, of course." In London they are convinced that Covent Garden is the best house of all, and down in Buenos Aires there is no doubt that the *Teatro Colon* is the first house in the world. Strange, isn't it? Only first opera houses on earth — no second house.'

The question of the first opera house is no longer important. Owing to the limited supply of first-rate conductors, producers, and singers, the same people now perform the same operas in various 'first' houses all over the world. The aeroplane and the star system have created a deplorable *Gleichschaltung* of repertory, casts and artistic apparatus, and the great houses are losing their sharply drawn, artistic profile of their own. Even the orchestras begin to sound alike, owing to the levelling influence of recordings and the strong hand of conductors. In fact, the only distinguishing element among the world's leading opera houses are the listeners.

People come to the opera for different reasons. Italians love opera; the lyrical theatre is in their blood; they want excitement. People in Austria and Germany were brought up on it; they look for enlightenment and inspiration. English audiences are getting close to the Continental state of mind; in the last few years there has been a complete change of attitude at Covent Garden. London is fast becoming an 'opera town', and there is the same churchlike atmosphere on a great evening in Covent Garden

An Indian princess with a hookah listening to the music
of her attendants, an 18th century miniature

that envelops a memorable night in Vienna or Munich. And the French love their Wagner; the French contingent in Bayreuth gets larger year after year.

American audiences haven't reached the exalted stage yet, but there are signs of a change between New York and San Francisco. We may yet see the time when people will come before the overture and leave after the end, when they will not be permitted to enter during the performance and the ushers will no longer use their flashlights as in Radio City Music Hall. There is already a widespread feeling that there is more to opera than powerful voices and sustained high Cs, that such intangibles as style, intensity and the integration of all elements create a truly artistic performance, a work of art.

The judicious opera lover who wants to derive the greatest pleasure from listening will carefully choose his operatic dishes. Italian opera is best performed at La Scala. In Italy opera has always been the national religion, and the *Teatro alla Scala* ('Theatre at the Stairs') is the national shrine. A square, brown, not particularly inspiring building from the outside, La Scala has a beautiful, gilded auditorium with fine acoustics and an electrifying atmosphere. The quality of the performances is uneven — a shortcoming which La Scala shares with all 'first' houses. Gustav Mahler, who directed the Vienna Court Opera during its 'golden' epoch in the early years of the century, used to say that one really good evening a week was a pretty good average.

La Scala's audience is made up of experts who are sure of their opinions and express them without restraint. Ladies and gentlemen in evening dress have been known to get involved in vitriolic arguments, and no holds are barred in the galleries. A few years ago a tuxedoed gentleman in a front row threw one of his shoes at the stage in a moment of violent disapproval, and a lot of ketchup could have been made out of the ripe tomatoes that were thrown at bad performers.

The audience is often carried away by its inborn flair for drama and melody. People hum the aria while the great tenor sings it, which would be impossible in the colder emotional climate of a German opera house. But the Italian *brio* is infectious: after a while the disciplined listener from the northern latitudes finds himself humming too. La Scala is the only house on earth that has a full-time, professional school for young singers. At *La Piccola Scala* intimate works are performed in an intimate frame for audiences of connoisseurs.

Vienna's State Opera has gone through ups and downs since the golden days of Mahler. It is supported financially and enthusiastically by Austria's entire population. Most Austrians never go to the *Staatsoper* but all have a close personal feeling about 'their' opera house and consider themselves its joint owners. There are many people in Vienna who have never heard *Figaro*, but few who don't know what happened backstage at last night's *Figaro*. Life and the theatre are inseparable in the musical capital of the world with its constant interplay between reality and stage illusion. Elderly Viennese remember the local aristocrat whom Hugo von Hofmannsthal, with poetic licence, transformed into the immortal Baron Ochs von Lerchenau in *Rosenkavalier*. The *Feldmarschallin*, the most feminine heroine in the entire operatic literature, was invented by Hofmannsthal and brought to life by Strauss, but the illogical Viennese show you the Palais where the charming adulteress lived. Perhaps she existed, under a different name. Truth and fiction are always merged on this city-wide stage.

The *Staatsoper* has the best operatic orchestra on earth, the Vienna Philharmonic. They make music (which is not the same as performing it) and have a great feeling for beautiful sound. The standards of the performances vary from sloppy improvisation one night to impeccable style the next. There is always surprise — one reason why opera never bores its addicts. Great singers love to sing in Vienna. 'The audience gives you so much,' one told me recently.

European opera lovers have learned at last that New York's Metropolitan is neither a 'second-class' house nor a very rich one. On the contrary, it's first-rate and poor. The Met's management spends much time and energy collecting money from rich patrons or not-so-rich radio listeners. With its lack of permanent subsidies, the high cost of unionized labour and the demand for expensive voices, the Met is often on the brink of financial disaster and cannot afford costly experiments like the luckier, state-supported houses in Germany or Austria. Between 1943 and 1957 it performed no world première of any new work; unpopular works are rarely revived. The repertoire consists mainly of sure-fire box office favourites that people want to hear over and over again. Lately, however, courageous forays into virgin territory were made. Who would have thought that the Met would ever dare perform Alban Berg's *Wozzeck*, or Richard Strauss' *Ariadne auf Naxos*? Both became popular successes. And a production of Strauss' difficult-to-perform masterpiece, *Die Frau ohne Schatten*, would have been considered impossible ten years ago.

The Met is a house of fascinating extremes. The sets are terrible one night and wonderful the next. The orchestra plays indifferently or superbly, depending on the conductor. Vocally no other house can compete with the Met's array of great voices; the Met gets the best singers from both Europe and America. It is still primarily a star theatre, with a sense

42

Beckmesser, an unsuccessful candidate in the
prize-competition from *Die Meistersinger*

of unity lacking in many productions. It will remain that way until the listeners learn that a night at the opera is more than a social duty or just an evening's entertainment. Grand opera is a demanding art that gives itself only to those who give much to it.

London's Royal Opera House, Covent Garden, is proud of its memories and traditions. Outside, rough crates with carrots and oranges are placed against the walls; inside there is elegance in the grand manner and a festive mood. The usually tranquil English climate of appreciation has lately been interrupted by wild cheering and loud booing — healthy symptoms of operatic libido. Some people were very shocked about this display of positive and negative enthusiasm, but the English are still very well behaved compared to the *aficionados* in Parma's *Teatro Regio*. In Parma the real drama is always this side of the orchestra pit. The greatest singers were booed there when they were not in top form. Toscanini once swore he would never go back there. Railway porters in Parma once refused to carry the luggage of a famous tenor who had cracked his high C the night before.

One beautiful opera house which provides no pleasure of listening is the Opéra in Paris. The *Théatre National de l'Opéra*, as it is known officially, is 'national' in name only. In France opera is not yet one of the national arts, like painting and cooking. Many Frenchmen consider the Opéra a stuffy musical museum. Jean Louis Charles Garnier, the architect of the Second Empire, put everything that was expensive into the building, maybe a little too much of it. The pomp and marble, the staircases and sculptures, leave you cold; so do the performances. Conductors, orchestra members, singers and the rest of them go through their routine with a lack of enthusiasm that would not be tolerated in the kitchen of La Tour d'Argent. The ballet is good but the scenic and choreographic possibilities are rarely used. The most popular work is Gounod's *Faust* which is performed almost every week. The French are mad about Wagner who spent several weeks in a debtors' prison in Paris, and lived through a terrific scandal after the unhappy première of the revised *Tannhäuser* on March 13, 1861, after 163 rehearsals and after M. Adolphe Sax had been called in with his saxophone to supplement the stage horns.

Among the opera houses of Germany the West Berlin *Deutsche Oper* and the Hamburg State Opera rely on solid ensemble art, and pioneer many modern works. Munich considers itself the artistic home of Richard Strauss, and has good Wagner and Mozart performances. Stuttgart has a well-integrated ensemble. Peregrinating opera fans love Venice's beautiful *Teatro Fenice*, Naples' San Carlo, the Opera in Rome, the small, lovely Monte Carlo Opera, the Royal Opera in Stockholm, Lisbon's *Teatro Sao*

Covent Garden has elegance in the grand manner. *In the Front Row at the Opera* by William Holyoake

Carlos, Barcelona's *Liceo*, the *Teatro Colon* in Buenos Aires, the San Francisco Opera.

And there are important theatres and orchestras behind the Iron Curtain – particularly in East Berlin, Dresden, Prague, Warsaw, Budapest, Moscow and Leningrad. The East Berlin *Staatsoper Unter den Linden* was opened in 1742 during the reign of Frederick the Great. It was a fine example of the Berlin 'Forum' style with its austerely classical façade, and with many baroque and rococo touches. An official East German publication now explains that the opera house then was 'the salon of the feudal régime, with no inner meaning for the people'. During the Seven Years' War the house was closed, and in the period of Napoleon's occupation it became a

45

storage house for bread. In 1843 it burned down and was quickly rebuilt. After the beginning of our century it was one of the 'first' houses on earth. Muck, Strauss, Kleiber, Blech, Furtwängler conducted there. It was bombed in 1941, rebuilt and reopened by order of Goering, bombed again in 1945, and rebuilt once more, with Soviet aid.

Unter den Linden, once the *via triumphalis* of an empire, has become a ghost street. The State Opera is still flanked by grey ruins, and one is not prepared for the profusion of marble and mirrors, of chandeliers and carpets that one finds inside. The performances are not basically different from those in the western world—the *Staatskapelle* is a very good orchestra; the staging is sometimes curiously old-fashioned — but one becomes aware of a different mood in the auditorium when the lights go on during the intervals. There is a strong contrast between the auditorium's warmth and intimacy and the audience's restraint and self-consciousness. People don't look happy. All the gold leaf and cold marble can't hide the listeners' bad shoes and rough shirts. More than under the reign of the Prussian kings the *Linden-Oper* is now 'the salon of the régime, with no inner meaning for the people'.

Neophytes in the art of listening should begin with the kind of music that appeals to them most. Some begin with jazz and wind up with Mozart and Bach. One doesn't have to be 'musical' to enjoy a Schubert song or a waltz by Johann Strauss or a Gershwin melody — very fine music. It's more difficult to enjoy the symphonies of the classic and romantic composers; and the giants — Bach, Beethoven, Bruckner — should be approached with an open mind and an open heart. Great music improves with repeated hearing, and bad works get worse.

Recordings, radio and television have widened the circle of music lovers everywhere. But they will always remain substitutes. Even the best recordings — and the best are very, very good — lack the breath of life of a great performance just as the finest canned fruit will never approach the flavour of the freshly plucked one. I prefer the real performance with its imperfections to the glossy engineering miracles of modern recording. No recording can convey the sense of enthusiasm and feeling of gratitude that one has after a great evening in the opera house or the concert hall.

The experienced listener often has a premonition of either exultation or failure even before the evening has started. As he takes his seat he senses boredom hanging over the auditorium like an invisible cloud; there is a deadly stillness around him. The experienced listener would like to get out. He hopes against hope: perhaps an extraordinary conductor or an exciting artist will perform the miracle — pull the audience out of its lethargy, make them sit up straight, cast a spell. Alas, usually the evening that started under bad auspices ends in disaster, under the steamroller of mediocrity.

And there are nights when the experienced listener feels a subdued sense of excitement even before he enters the auditorium. It reaches out into corridors and cloakrooms — an electrifying feeling of anticipation. The lights seem to be brighter and the tuning sounds of the orchestra are a few decibles sharper. It is as if invisible high-tension wires were strung up all over the place. At last the house-lights dim. For a few seconds only the lights in the rows of boxes remain, making the auditorium look like a mystic, mediaeval cathedral. A torrent of applause greets the conductor, and as he lifts his hands and the first sound is heard, you feel — no, you *know* — that this will be an unforgettable night. You close your eyes and lean back. Time and space recede; there is nothing but bliss and beauty all over the large auditorium. It took you many hours of patient listening to became an active part of this glory, but it was worth it.

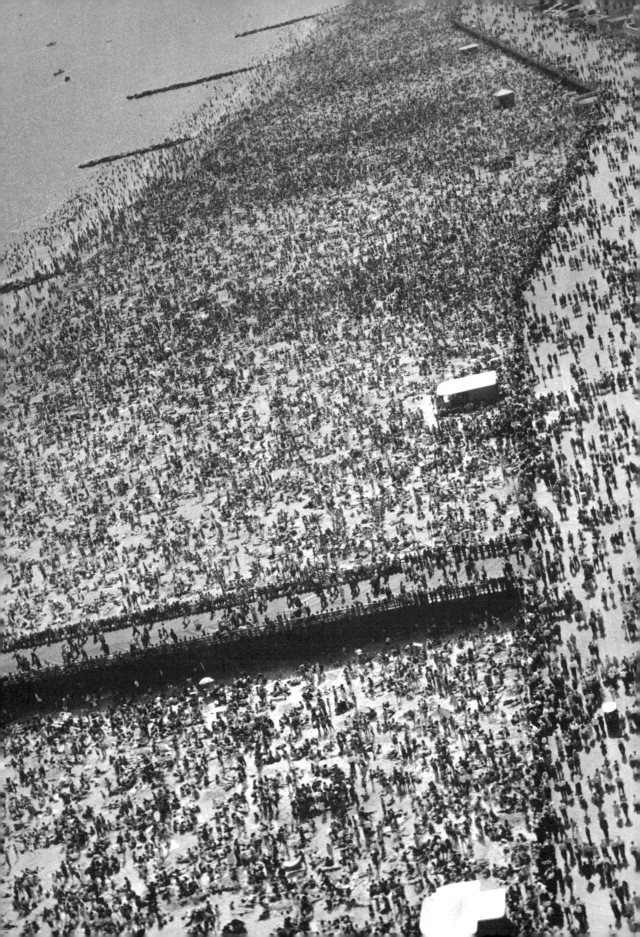

The Meaning of Travel

I SPENT the summer in the peaceful solitude of my study but was kept posted on the merry-go-round of the noisy, jammed highways of Europe by Frau H., the charwoman, who comes to the house three afternoons a week to help with the chores. Except in summer when she drives off in a brand-new Opel with husband and son. This year they went all the way down to Yugoslavia and Greece.

The people who used to travel now stay at home during the summer vacations when the Continent is too crowded for the man who likes to relax in tranquillity. The whole picture has changed. Travel, once the prerogative of what romanticists called 'the moneyed class', has become a compulsion with people who go now and pay later. A gratifying sign of progress, according to the economists, but perhaps not an unmixed blessing. More people than ever are travelling but fewer than ever know why they go.

I asked Frau H. Her answer was characteristic. 'Why shouldn't we go? *Every*body is going some place this summer.'

I heard the resentful, social-injustice undertone, and quickly dropped the subject. I want Frau H. to go; above all I want her to come back. She's a pearl about the house — though not always a cultured one — and what would we do without her?

I have a hunch, however, that the Frau H.s of this world are not going some place. They are just running away, afraid to miss something, terrified of being left behind. They leave panicky and return defeated. They are always on the run. In this morning's newspaper I read three significant stories. In Venice's Piazza San Marco a German couple was arrested for 'unlawful mendicancy'; they told the Italian police they had come by car but had run out of their money. In a town in Carinthia, one Navratil

The beach at Coney Island, New York.
Togetherness has become the symbol of modern tourism

robbed a woman of her purse 'because my vacation was more expensive than I'd expected'. And in Vienna a woman was arrested for stealing, and admitted tearfully she would have liked to go to the Riviera, 'where everybody went this summer'.

The classic nineteenth-century travellers – I think of Goethe, the Humboldts, Mark Twain, Gauguin – had a definite idea in their mind and a special purpose in their trip. They had a good reason for going somewhere and methodically followed the pursuit of peregrinating happiness. Time didn't matter. Speed was unknown. It took Beethoven seventeen days to make the journey from Bonn to Vienna by stagecoach. Nowadays people go around the world in less time but they find it hard to explain why they went in the first place.

Beethoven, always an inner-self traveller, an Ahasver driven by his restless genius, never stayed long in one place. His way of travel was to move out of a rented room where he was no longer welcome to a place three streets away. But though he never went far, he left us some immortal travel notes. A journey to Baden, less than ten miles away, gave mankind his Ninth Symphony.

Today travel is not rated by content and inner experience but by mileage and haste. It's no longer a custom-made adventure but a mass-produced business. As always in such a case, quantity has not improved the quality of the product. The popularization of travel has debased its technique to an appallingly low denominator. Once the element of surprise was one of travel's great attractions. After the routine of all-year-round life, the daily drudgery at the office, the glorious holiday meant getting away from it all, the lure of the unknown, excitement of exotic places, a change in one's emotional climate and intellectual outlook. The pleasure of travelling meant both the pleasure of going away and the greater pleasure even of coming back; for there can be no pleasure on a journey that has no happy destination.

Now the efficient organizers have taken the joy of surprise out of the journey. Ubiquitous experts compete for the privilege of making your trip devoid of all worry and rob it of all wonder. The whole journey is delivered like deep-frozen food – wrapped in cellophane, clean and dull. Instead of an adventure, the entire voyage is a predictable venture, with a programme as tight and unexciting as a railway schedule. There is no room in this schedule for pleasant improvisation.

Many people now make their grand tour for the sole purpose of checking off sights and side-trips, excursions and meals, antiques and sunsets, as if they were items on a laundry list. The old *Simplicissimus* cartoons of earlier Baedeker tourists – some with stiff German collars and others with

Tourists were as unmistakable in the 1890s
as they are today, a cartoon from *Simplicissimus*

tweedy English knickers — are being revised by European cartoonists in different form. Today's wanderers carry guidebooks that sell better but are less reliable than the old Baedeker. The new tourists are immediately spotted even if they don't wear a couple of cameras dangling over their stomach, for they are just as conspicuous as their predecessors. The native population watches them with mixed reactions that range from greed and false courtesy to amusement or outright antagonism.

The efficient organizers provide everything except what matters most: contact with the local populace. That is considered somewhat insalubrious, like drinking the local water. And so the travellers see everything and meet no one but waiters, porters, sales clerks and guides. No wonder the thoughtful wayfarer feels frustrated and tries to compensate by speed and scope. But speed is an illusion: the supersonic plane of the near future will deliver you at your destination at an earlier hour than you departed from your last stop. And scope is meaningless, measured by the number of minutes it takes you to 'do' a place. Two-dimensional peregrination, with no sense of depth. I'm told the record of 'doing' the Louvre now stands at thirty-four minutes and twelve seconds. This includes a side-trip to the Venus of Milo but not a minute of blissful introspection in front of Giorgione's *Concert in the Open Air*. That's known as the 'if-this-is-Tuesday-we-must-be-in-Paris' school of travelling. On cruises the travellers rush from one thing to the next. The trip is organized down to the last half-hour. There is no time for improvisation, relaxation or meditation. The client must be on the go all the time. If you were bored for ten minutes, your trip, like a Broadway show, is considered a flop. Togetherness has become the symbol — and the curse — of modern tourism.

Looking at these exhausted excursionists who secretly wish they were back home again, I've often wondered what made them come here in the first place. Was it a healthy thirst for knowledge, or man's eternal wanderlust? Curiosity perhaps, or an inborn sense of adventure? Do they come for the sights and sounds, or just for the fun of doing some shopping? Because they love the mountains or the sea, the battlefields or historic places? Is it beauty of nature they're looking for, or the pleasure of meeting folks from back home in unexpected places? Or, could it be that they go for the primary purpose of travel — to find out what makes other people tick?

Whatever it is, wanderer, make up your mind why you want to go and then go after it, ignoring the unchartered reefs and treacherous shallows of two-star sights and one-way side-streets. Go on your own and without a schedule. I salute the courageous friend who dared refuse his wife's suggestion to accompany her to the Louvre. Instead, he spent the afternoon

The journey from Greenwich to Charing Cross for the Whitsuntide holiday in 1783. Once the element of surprise was one of travel's great attractions

at the small café, where he had a wonderful time. He came home with strong impressions, though of a different kind than those ordinarily gained at the Louvre. And I respect the man who never went near a hotel or restaurant recommended by hotel porters, professional guides or other kick-back specialists. What's the sense of going to that intimate bistro with sawdust on the floor, famous for its *poule au gros sel*, and then ordering steak and French fries? You might as well eat the sawdust. Or stay at home and get a better steak.

To meet people in a foreign country – not the questionable types that hang around hotel bars in search of gullible tourists but ordinary human beings whom the politicians call 'the man in the street' – is much harder than to

53

look at the famous sights but also much more rewarding. The sights and the sounds of a place, the works of art and relics of history, the city's mood and smell and feel are nothing but the reflection of its people — past and present generations. To go on a trip and miss the people is like attending a concert with cotton pads in your ears.

The very essence of travelling is communication. Meeting people is getting harder all the time because of the frightening breakdown in communications. Old language barriers are being torn down—more people than before are beginning to speak more languages — but new psychological barriers are being put up. People who speak the same language do not even try to understand one another. Disraeli said that 'travel teaches tolerance', but it seems to affect some people the wrong way. At home they were well-mannered and kind-hearted but when they go abroad they begin to throw around their weight and money. Americans take a condescending view of old European countries where the plumbing is less conspicuous than the culture; Europeans are just as wrong by expressing their belief that 'the Americans have plumbing without culture'; and both of them regard Africans and Asiatics as little children who must be patronized. There is always the assumption, conscious or unconscious, that 'the local people' are inferior.

Such an attitude will not help the traveller to establish a subtle inner rapport with 'the local people'; he will always remain outside the charmed circle, surrounded by a bleak wall of antagonism. After a while he will feel lost in the foreign country and will make up for it by being rude. The disaster will be total. Tact and tolerance are far more important than speaking foreign languages. Before the Second World War, I once travelled on the famous Shanghai Express, an unglamorous train, from Shanghai to Peking. I was young and impecunious and travelled third-class, and when people asked me why I went third, I answered, like the thrifty member of the Swiss Government whose name I've forgotten, 'Because there is no fourth class.' But going third-class turned out to be a break. My companions were the little people of China of whom God made so many that the exact figure is never known. I would have missed them if I had gone first-class with the well-heeled foreigners. I didn't understand a syllable of what my companions were saying and they certainly didn't understand me. But we had a wonderful time during two days and two nights, and parted as friends who know they will never meet again. Sweet oranges were shared as well as feelings of mutual esteem, and there was a constant communication of associations and impressions. I learned more about the Chinese on that trip than from half-a-dozen books I'd previously read on China.

I also learned that people react instinctively when they sense sympathy and good will. They will gladly forgive you your mistakes and 'eccentric' manners — eccentric from their point of view. On a journey from London to Scotland I've seen the proverbial reticence of the English melt like ice-cream on a midsummer afternoon. (There is no such reticence in the Mediterranean countries and the United States.) A casual meeting on a train with a Swiss led to a lifelong friendship.

Sometimes enterprise and ingenuity are needed to meet people. An American friend recently went to Moscow with a group of VIPs. Moscow is one of the hardest places on earth to get acquainted with the local people. There is distrust of foreigners and widespread fear to be seen with them; the not-so-distant past is not yet forgotten. When my friend met two men at a reception who spoke English he took a chance and invited them to dinner with their wives.

After some hesitation they accepted; each of them later admitted to my friend he wouldn't have dared if the other hadn't come along. By midnight, after many small glasses of vodka, the brotherhood of men was well established. They all stayed together until the early hours of the morning, and when they parted they made a date to meet again in the afternoon. By that time the thaw must really have set in, for my friend was asked to come home with them, and then they took him out to their favourite restaurant. The party broke up at three o'clock on an icy winter morning. My friend had absorbed much local color and local alcohol and felt slightly groggy. There was no taxi in sight, and his hotel was four miles away. At last the Russians stopped a city garbage truck. My friend passed out the last of the American cigars he'd thoughtfully taken along, which immediately established his excellent standing with the garbage men. He arrived in front of the hotel in style on the garbage truck, with more knowledge about the good people of the Soviet Union than his fellow VIPs who had spent the days listening to official briefings.

Since travel has become big business, the prospective traveller is showered with promises of glorified sights, tempted by pictures of enchanting women in lovely landscapes, fascinated by full-page ads of Technicolour sunsets. He is told Where to Go and What to See. By the time he leaves he knows everything in advance. Well — almost everything.

There is just one thing missing in this bewitching set-up: some sound advice to the eager wanderer on Where Not to Go and What Not to See. The lure of the unknown makes children out of sophisticates and enthusiasts out of misanthropes. New Yorkers who at home wouldn't dream of going near Radio City Music Hall ('That's strictly for tourists, Mac'), run

55

up the stairs of Paris' Eiffel Tower. And I know at least one worldly Parisian *boulevardier* who never goes to Montmartre *(C'est seulement pour les touristes, mon vieux)*, but was on the top of the Empire State Building an hour after his arrival in New York.

The fatherly, bewhiskered guides who wrote the old, red-backed Baedekers, had real *Zivilcourage*. They used to put down against the name of some city or site that they found not particularly worthwhile the forbidding phrase, 'Nothing need detain the tourist here'. Yet they never intended thereby to discourage the wanderer, and neither do I. I have little hope that the reader may be influenced by my discommendations. In travel, love and politics a man never learns from the mistakes of others. He has to find out for himself, and pay for it. But at least you cannot say that you haven't been warned.

My discommendations are of necessity highly subjective, a reflection of my personal prejudices. The Grand Tour of Europe (or of America, of Africa, of the Far East) is like a modern painting: it's interesting but people can't always agree exactly why. My suggestions are based on sound research and repeated experience, not on a sudden mood of irritation. These suggestions are for the relatively few travellers who care more about content than appearance, who prefer people to places. I may not win many friends but I hope to influence some readers.

I would never advise you to avoid certain countries altogether. There exist irritating national traits – gypping in France, tipping in Austria, suspicion in the Soviet Union – but despite what some superpatriots may say, there are objectionable people but no objectionable nations.

Generally, my discommendations fall into three categories.

First, the snobbish, fashionable, 'three-Os' – Overdone, Overcrowded, Overcharging. Portofino and Ischia in Italy, Cannes and St Tropez in France, Salzburg and Kitzbühel in Austria, Garmisch and Berchtesgaden in Germany, Ascona and Locarno in Switzerland, most summer festival cities and wide parts of Paris, belong in this category. When everybody who is anybody begins to talk about these places, the wise traveller knows he had better stay away.

Second, places where scenic beauty and native charm have been hopelessly ruined by commercial tourism. These days I would avoid the châteaux of the Loire, the wine villages along the German Rhine, Volendam in Holland and Killarney in Ireland, the Zugspitze and the Jungfraujoch in the Alps, Sorrento and Amalfi in southern Italy, Venice in midsummer, Munich during the Oktoberfest, and Capri all year round.

Third, the brash, uninhibited tourist traps set for exploitation by the unsuspecting sucker: Paris' Montmartre; Hamburg's *Reeperbahn*; Belgium's

The first Cook's Tour to the Rigi Kulm in Switzerland in 1863. In those days organised excursions were allowed to move at a more leisurely pace

Carnival de Binche; dilapidated, refurbished, castles all over Europe, run as hostelries by dilapidated, refurbished members of the local aristocracy; such macabre tourist attractions as Madame Tussaud's gruesome waxworks in London, Hitler's former residence near Berchtesgaden, the battlefield of Waterloo in Belgium. Also certain *spécialités de la région* — lovely-looking provincial inns in Merrie Olde England that don't serve anything to eat after eight pm; rural buses in Ireland and Spain; the Palace of Culture in Warsaw and Rome's Palazzo Venezia, which both violate the standards of good taste.

(Paris, the City of Light and greatest tourist attraction of all, offers Many Things Not to See. I discommend especially a night at the Opéra; the Latin Quarter, which addicts of Murger's *Scènes de la Vie de Bohème* will hardly recognize; and Place Pigalle where the food and the entertainments are less good and more expensive than elsewhere. But even wise men doing don't mind being fools once in a while, particularly on their first trip to Paris.)

Does all this mean that there is no place to go any more? Of course not. The world is wide and wonderful for the man blessed with the gift of enjoyment. But travel should remain a noble exercise in individualism, and every journey should be something of a discovery. Each of us has dreamed about places he wants to see. It may be the aura of the past, the sound of a name, the fragrance of the air. I've always wanted to go to Samarkand, and some day I shall go there in spite of what I've lately read about the place. I would like to see the deep-blue waters of a Norwegian fjord, and look up at the giant whiteness and majestic calm of a Himalayan peak.

And I want to go back to some places, although I realize that revisiting the scenes of one's memories may become a dangerous experiment in nostalgia that sometimes ends on a note of disappointment. Ex-student princes who went back to the Heidelberg of their exuberant, younger days have been saddened to find a noisy, crowded American Army headquarters town, as idyllic as a roller-coaster stadium. But the risk must be taken.

I want once more to stand in front of the Temple of Heaven in Peking. I was there thirty years ago and I can still see it, in all its brilliant colours. Three circles of snow-white marble rows surrounded the Temple, three garlands out of which the beautiful structure rose toward the deep-blue sky, a symphony in blue, gold, yellow, red colours. The priests used to sit in the marble rows. Only the Emperor, 'Son of Heaven', was permitted to go into the Temple itself. The building had been restored a few years before I saw it and the colours were vivid and brilliant. The composition was perfect, with its white marble foreground and the deep, dark blue of the sky in the rear. I was so enchanted that I went back that night, and when I returned to my hotel, I wrote something that was later published in my first book. I re-read it the other day and it all came back to me:

There are many beautiful wonders in this world of ours and it would be absurd to state that one of them is the most beautiful of all; but tonight I have seen the Temple of Heaven in the light of a full moon and I know I shall never see anything like it again. I experienced a strong sense of delicate, ethereal beauty. In spite of the finesse of its detail the building makes an imposing impression of grandeur. A friend once said to me he considered Agra's Taj Mahal the most beautiful 'moonlight miracle'. I don't know. The Taj Mahal made me feel sombre and sad. But there was no sadness tonight — there was tranquil charm — the smiling serenity of China. The Temple of Heaven had tenderness and warmth, and seemed to radiate an inner light of its own. Is it possible that 'in the course of the city's modernization program' some people suggested to turn the Temple into an open-air theatre, and others wanted to build a stadium around it?

The delicate, ethereal beauty of the Temple of Heaven

The Travelling Companions by Augustus Egg, 1862

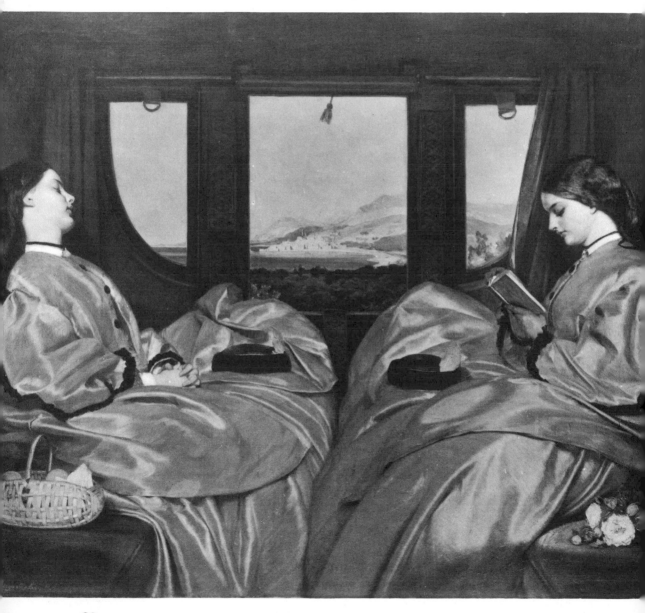

The genuine traveller is exhilarated every time he crosses a border. Every frontier opens up a new world, and in some parts of Europe the frontiers come fast. You follow the Rhine Valley between the Vosges Mountains and the Black Forest and you will find old people in the Alsatian villages whose nationality was changed by wars and peace-treaties five times in their life-time though they never left their village. French and German and French and German and now they are French again — but mostly they feel like Alsatians, and you can't bame them.

Or go down to the Balkans where there is more linguistic confusion than one ever thought possible. Of Yugoslavia's eighteen million in-habitants some fifteen million in Serbia, Croatia, Montenegro and Bosnia-Herzegovina speak Serbo-Croatian, one and a half million Slovenes speak Slovenian, and the people of Macedonia speak Macedonian. All these languages are similar, though with distinctive qualities, and several dialects among them. There are also minorities who speak Hungarian, German, Slovak, Czech, Italian, Bulgarian, Albanian, Rumanian.

Further complications arise since the Serbians, Montenegrins and Mace-donians use the Cyrillic alphabet, while the Slovenes and Croats use a modified Latin one. And though Macedonia was the homeland of Alexander the Great who briefly made it a world empire, its literary language is the youngest on earth, exactly twelve years old. This is indignantly denied by the Greeks who gave Macedonia its early culture and consider Macedonian 'nothing but a Greek dialect'. In Greece there is an Aegean-Macedonian minority. Both the Yugoslav Macedonians *and* the Greek Macedonians are bitterly opposed by the Bulgarian Macedonians who consider Macedonians 'just another Bulgarian dialect'. They have a good argument: in the old days Cyrillic Church-Slavonic was also know as 'Old Bulgarian'.

Didn't I tell you there is still excitement in crossing a border?

At the tender age of eight, for reasons I no longer remember, I made my first journey all by myself. I went from Merano, a lovely town in the South Tyrol, a paradise of orchards and vineyards surrounded by high mountains at the end of a beautiful valley, to the nearby town of Bolzano. The trip took fifty-five minutes but I had hardly slept the preceding night and was at the railway station one hour before the departure of the train.

When I stepped up to the ticket counter and asked for a ticket, 'half-fare, third-class', my hands were wet and the coins stuck to my palms. The small train with two coaches stood outside, and I stepped into the third-class coach and sat down. My heart was beating wildly. My mother had warned me not to sit near a window (there might be a draught), to keep away from the doors (which might open), to watch my wallet (which contained practically no money), and not to talk to strangers (all mothers

61

give the same advice). I had received half-a-dozen additional instructions, and as I sat in the empty coach I reeled them off in my mind like a Tibetan monk mechanically reciting his prayers. I watched the door for suspicious people and the sidings for possible railway disasters. After sitting there all by myself for half-an-hour I began to have serious doubts that the train would ever leave. At last I got off and asked the conductor. He was an un-friendly man who gave me a hard stare and said, 'Of course the train will leave, but there is plenty of time.' I decided that when I grew up I would always arrive at the station only half-a-minute before the train's departure, a sophisticated traveller.

At last the coach became quite crowded with suspicious-looking men and chattering women, the doors were closed, a whistle was blown and then the train started to move. I could hardly believe it: here I was all by myself with no one to watch me, and the train was going! I leaned back with a sense of pride. I'd done it. I decided to become a great traveller, a discoverer like Livingstone, or Admiral Byrd, or –

'Your ticket!'

The unfriendly conductor stood in front of me, a forbidding figure of authority. My ticket! I'd held it in my hand all the time until I'd gone out to ask him about the train. I was sure I'd put it into my right trouser pocket but it wasn't there. I went through all my pockets while the conductor stood there, and I felt the stares of the people around me like stabs of a knife in the back of my head. I tried to keep back the tears and told him that I had *really* bought a ticket. He said that I was to get out at the next station, and he would 'talk to the station master'.

Cold sweat broke out behind my neck. My hands trembled. An elderly woman said, 'Why don't you look once more in your pockets? Take your time. You had your ticket. You'll find it.'

I found it at last inside my handkerchief.

Thinking back, I am sure it was a more exciting trip than my last cross-ing from New York to Europe when I had excitement of a different sort. On the way to the boat I got tied up in crosstown traffic and it was getting late. The big gangway was already up, and I had to hurry over the narrow one that is used by officials and shipping company people coming ashore shortly before the boat sails. I arrived in a breathless state. It was not the happy intoxication of my earlier trip from Merano to Bolzano.

But fortunately I've never quite overcome the pleasant affliction known as travel fever. True, I no longer practise 'rehearsal packing' which was standard procedure in our home. My mother would always pack her bags two or three days in advance, 'to see whether everything would go in', and then she would unpack again. She felt reassured now, but it was a futile sense of security. On the day of her trip, when she packed in a hurry, the bags seemed to have shrunk. There would be a big crisis when it was high time to leave for the station and we couldn't get her bags closed.

Nowadays my symptoms of travel fever are different. There is the delight of recognizing the familiar contours of a landscape that hasn't changed or to see friends again that haven't aged too much . . . Arriving on a rainy night in the mountain hotel when the clouds are low and nothing is cheerful except the warm radiators, and then stepping out on the balcony the next morning into sunshine and blue skies and the wonderful panorama of towering glaciers . . . Standing high up on the sun-deck of a great liner and watching the infinity of the ocean, the everchanging play of lights and shadows and iridescent patterns of colour . . . Walking leisurely through the streets of a small town where one finds oneself quite unexpectedly, and discovering the small sights and smells that give you the feel of the place . . . The moment of arrival as the 'plane comes down or the train's brakes are applied and one sees someone very dear standing there, waiting for you . . .

Or the ship's foghorn giving three long blasts – the sign that the last visitors have gone ashore, the last ropes are loosened, the slight trembling under one's feet indicating that we are on our way. There is a heightened awareness of things to come – as in the theatre when the curtain goes up. This time perhaps there will be a real adventure . . .

Standing between the lifeboats I watch the pier recede. I am quite sure now that the journey will be wonderfully exciting, unlike any other previous one. And I can't help feeling sorry for the fellow who is busily clicking his shutter and sees the world only through the range-finder of his camera – or the man downstairs in the bar who doesn't care. Poor people – they will never know the happiness of travel fever.

Je pars de BORDEAUX
et vous envoie mes Amitiés.
N. G. Dépôt.

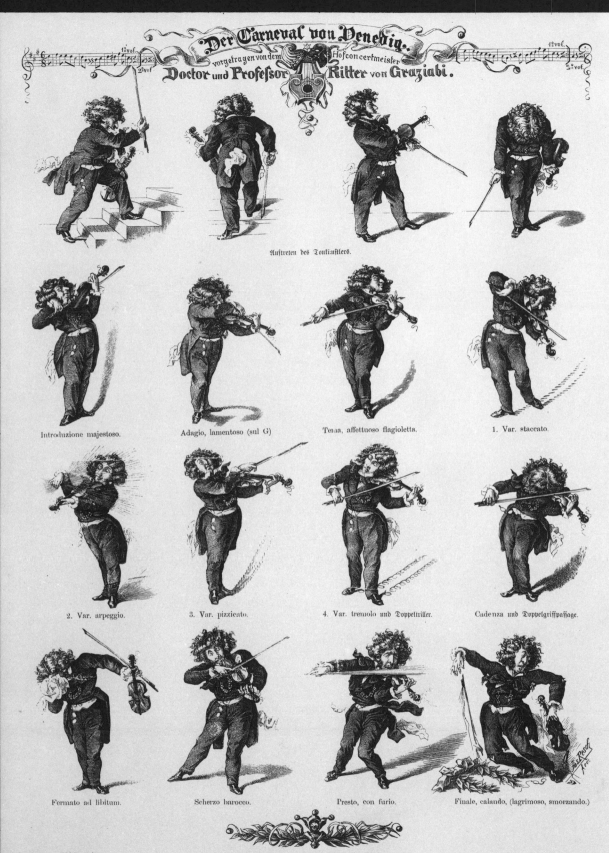

Der Carneval von Venedig,

vorgetragen von dem Hofconcertmeister

Doctor und Professor Ritter von Graziabi.

Auftreten des Tonkünstlers.

Introduzione majestoso.

Adagio, lamentoso (sul G)

Tema, affettuoso flagioletta.

1. Var. staccato.

2. Var. arpeggio.

3. Var. pizzicato.

4. Var. tremolo und Doppeltriller.

Cadenza und Doppelgriffpassage.

Fermato ad libitum.

Scherzo barocco.

Presto, con furio.

Finale, calando, (lagrimoso, smorzando.)

Münchener Bilderbogen.
5. Auflage.
(Alle Rechte vorbehalten.)

Nro. 717.
kgl. Hof- und Universitäts-Buchdruckerei von Dr. C. Wolf & Sohn in München.

Herausgegeben und verlegt von Braun & Schneider in München.

My Stradivari

FOR THE first fifty years of my life I only dreamed of having a Stradivari. Now I own and play one, and it has been sheer joy. A house, a car, furniture, jewellery, savings-books, stocks and bonds, collections of all kinds – china or postage stamps or neckties or dirty postcards – are, at best, mixed blessings. So are, I suppose, a boat, a race horse, a castle, a swimming-pool surrounded by pretty, complaisant girls, an aeroplane, a factory, a farm, a grouse-moor and other things I wouldn't want to have if they gave them to me.

Possessions cause trouble. They need attention. I love books and I would like to own certain paintings which are beyond anybody's reach. But even books and paintings, though not exactly silent, cannot speak to you as a fine violin does. In fact, the only things I can think of in connection with my Stradivari are wines and flowers. They too are living things; they have to be lovingly cared for to be fully enjoyed. But wines and flowers are too closely related to the eternal cycle of life and death. An empty wine bottle, a withered rose, create an unpleasant reminder of The End. *Memento mori.* Yes, we know, but we don't want to think of it.

The life of a great fiddle outlasts a man's life-span; a violin is almost immortal. My Stradivari has a distinguished pedigree of previous owners, among them a millionaire-embezzler; a man who was locked up in an asylum by his relatives because in their opinion he spent too much money on women and fiddles (an ideal combination that proves how eminently sane he was!); and a crank who kept it under his bed and never played it, poor fellow.

My Strad is beautiful. Violins age gracefully. I know – I've had quite a few. In the violin world, as in the world-at-large, you work your way up from rags to riches. Every time I exchanged my fiddle for a finer one, I

Attitudes of a 19th century virtuoso, from a German print

had an acute sense of loss. It was like saying goodbye to a dear, dear friend. Before my Strad I had a lovely, frail, slim, feminine fiddle made in 1608 by the brothers Antonio and Girolamo Amati in Cremona. The Amatis were the noblest violin-making dynasty of all, not-withstanding the personal fame of Antonio Stradivari and Giuseppe Guarneri del Gesù. The patrician Amati family has been traced back to 1007. The oldest maestro of the clan was Andrea, born probably in 1535, who is now regarded by many experts as the creator of the modern violin. Some experts make the same claim for Gasparo da Salò from the Lake of Garda, the founder of the Brescia school of violin-making, and there are those who state that Kaspar Tieffenbrucker, a German who worked in Lyons around 1550, made the first violins. At any rate, no one made them as beautifully as the Cremonese, and Andrea Amati was doubtless the first great Cremonese master.

Andrea Amati was primarily concerned with sweetness and beauty of tone, while Gasparo da Salò cared more for power and resonance. Andrea left very few instruments. His two sons, Antonio and Girolamo (Hieronymus), continued their father's art and copied his models. One of Girolamo's fourteen children was Nicolò, the most famous of the Amatis, who lived to be eighty-eight, gave us some of the finest violins on earth and became the teacher of Antonio Stradivari.

My Amati was made by the two brothers in Cremona in 1608 (the very year in which Claudio Monteverdi, another genius from Cremona, mentioned a *violino piccolo à la francese* in the score of his *Orfeo*.) Considering that very few violins exist which were made in the sixteenth century — there are only two early Andrea Amatis, whose labels are dated 1551 — my fiddle was one of the oldest in the world, over three hundred and fifty years. But no one who listened to its soft, melodious voice would have said so; it was the voice of a young, happy, lovely girl. I hope my successors will treat the Amati as they ought to treat a lovely young girl. It might live another three hundred years and will sound better then ever. No other living thing, no bottle of wine, lasts that long.

The Amati's successor in my violinistic affections is a beautiful Stradivari made in 1730 in Cremona when the master of masters was eighty-six years old. Perhaps it was Cremona's healthy climate that kept the great violin-makers young and energetic, or it was their stimulating yet tranquil work which they loved so much. My Strad still has its genuine label in it, which is rather rare, although somebody fooled around with the date, altering it to 1716 — a practice as common in certain circles of dealers and collectors as the practice of altering one's birth date in a passport is among ladies of a certain age.

In this case it was not a matter of feminine vanity but of masculine

The certificate of authenticity of the author's Strad, with photographs of the instrument, signed by the dealer and expert Emil Herrmann. The portrait of Stradivari is pure fantasy

I Certify that the violin sold by me this day to Mr. Joseph Wechsberg of Vienna, Austria is in my opinion a work of Antonio Stradivari of Cremona Period 1729/30 and bears a label 1716.

ex Oscar Mez.

Description The back is in one piece of handsome maple of medium curl, the sides and scroll to match. The top is of pine of medium grain. The varnish of an orange reddish brown color and of fine quality. The instrument is in a good state of preservation and repair. Four original letters of Gustav Bernardel of Paris and dated Jan. 12, 18, 22 & 24th, also certificate of Jan 24th 1895 accompany the instrument.

Photographs overleaf

#1331

Emil Herrmann

Easton, Conn. October 31st 1961

greed. Dealers and collectors often changed the dates on labels in works of Stradivari to pass off violins of the 'early' period (from 1666 to 1700) as works of his 'golden period', (from 1700 to 1720). They also falsified the dates in works of his 'late' period, especially after 1727, to bring them back to the 'golden period' which is rated the best.

At the age of two hundred and thirty-four years my Strad shows no signs of senescence. It responds easily to the slightest touch of the bow and combines beauty of tone with carrying power. We amateurs and chamber-music players prefer beauty of tone to beauty of appearance, while collectors are more interested in the impeccable condition of an instrument than in its tonal qualities. The most valuable Stradivaris such as the famous *Salabue* are violins almost without a scratch, that look as if they'd just left master's workshop; but their tone is rather hard, for great fiddles need to be played, and treated with knowledge and affection in order to mature and develop; in that respect they resemble women.

My Strad has been played a lot. The certificate of authenticity says, 'The instrument is in a good state of preservation and repair.' This certificate, the violin's passport, includes full-size photographic reproductions of the violin's f-holes and scroll, and reduced photographs of its front, back, and sides. It says, 'The back is in one piece of handsome maple of medium curl, the sides and scroll to match. The top is of pine of medium grain. The varnish of an orange reddish brown colour and of fine quality.'

I've learned by bitter experience that possessions tie you down. They often adversely affect one's decisions in crucial moments. But my Strad is an exception. If the worst comes to the worst, I can always take it along, and I will. I expect the love-affair between my Strad and myself to last until the end of my earthly days.

The French language, particularly subtle in expressing the hidden nuances of the inner life, calls the violin's sound post *l'âme*, 'the soul' of the violin. The sound post is the slender, cylindrical rod that supports the right foot of the bridge and transmits the vibrations of the belly to the back. (The left foot of the bridge is supported by the bass-bar which is attached to the belly and helps to maintain a balance between the vibrations of the belly and the vibration of the G string. There is more to a violin than meets the eye.)

The smallest change in the position of 'the soul' will alter the sound and character of the violin. Only a thoroughly skilled craftsman should be permitted to perform this delicate operation — and only if the player is convinced that the tonal problem that bothers him is caused by the instrument and not by himself. Great artists no longer in their prime often attribute their failing powers to mysterious maladies inside their violins instead of blaming themselves. A once-great violinist who owns one of the once-finest fiddles in the world had it opened, inspected and 'improved' so many times that the emasculated instrument has changed its personality; every time an instrument is opened, a little of the invaluable varnish and wood gets lost, and also a little of its character.

It is this resemblance to a living being that makes a violin – and every other string instrument – a very special work of art. Great paintings reflect the personality of their maker, but certain paintings have detached themselves from the genius of the maker and lead a life of their own. People think of the *Mona Lisa* as if she were alive, no longer in connection with da Vinci. Every Renoir breathes the genius of Renoir, but some Renoirs – think of his enchanting *Moulin de la Galette* – have won independence from their creator; such paintings speak to you with eloquence and conviction. And so does every great violin.

I say every great violin because not two are alike. They may seem similar to the untrained eye, as two Chinese or Tibetans seem similar to us. But to the expert they have different faces. The experts can recognize a violin which they haven't seen for many years although they may not always recognize people. Of Stradivari's three thousand instruments which left his workshop, some six hundred are believed to have survived – wars, revolutions, fires, various disasters have taken a heavy toll – and not two closely resemble each other. Each Stradivari instrument has its own personality, but each reflects the spirit of the Master's genius.

I once brought my Strad for a very minor repair to a well-known violin-maker in a big city in Europe. He knew neither me nor my instrument, and I still remember his astonishment when I opened the case. He cast one short, excited glance at my violin, took it out lovingly, held it away from himself with the left hand and smiled.

'Wonderful,' he said. 'You're lucky to own such a Strad.'

I asked him how he could recognize the instrument in a second.

He gave me a pitying look. 'Why, it couldn't be anything but a Stradivari,' he said, reproachfully. 'Can't you *feel* it? Stradivari's genius is all over it.'

Of course I couldn't. I've learned that there are few such experts, perhaps not more than a dozen in the whole world who can pass judgement on the authenticity and merits of old violins and really make their judgements stick.

When such an expert looks at a beautiful old violin for the first time, he is something to look at himself. He holds it up in front of him, getting the feel of it and noting its shape. If he cannot identify a reputedly good violin within half a minute, the chances are that something is amiss. In doubtful cases his extensive scrutiny begins with the back, where he examines the texture of the wood and the quality of the varnish. Then he studies the front, with its f-holes, and the scroll, the sides, and the ornamental purfling along the edges. Every great master had certain peculiarities of design, and they are as obvious to the eye of the expert as the characteristics of a man's signature are to a bank teller; the cutting of the scroll and f-holes is particularly revealing.

Even aberrations sometimes provide a key; Stradivari's eyes grew weak

in his last years, with the result that the curves and f-holes of the violins he then made lack the dynamic sweep of his earlier ones. Some violins display the touch of more than one maker. A number of the last instruments made by Nicolò Amati show the hand of Stradivari who started out as an apprentice in Amati's workshop. In his great book, *Antonio Stradivari, His Life and Work*, the late Alfred E. Hill, a violin dealer in London and one of the great violin authorities of all time, mentioned an authentic Stradivari with a label reading, *Alumnus Nicholai Amati, Faciebat Anno 1666*. This would mean that Stradivari was then in his early twenties,

An 18th century instrument-maker's workshop, an engraving from Diderot's *Encyclopédie*

71

which is entirely plausible, for the great violin-makers started early and finished late. Andrea Guarneri made one of his outstanding violins when he was fifteen.

In some of Stradivari's last violins, the co-operation of his sons Francesco and Omobono is evident. Experts love to argue about certain violins which were made around 1720, when Andrea Guarneri's son Giuseppe Guarneri had his younger cousin Giuseppe Guarneri del Gesù (the genius-member among the Guarneri dynasty), Carlo Bergonzi and Lorenzo Guadagnini all working side by side in his workshop. Bergonzi and Guadagnini became famous violin-makers, and there is endless speculation among the experts about who made what on a certain instrument of that period.

Some years ago my friend Emil Herrmann — another all-time great violin authority who sold me my Amati and later my Stradivari — identified an alleged Giuseppe Guarneri del Gesù as the work of Giuseppe Guarneri. On the other hand, del Gesù used his own labels only after 1726, and some of his independently made earlier violins bear his cousin's label. In Herrmann's vault is a violin labelled *Nicolò Amati, 1646*, which is known to have actually been made by his less famous son, Girolamo. It was the favourite violin of Benito Mussolini who always thought he had a genuine Nicolò Amati. Obviously, no one dared disillusion him.

The collection started by Rudolph Wurlitzer, of the musical instrument company, used to contain a violin with belly and label by Stradivari, and back, ribs and scroll by Alessandro Gagliano (who was not in the same class). Hill once bought a fine Stradivari of 1710 with a scroll by del Gesù (who was definitely in the class of Stradivari), and soon thereafter came into possession of a fine del Gesù with a Stradivari scroll. Perhaps an anonymous violin-maker had both violins in his shop for repair and accidentally changed the scrolls.

Dealers have occasion sometimes to match up violins with their proper labels. Labels often tell a story. On the labels of G. B. Guadagnini, for instance, one can follow the maker's wanderings from Piacenza to Milan to Cremona to Parma to Turin. A meticulous man, Guadagnini always changed his labels with his place of residence. Stradivari changed the typeface of his labels but never their wording, although after 1729 he changed the Latin *u* in *Stradiuarius* to the Roman *v*.

The life of a violin sleuth is full of excitement and there are plenty of clues lying around, but this is no game for amateurs. Almost anyone with a reasonable amount of discernment and taste can in due time become a connoisseur of old furniture, paintings or china by study, but no one can become an expert on violins simply by reading books about them. An expert on violins must have not only an academic knowledge of the instrument but also an eye and an instinct for them. He must also have a sound sense of economics.

Stradivari's violins, for instance, vary considerably in value. Although his genius is evident in everything he did, there is a difference in quality and price between the instruments of his early, Amati period (they are called Amatisé) and those of his 'golden' period. Of the approximately five hundred and forty violins (and eleven violas and fifty cellos) that have survived, there are a dozen that are regarded as supreme. At the head of the list is the *Messiah*, which was made in 1716, when Stradivari was seventy-two, and which is now at the Ashmolean Museum at Oxford, a gift of the Hills who stated in their will that it must never leave England. Among the distinguished Stradivari violins are the *Alard* of 1715; the *Cessole* of 1716; the *Parke-Kreisler* of 1711. Some are owned by great artists: Heifetz plays the magnificent *Dolphin* of 1714 (if he gets bored with it, he can always play his magnificent Guarneri del Gesù, of 1742); and Menuhin owns the *Soil* of 1714. Herrmann once sold the *King Maximilian* of 1709, 'a notable example, unique in being in unblemished fresh condition', according to the late Ernest N. Doring, to Frau R. Loeb, the wife of a Berlin banker for 300,000 marks, which was then $71,000 and is the highest price he ever got for a violin. Today, prices of Stradivari violins range from around $15,000 to around $60,000. The *Duport* and *Batta* celli were sold for over $80,000.

The violin market, though not as topsy-turvy as the art market, has had violent ups and downs. There have been times when a fine violin offered at a ridiculously low price has gone begging, and at other times a fine violin could not be had at any price within reason. Henry Ford, who never played the violin but was a zealous collector — because he considered the violin an achievement of perfect engineering and a triumph of the human mind — once offered $150,000 for the *Alard* Stradivari of 1715, 'an outstanding specimen', named after a great French violinist, Delphin Alard. (How nice to become immortal through the mere acquisition of a great violin!) Ford didn't get it.

Some men who want to select a violin behave as if they were going to choose a bride. They bring along their friends and relatives, ask them to listen to the violin, and afterwards want their opinion. As though anyone could pick somebody else's wife!

Violinists disagree about fiddles as men disagree about women. One man likes the sweet, nightingale sound of an Amati, another the robust, clarinet tones of a Guarneri del Gesù, while a third prefer the rich, oboe timbre of a Stradivari. Amateurs and chamber-music players prefer beauty of tone

73

Two of Antonio Stradivari's violins —
the 'Messiah', his greatest masterpiece,
made in 1716, and *Il Cremonese*,
now preserved in his native town

rather than powerful sound. Orchestra musicians want an instrument with a strong tone that will enable them to make themselves heard over the din raised by their fellow-players. Soloists and great concert virtuosos need instruments that respond easily, combine beauty of tone with carrying power, sing out with an almost human voice and can be heard in large halls even when then the softest *pianissimo* is played on them.

Even the world's great violinists don't always sound as brilliant when they are trying out violins as they do on the concert stage. Few players are able to make all violins sound right, even the good ones. For a while the friends and relatives (most of whom happen to be fiddlers, otherwise they wouldn't have come along) listen to the prospective buyer trying out the prospective bride — but after a while they forget that they came here merely to listen. They get overwhelmed by the sight of all the beautiful fiddles lying around though they know they may never own one. The desire to play a great violin always exceeds one's ability to pay for it.

For a true-blood fidder it is hard to resist grabbing a bow when a Stradivari lies within reach. In no time he holds a fiddle under the chin and wanders around playing it. The result is acoustic pandemonium, with two, three or more people playing fine violins. The air becomes filled with discordant opinions and dissonant sounds.

I've spent many happy afternoons in Herrmann's bomb-proof study, trying out one violin after the other, while other people were milling around. We all tried frantically to outplay one another. After a while we were all so mixed up that no one knew any longer who was playing what violin. I know today that one must never try out a fiddle for more than fifteen minutes at a time. After a quarter of an hour even musicians with an expert ear loose their ability to discriminate.

As a rule the last violin always sounds the best; alas, it is nearly always the most expensive one. Many people make the mistake of letting someone else play the violin they have selected 'to hear how it sounds'. Wrong. It will never sound under somebody's hands as it sounds when you play it yourself. The same violin played by three great players sounds utterly different. In the last analysis it is not the violin that creates the sound, but the man who plays it. A bad violinist will sound bad even when he plays the finest Stradivari. A great violinist will sound good even on a mediocre violin but he may be helped by a great instrument.

It took me a long time to learn that a man must select an instrument which he himself likes and loves, not one that his friends and relatives think is right for him. Often I tried out a fiddle in the study where it sounded beautifully, but when I took it home and tried it out there, the magic seemed to have gone out of it.

'A man testing violins gives himself away without knowing it', Herrmann once told me. 'He takes one in his hands, puts it down, and tries another, and so on. But soon it becomes apparent that there is a violin which he instinctively likes best — and he may not even be aware of it. In nine cases out of the ten, that's the violin for him. Another problem is the customer who buys an expensive instrument and after a while begins to think he's made a mistake. He paid forty thousand dollars perhaps, and suddenly, for no particular reason, he feels that the violin "doesn't sound the way it should". The only way is to ask him to bring it back to the office and try it out in comparison with other masterpieces, and just as suddenly it sounds all right to him again.'

Unfortunately, good violinists cannot always afford the instruments they ought to have. In earlier days, the ratio between a concert artist's earnings and the price of a fine violin was more in the artist's favour. When Nicolò Paganini gave a series of fourteen concerts in London's Covent Garden in the summer of 1832, he collected eight thousand pounds in ten weeks — almost three thousand dollars a concert. Yet Paganini paid the equivalent of only a thousand dollars for his famous viola, made by Stradivari in 1731 — the viola that led Hector Berlioz to compose *Harold in Italy*.

Describing how this came about, Berlioz later wrote, 'Paganini came to me and said, "I have a marvellous viola, an admirable Stradivari, and I wish to play it in public, but I have no music *ad hoc*. Will you write a solo piece for me? You are the only one I can trust for such a work."' To be sure, after Berlioz had completed *Harold in Italy*, Paganini was displeased with it because 'it contained too many rests for the viola'. The marvellous 'Paganini' viola of 1731 is worth over sixty thousand dollars now.

Musicians often bitterly object to collectors who buy up fine violins and put them away where they do no one any good. But in all fairness it must be said that the world is indebted to collectors for the preservation of many fine instruments that would otherwise have deteriorated. If all the great violins had always been in the hands of professionals, there would be fewer of them today. Some great artists — notably Heifetz, Stern, Milstein, Menuhin and Francescatti — keep theirs in perfect condition. They always clean them carefully and 'put them to bed' after using them. But other musicians take shocking care of their instruments — exposing them unnecessarily to the rigours of climate, getting them scratched and neglecting to remove rosin dust, which eats into the varnish.

It is true that a violin becomes less responsive in its vibrations and tonal qualities if it is seldom played over a period of ten or twenty years, but after a few months of expert playing it sounds as good as before, and sometimes better. No one should feel that it is his privilege to mistreat a violin simply because he paid for it. The owner of a fine violin is merely the trustee for future generations. His ownership is temporary. He has the duty of preserving his instrument for posterity.

There are sometimes strong bonds between a reader and a book, or between a collector and a certain painting, but they cannot be compared with the close relationship that exists between a fiddler and his fiddle. I've long held the theory that musicians reflect temperamentally the type of instruments they play. Bass-fiddlers are usually placid, oboists are nervous, bass-tuba players are relaxed and fond of beer, cellists serious and moody, and violinists sensitive and intense. We fiddlers feel that a fine fiddle reacts to the subtle wishes of our minds as to the subtle pressure of our fingers. String players generally agree that their instruments have a soul. The viola has one, and so has the cello, and even the double bass, clumsiest member of the family which may surprise you with the sudden vehemence of its emotions. (Fat, old men resembling a double bass do strange things once in a while). But on the whole they are reliable and it's good to have these deep-voiced, sturdy fellows around the orchestra among its more nervous, temperamental, shrill-voiced members. (Compared to a violin, the piano is at best a beautifully conceived and ingeniously constructed machine, that sounds almost human under the hands of a great player. But it always remains a machine. Even its greatest masters cannot create the soul of the piano because it has none. A piano will never sing out like a human voice, or like a violin.)

At long last the Stradivari is yours but it will take you a long time to get used to it – and for the fiddle to get used to you. There is no over-all method for winning the heart (and 'the soul') of a violin. Some have to be charmed and others must be caressed. Some prefer a long courtship and others become quickly attached to you. My Stradivari was a real lady; she wanted to be courted properly and for a long time pretended to be untouched by my affections. She disliked pressure of any kind, especially pressure of the bow. As I learned to treat her gently, she began to care for me. I know now that I must never force her to do anything she dislikes doing. Play her gently, and she will sing out beautifully; use force and she will resent it. Singers will understand what I mean; they, too, have learned not to strain their voices.

A violin is as unpredictable as a capricious woman. When it isn't in the right mood, you cannot force it to make beautiful music. It will sound dull and bored. Put it back and wait for a happier mood. My violin gets irritated by extreme heat and cold, it doesn't like cigarette smoke, and hates bright lights. It reacts to sudden changes of climate and long trips, it revolts against rosin dust and bad strings. It makes demands upon you which you'd better give in to. No use fighting back fiddles and women. Life has become too short.

Emil Herrmann once showed me a letter that Yehudi Menuhin wrote him in 1939, after buying from Herrmann his Guarneri del Gesù of 1742.

> You can well imagine how happy I am with the Guarneri. It is useless to describe to *you* the glory of this instrument. It is fitting that I should find another lifelong friend through you . . . I know that now, with two of your adopted children in my possession, an even greater attachment will ensue between us.

The first adopted child Menuhin had received from Herrmann was the *Prince Khevenhüller* Stradivari of 1733, whose label bears the notation, in Stradivari's own hand, *d'anni 90* (at the age of ninety). The old master took a justifiable pride in producing such a masterpiece at that age. Herrmann had lent the violin to Menuhin, who was then thirteen years old, for a concert at Carnegie Hall in 1929. In the audience was the late Henry Goldman, the blind New Yorker banker and art collector. Goldman was enchanted by Menuhin and the violin, and thought it would be a fine thing to bring them together permanently. He asked Adolf Busch and Fritz Kreisler about Herrmann. When he was assured that the dealer's judgement could be trusted, he bought the *Prince Khevenhüller* for Menuhin. In 1952 Menuhin bought another great fiddle from Herrmann, the *Soil* Stradivari of 1714, named after M. Soil, a nineteenth-century Belgian collector.

Jascha Heifetz once wrote to Herrmann who had picked out the magnificent *Ferdinand David* Guarneri del Gesù, of 1742 – David was a concertmaster of the Leipzig *Gewandhaus* Orchestra who once owned it – 'I have wanted to tell you how much joy my "David" Guarneri is giving me. It is a most wonderful violin under any kind of playing conditions and I am continuously delighted with it . . . I feel warmly toward you for bringing us together.'

Lesser violinists feel just as warmly about their violins. Buying a violin isn't a cold financial transaction like buying shares or a big diamond. There is excitement prior to the first meeting. The first happiness is usually followed by nagging doubts. There are moments of uncertainty, of hope, of dejection. Collectors in the early, innocent stage know the sweet doubts of unsureness; later they become hard-boiled and collect for the sake of out-collecting their competitors; what began as an exciting vocation becomes mere routine.

Trying out fine violins is an elusive pastime, especially when done with the purpose of buying one. When for the first time I stepped through the massive steel doors that lead from Emil Herrmann's bomb-proof study in

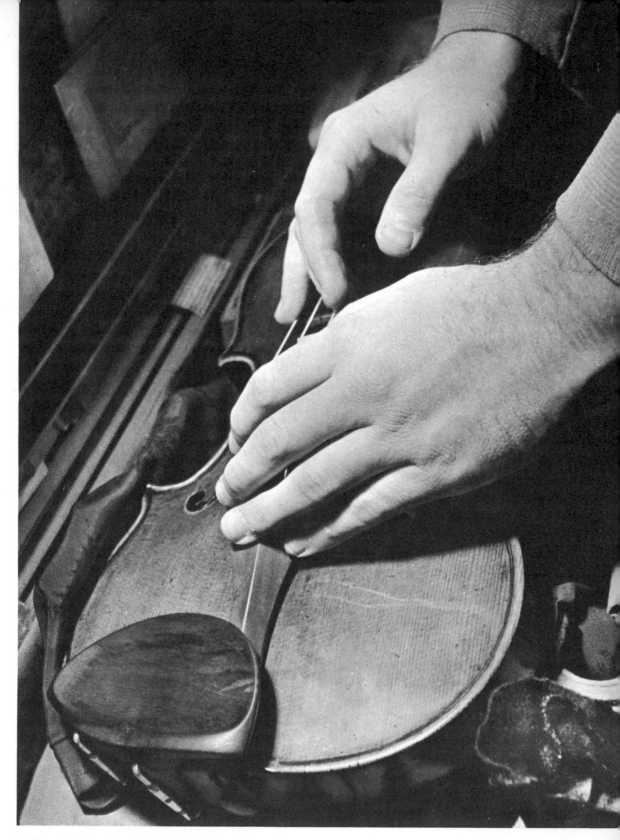

The sensitive hands of Yehudi Menuhin 'putting
to bed' his *Prince Khevenhüller* Stradivari of 1733

the basement of his Connecticut house, *Fiddledale*, into the vault where he keeps his precious violins, my heart beat faster. Other people may feel that way when they step into a limousine, or walk into Cartier's.

The showcases of Cartier may contain glittering treasures but many others of greater value rest in the company's safe. There were often a few lesser Gaglianos or Guadagninis lying on the table of Herrmann's study which someone had just tried out, but the great treasures were in the vault. Resting on their sides, in small, velvet-lined compartments were the wonderful violins. To the left of the entrance were rows of violins by Stradivari, the Guarneris, the Amatis, Bergonzi, Montagnana and Ruggieri. To the right were the less important violins, which were sometimes crowded out by an overflow of Guadagninis, Gaglianos and Gofrillers from the left.

The hundred and eighty compartments built into the vault were not enough to house all the stock, and dozens of minor fiddles were stored on shelves above and below the big show. The climate had to be carefully controlled: during the summer an electric dehumidifier was put to work; in the winter a trayful of water stood in the vault to moisten the air. Somewhere in the vault there was a register of the most important violins known to exist. It listed the exact measurements of each; provided a set of photographs showing its front, back, sides, scroll and f-holes; described its wood and colour of the varnish; gave its history, and a record of its ownership at the present.

Something seems to happen to people the moment they pick up a great violin. Some are so afraid of dropping it that they can hardly put a bow on it. Some are awed by the thought that the small piece of varnished wood in their hands is worth more than a town-house in Manhattan or a villa on the Riviera. Some get an acquisitive gleam in their eyes of the sort familiar to croupiers at Monte Carlo, to bookies and to jewellery salesmen. In 1938, a man who got that gleam, took a violin at random from Herrmann's vault, and walked out with it under his jacket. There were plenty of Stradivaris and Guarneris del Gesù in the vault that day, but the untutored thief happened to grab the least expensive violin of the lot, a Giuseppe Gagliano, worth fifteen hundred dollars. It was recovered when the thief sold it to an instrument dealer for sixty-five dollars and the police discovered it while making a check of music shops.

A few years later, a fine G. B. Guadagnini viola was stolen on New York's Sixty-seventh Street from a locked car owned by a member of the New Music String Quartet who had borrowed the instrument from Herrmann. It has not been found. The whereabouts of every really important instrument is well known in the violin dealer's fraternity, and it can never be sold for anything like its real value but could only be passed off as a cheap factory fiddle. Violin dealers say it is harder to get rid of a fiddle than of a stolen baby.

But violins strongly appeal to fanatics who don't want to sell it, and there have always been mysterious thefts. One night in 1908 the *Hercules* Stradivari of 1732, which then belonged to the great Belgian violinist Eugène Ysaye, was stolen from the artist's dressing room at the Maryinski Theatre in St Petersburg, while he was on stage playing his Guarneri del Gesù. It has never been seen since. Perhaps it is hidden in the backroom of a fanatic who guards it with that gleam in his eyes.

In 1919, Bronislaw Huberman's celebrated *Gibson* Stradivari of 1713 was taken from his hotel room in Vienna. Within a few hours it was offered to a dealer who notified a detective agency and the thief was caught. Then in February, 1936, the same violin disappeared from Huberman's dressing room in Carnegie Hall; no trace of it has ever been found. Huberman collected thirty thousand dollars insurance on it but that was small consolation. The money would not bring back his beloved Stradivari. Experts believe that Huberman's Strad is hidden somewhere in America, watched over by someone who wouldn't sell it for a million dollars.

Once in a while the newspapers come out with a story about the discovery of an allegedly old and priceless violin. When that happens, dealers are deluged with telegrams, long-distance calls and letters from people who are convinced that they, too, have a master instrument. An old violin has been cluttering up the attic for a long time. Upon reading of somebody's lucky find, they open the case and inside is a violin bearing the label, *Antonius Stradivarius Cremonensis Faciebat Anno 17––*. They recall that their parents once said Grandpa had brought a violin with him from Europe in the eighteen-fifties, and they are convinced they own a fifty-thousand-dollar instrument. (Fifty thousand dollars – that's what it said in the paper!) The unfortunate truth is that their violin is probably worth between twenty and thirty dollars. Almost certainly it is a cheap 'factory fiddle'. In the past hundred years tens of thousands of them were made, in assembly-line style, in Markneukirchen, Saxony; Graslitz, Bohemia; Mittenwald, Bavaria; and Mirecourt, France. Almost the entire population in these communities works at turning out inexpensive musical instruments. The men cut bellies and backpieces and make the sides, scrolls, and f-holes. The youngsters apply the varnish and chisel bridges and pegs. The women make fingerboards and cases, and print beautiful labels bearing the name of Antonius Stradivarius. I once spent several days in Mittenwald, and it was a macabre experience. One mechanical-minded enterprise had

Ingres del.
anno 1819.

designed a machine that cut several bellies at one time, the way they cut dresses in New York's garment centre. Most of the people got little money for their labour; the profits, I discovered, went to the exporters. It is no coincidence that before the Second World War Markneukirchen had more millionaires than any other German town of comparable size.

The chances of finding a genuine old fiddle in an attic are infinitesimal. It is true that many precious violins disappeared during the Napoleonic invasions of Italy, Spain, and Austria, during the Franco-Prussian War, and during the two World Wars. But the experts are convinced that they were destroyed. The history of almost all the remaining great violins can be traced back for forty or fifty years; in the case of some instruments, the entire history is known, from the time it left the workshop of its maker.

The *Salabue* Stradivari of 1727, for instance, was bought from the Stradivari estate by Count Cozio di Salabue, who sold it in 1817 to Paganini for a hundred louis d'or, approximately four hundred dollars. Subsequent owners were Paganini's son, Baron Achille Paganini; the dealer J. B. Vuillaume; the Conte de Vireille; the dealers Gand and Bernardel; the Italian collector Ernest Nicolini, the husband of Adelina Patti; the dealers Hart & Son; the British collector Frederick Smith; the dealers W. E. Hill & Sons in London; the American collector Felix Kahn; Emil Herrmann; and Mrs Anna E. Clark, of New York, who bought it from Herrmann together with three other Stradivari instruments once owned by Paganini – the *Desaint* violin of 1680, the *Paganini* viola of 1731, and the *Ladenburg* cello of 1736. (During its tortuous journey through the centuries the price of the *Salabue* went up a hundredfold – to forty thousand dollars.)

Mrs Clark later turned over the four Paganini instruments to a professional quartet which named itself, not surprisingly, the Paganini Quartet. To assemble a quartet of four Stradivari instruments is an impressive achievement but to bring together the four Stradivari instruments that were once owned by Paganini, the most celebrated violin virtuoso of all time, is an achievement that borders upon a miracle. Theoretically, only eleven Stradivari quartets could be formed because only eleven Stradivari violas exist.

It is possible that a few great Strads are still hidden somewhere – but not in the attic of your house. Perhaps they are in the possession of wealthy, aristocratic families in Italy, France or England, who know all about their treasure but say nothing about it. During the Russian Revolution some fine fiddles must have found their way from glass cases in noblemen's houses to the vaults of the State. In the Soviet Union the State owns many important instruments and lends them out to 'reliable' artists.

83

Nicolo Paganini, the greatest virtuoso of the violin, who had a quartet of Stradivari instruments. From a drawing by Ingres

Isaac Stern, who plays violins by both Guarneri and Stradivari

The finest Stradivari in Russia is thought to be the one played by David Oistrakh, the Kremlin's favorite violinist.

Paradoxically, there are now very few old violins in Italy, where almost all of them came from originally. This is attributed chiefly to the activities of several Italian dealers during the past century, the most assiduous of whom was Luigi Tarisio, who between 1800 and 1845 bought up fine Italian violins by the score and sold them in France. Today the Italians are unhappy about the loss of their national treasures. On my first visit to the town of Cremona, years ago, I was shocked to discover that the birthplace of the world's greatest violins owned not one of them.

The great violins have glamorous names which have helped to preserve their identities. To an expert or connoisseur the name immediately conjures the sound and beauty of a certain instrument. The names of the famous violins are a register of man's eternal search for beauty and his constant addiction to vanity. Some were named for former owners of prominence (several Strads are named *Paganini*, *Auer*, *Récamier*, *Morgan*, *Joachim*, and *King Maximilian*). Other names refer to the violin's physical or tonal characteristics (*Titian*, *Apollo*, *Red Diamond* and *Nightingale*), or to a memorable place or event connected with the instrument, *Irish*, *Siberian*, *Rochester*, *Berliner* and *Swan Song*, which is the name of Stradivari's last known violin, made in 1737.

Sometimes the names have no significance at all. There is a violin called *Lord Nelson*, for instance, simply because it was found in an officer's stateroom on Lord Nelson's flagship after the Battle of Trafalgar. Lord Nelson never played a violin and never owned one.

The most famous Stradivari, the *Messiah* of 1716, owes its name to Tarisio, the super-dealer 'who spoke in enraptured tones of a Stradivari, which he claimed to possess but would show to no one because it was so beautiful'. Tarisio's super-violin, much talked about and never seen, like the Messiah, became famous under this name.

Very little is known about Antonio Stradivari. We don't know exactly when or where he was born. He was married, had two sons and lived in Cremona. The date of his birth was later deduced from information supplied by Stradivari himself on his labels inserted in several instruments during the last ten years of his long life. The first official document showing Stradivari as a resident of the City of Cremona was the record of his marriage with Francesca Feraboschi in 1667. There is no documentary evidence that Antonio Stradivari lived at Cremona or elsewhere before that year. There is very little evidence of anything. In the Hill book on the Guarneri family, there is the sentence,

. . . statements were light-heartedly made at the beginning of the last century, accepted and repeated as time sped on, without any attempt being made to verify their correctness either by the light of experience or renewed research.

That goes for almost everything concerning all the great violin-makers. The identification of Stradivari's date of birth by means of his labels has caused considerable confusion. The most famous case is the notation of the *Wiener* Strad (named after a Mr Wiener from Prague who resided in England after 1850 and was well known in musical circles) where it says after *Faciebat Anno 1732*, in Stradivari's shaky handwriting *de Anni 89*. For over a century and a half the figure 9 was read to be a 2, which confounded the experts. The mystery was cleared up only by the Hills, who discovered that what looked like a 2 was really intended to be a 9. The old man's eyes were weak; he was better at making great fiddles than writing figures, and he didn't care much about spelling. On the Wiener Strad he spelled it *de Anni 89*, and four years later on a violin made in 1737, he wrote *d'Anni 93*. 'Read it *de Anni 89*, and it tallies with all other inscriptions, as the master, though eighty-eight years of age in 1732, obviously celebrated his eighty-ninth birthday during the year, and this instrument was made after that event,' writes Hill.

Confusion was worse confounded by the diaries of the afore-mentioned Count Ignazio Alessandro Cozio di Salabue, a Piedmontese nobleman from Casalmonferato, who bought over a hundred Stradivari instruments and many memorabilia from Antonio Stradivari's youngest son. Paolo Stradivari, a textile merchant, took absolutely no interest in his father's work. My friend Renzo Bacchetta, one of Italy's leading experts, thinks that the good Count was not only an ardent collector but also a shrewd businessman. Cozio admits in his diaries that he altered the year on the labels of several Strads from 1727 to 1737 and from 1730 to 1736.

No one knows who made the first violin, but it remains one of the great miracles of human achievement. The violin didn't pass through various stages of evolution but emerged from its very beginning in its final, perfect form, combining the quintessence of physical laws with incredible beauty of architectural form. It is one of the rare things in this world that cannot be improved — a model of perfection. 'It is so beautifully balanced that it would be impossible to change the smallest detail in its design without disturbing its peerless symmetry', writes Franz Farga. Whoever designed the first violin was clearly a genius, and it was to be expected that legends would embroider the few facts that we know. It has been written that Leonardo da Vinci, who is credited with so many 'firsts', made the first design of the violin and cut the f-holes 'to honour his patron' Francis I, King of France'. A nice story but completely unauthenticated.

But there can be no doubt that the *genius loci* was very strong in Cremona, the two-thousand-year-old town in Lombardy, where most of the great violins were made. The Cremonese School began with Andrea Amati in the sixteenth century, reached its peak after 1700, when several Amatis, Guarneris and Stradivaris were working there, continued with the prominent disciples of the great masters, Carlo Bergonzi and Francesco Ruggieri, and ended in 1883 with the death of Enrico Cerutti, the last master in the Stradivari tradition. The Cremonese School gave the world its finest stringed instruments and some exciting legends.

Most of them concern Stradivari himself, who never gave away his secrets. He was perhaps the only human being able to understand com-

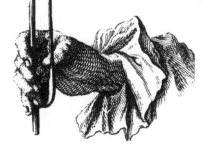

The correct way to hold the violin bow,
from Leopold Mozart's *Violinschule*

pletely the miracle of sound that he created in his instruments. He never made a bad instrument; while Guarneri del Gesù, who comes closest to Stradivari's genius, has left some violins that are far from being perfect. Unfortunately Stradivari never bothered to write down formulae or make blueprints. That is how all the talk about his 'secrets' started. Obviously Stradivari knew all about the vibrations of various types of wood, or the elasticity of the varnish, and he saw no necessity for putting down what to him was no secret. Perhaps there weren't such friendly feelings of comradeship in Cremona's Contrada dei Coltellai as has been claimed by some romanticists; perhaps the members of the violin-makers' guild did not share their discoveries.

The exact definition of Stradivari's varnish has defied all modern methods of analysis. Experts know that varnish is a mixture of oils, gums and alcohol, but no one knows how much of each ingredient Stradivari used, whether the mixture was cold or boiled, and whether he used, as has been claimed, dragon's blood — a dark-red, gummy substance derived from the fruit of a Malayan palm tree that Marco Polo brought to Venice. Stradivari's varnish remains an unsolved mystery.

The English novelist Charles Reade, a fellow enthusiast on the subject of old violins, writes about the 'lost art' of varnishing:

> The way to discover a lost art, once practised with variations by a hundred people, is to examine very closely the most brilliant specimen . . . the most extravagant specimen — if you can find one. I found in the chippiest varnish of Stradivarius, his dark-red varnish, the key to all the varnish of Cremona, red or yellow . . . Look at this dark-red varnish, and use your eyes. What do you see? A red varnish which chips readily off what people call *the bare wood*. But it is *not bare wood*. Bare wood turns a dirty brown with age; this is a rich and lovely yellow. By its colour, and by its glassy gloss, and by disbelieving what "echoes of echoes" say, and trusting only to our own eyes, we may see at a glance that it is not bare wood, but highly varnished wood. This varnish is evidently oil, and contains a gum. Allowing for the tendency for oil to run into the wood, I should say *four coats of varnish*; and they call this bare wood . . .

I made a pilgrimage to Cremona a few years ago hoping to find something of the *genius loci* that inspired the greatest violin-makers of all times. I should have been warned by a note in an Italian guidebook that Cremona was known 'chiefly for its gastronomic specialties, such as butter and cheeses, mustards and sausages, marmalade and *torrone*', which is an Italian sweetmeat made of nuts, fruits, honey and sugar. I soon discovered that the Cremonese were much more interested in the production of cheese than in the memory of Stradivari.

'If Stradivari had invented a cheese, the Cremonese might have built him a monument,' Renzo Bacchetta said to me bitterly. 'But he only made the finest violins on earth.' Rather reluctantly the city honoured Stradivari in 1937, the bi-centenary of his death, by an exhibition and by founding a school for violin-making.

The house in Piazza Roma where Stradivari lived and had his workshop was torn down in 1928 to make space for a large office building in neo-classic style with a pretentious marble façade. Where Stradivari's workshop is believed to have stood, there is now a large café with advertisements of a vermouth firm and posters of the Cremona Football Club. After a while one discovers above one window a small marble panel with the words,

Qui sorgerà la casa dove Antonio Stradivari recando a mirabile perfezione il liuto levava alla sua Cremona nome imperituro di artifice somo.

Standing there I had a brief, fleeting vision of the simple two-storey building I'd seen on some photographs. Old Cremonese remember a tailor shop there and next to it a pool-room with billiard tables. The house had a flat roof where Stradivari may have hung his newly varnished instruments in the sunshine to dry. Perhaps his workshop had a beautiful smell of aged wood, varnish and rosin. Perhaps . . .

There exist several paintings of Stradivari but they are works of pure fantasy. No one knows what he looked like and no description has been left to us. On my first visit to Cremona I met Stradivari's great-great-great-great grandson, who then lived in the town (and died only two years ago). He was Maestro Mario Stradivari, a well-known *avvocato*, famous as a criminal lawyer, a wonderful character, full of brio, cheerfulness and that zest for life that makes Italians such amusing talking and drinking companions. The *avvocato* didn't like to discuss Antonio Stradivari and he strongly discouraged my romantic notion that he looked a little like his celebrated ancestor. The *avvocato* was a tall and colourful man with a furrowed Renaissance face, a high-domed forehead, a large, aquiline nose, a curved mouth. I still like to think that that's the way Antonio looked.

The *avvocato* didn't play the violin. In fact, he'd never owned one. He was a good piano player though, and well known as a composer of operettas. His father, Libero Stradivari, had played the flute and was a great friend of Puccini who often came to Cremona for a few days. They would drink and sing all night long, waking up everybody, raising hell and getting in trouble with the police.

'There was one night when they wandered through the streets singing the "Christmas" song from the second act of *Bohème*,' Mario Stradivari remembered. 'At the Piazza del Commune they were stopped by a policeman who told them to be quiet. Papa pointed at Puccini and asked the policeman what had become of Cremona where a man couldn't even sing his own melodies any more. The policeman who knew all about opera, as does every policeman in Italy, got angry and said, "What do you mean, his melodies? That was from *Bohème*. Next thing, you'll tell me that he is Maestro Puccini." At that Puccini took off his hat, saluted elegantly with his cane and said, "I *am* Puccini". The policeman got so angry — he said that was an impertinent impersonation — that he arrested them and took them to jail where they spent the night, singing opera and keeping everybody awake.'

The family grave of the Stradivaris had been in the Rosario Chapel of the Church of San Domenico. After his death on December 18, 1737 — *that* date is certain — Antonio Stradivari was buried the following day. Later most of his children were buried near him. But in 1868 the church was demolished; some people in Cremona say that the land was needed for a public playground, and others remember that a wrecker from Milan paid some politicians forty-two thousand lire for the privilege of tearing down the church and selling the materials at a good profit. In the course of the demolition the grave of Stradivari was opened and the bones were taken out. No one knows what happened next. Perhaps they were buried in a common grave at the local cemetery. Or perhaps the tired workmen walked down to the nearby bank of the Po and threw the bones into the river . . . Does it really matter? We don't know where Mozart was buried, but he and Stradivari will be gratefully and reverently remembered as long as there are people on earth.

The former site of the church was later turned into the small park near Piazza Roma, across the street from where Stradivari, Guarneri del Gesù and the rest of them lived. Between flower-beds, on the former site of the grave, the old tombstone has been placed into the ground. It says, *Sepolcro di Antoni Stradivari e. Svoi Eredi, Anno 1729* (the year when Stradivari bought the grave), and next to the letters is the small cross with the initials A.S., the same circled monogram that is on the label of my violin.

At the nearby Palazzo Communale they now proudly exhibit a Stradivari under glass. Made in 1715, it was later played by the great violinist, Joseph Joachim, and is known as one of the *Joachim* Strads. The City of Cremona purchased it from Hill in London, and renamed it *Il Cremonese.*

And so, at long last, one of Antonio Stradivari's masterpieces has come back to the place where it was created.

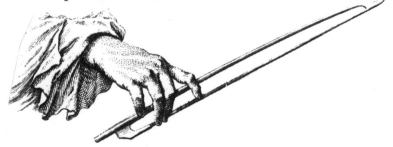

Epicureanism

BY AND LARGE, Anglo-Saxons regard gastronomy with suspicion. To descendants of the Puritans it is all but inconceivable that a man should spend hours talking about the great meal he plans to have, enjoying the meal, and then talking about how wonderful it was. There is still hunger in many parts of the world, and the mere notion of a great meal gives many people a feeling of actual guilt.

By and large, the French are different. It is no longer true, as it once was, that large numbers of Frenchmen live to eat. The younger people have learned that to eat well is to eat wisely, and the sensible American eating habits, with their emphasis on fruit-juice, salads, and grilled meat, have been widely accepted, along with some practices that may not enhance gastronomy, such as deep-freezing. But if most Frenchmen eat less than their fathers and grandfathers did, every Frenchman will nevertheless go on a culinary spree once in a while, and have that great meal – and he will talk about it for weeks afterwards, too. In France, food and wine are still major topics of conversation, and gastronomy is still seriously respected.

'Gastronomy,' writes Jean Anthelme Brillat-Savarin in *The Physiology of Taste*, the classic work on the subject, 'is the intelligent knowledge of whatever concerns man's nourishment.' The emphasis is on 'intelligent'. Gastronomy is a matter of education, experience, taste, style. The French have always made the distinction between the man who feeds himself (*il se nourrit*) and the one who knows how to eat well (*il sait bien manger*).

Gastronomy is the inner sanctum in the temple dedicated to the art of good living. Many arrive at the entrance of the temple but few are admitted to the inner sanctum. In matters of love and eating, every man must decide what he likes best, and to proclaim the superiority of certain dishes would be as absurd as to state the supremacy of brunettes. But the standards of

Fernand Point of *La Pyramide*, the greatest practitioner of *la grande cuisine* in our time

This illustration from Antonin Carême's gastronomic treatise *Le Maître d'Hôtel Français* bears witness to his study of Classical architecture

gastronomy have been set down objectively, with almost scientific precision. There can be disagreement about what is good eating but none about gastronomy.

According to Brillat-Savarin, gastronomy is closely bound up not only with cookery ('because of the art of adapting dishes and making them pleasant to the taste') but with natural history, physics, and chemistry ('by its classification of alimentary substances', and 'its investigation into their composition and properties'); with business and political economy ('because of the sources of revenue that gastronomy creates and the means of exchange that it establishes between nations'); and even with politics (because 'meals have become means of governing, and the fate of whole peoples is decided at a banquet').

The latter definition hardly applies to contemporary political banquets. Our statesmen, beset by anxieties and ulcers, prefer an austere diet of steak and salad to the opulence of the past, which is a regrettable development. It was a different story at the time of the Congress of Vienna when Charles Maurice de Talleyrand, Minister of Foreign Affairs to Louis XVIII, and one of the greatest French practitioners of political gastronomy, told the King prior to his departure for Vienna, 'Sire, I have more need of casseroles than of written instructions.' The King, a true gastronome, nodded understandingly.

With the help of Antonin Carême, his celebrated chef, Talleyrand often

92

achieved at the dinner-table what he failed to accomplish at the conference table. Anatole France quotes Carême as having said, 'The fine arts are five in number, to wit: painting, sculpture, poetry, music, architecture – whose main branch is confectionery.' And, indeed, Carême, who had studied classical architecture, made regular blue-prints for his enormous galantines, *pièces montées* and fruit-baskets.

He was by no means alone in his exalted opinion of his *métier*. In France, cooking has always been considered an art. Carême, who called cooking 'the most indispensable art', wrote with sarcasm about an anonymous 'gastronomic painter' (presumably the man knew less about gastronomy than about painting, or Carême would have called him a 'painting gastronome'), who complained that art critics used culinary terms in discussing painting – *cuisine, couleurs, pâté savoureuse, jus, tons crus,* even *rissolés.* To Carême, this complaint merely proved that the man was indeed no gastronome but just a painter. Why shouldn't a French art-critic recognize the close affinity between the art of cooking and the *beaux-arts*? Brillat-Savarin, who worked thirty years on his masterpiece, calls cooking 'the oldest of arts [and] the one that has done most to advance civilization, for the needs of the kitchen were what first taught us to use fire, and it is by fire that man has tamed Nature herself.'

The Greeks had more than a word for the art of cooking. Homer, in the ninth book of the Iliad, describes how Achilles entertained Patroclus, Ulysses, Ajax, and Phoenix in his tent with what Brillat-Savarin describes as 'a heroic feast of bread, wine and roast meat'. The Greeks were the first Europeans to have a literature of gastronomy (Plato, Athenaeus and others made references to cooking), and most French students of the subject have recognized the historical significance of Greek cooking, but latter-day French critics doubt whether the Athenians ever knew great cooking in the French sense of the term. (In France, 'great cooking' is entirely distinct from mere 'cooking', and even from 'good cooking'.)

There is also some doubt in France about the quality of the cooking in ancient Rome. Brillat-Savarin speaks well of the Romans, 'who put the whole world to gastronomical use . . . [bringing] guinea-fowl and truffles from Africa, rabbits from Spain and pheasants from Greece, the apricot from Armenia, the peach from Persia, the quince from Sidon, the raspberry from the deep slopes of Mount Ida, and the cherry, one of Lucullus' spoils, from the kingdom of Pontus.' But supplies alone won't make a great meal. The markets of London compare favourably with those of old Rome, but they are rarely put to gastronomical use. Carême, who made a very thorough study of Roman cooking wrote that it was 'fundamentally heavy and without refinement'.

Carême himself was hardly a practitioner of what one would call light cooking. Preparing fifty-odd rich entrées for a dinner party of Talleyrand's meant nothing to him. We still have Carême's formidable menu of the unforgettable lunch given one day in January, 1817, by the Prince Regent at Brighton for forty guests – three large, closely printed pages, with a hundred and twenty-four different dishes, almost all of them opulent and some quite spectacular, such as *escalope de faisan aux truffes de France*.

Nowhere in the works of prominent French authors on gastronomy and the culinary art is there any mention of China, where great cooking – though not in the French style – was known even before Homer wrote his Iliad. Doubtless the Chinese did for the culinary art in the East what the French did for it in the West. But great Chinese cooking is now a thing of the past, and French gastronomes, who know more about the subject than the experts of any other nation, acknowledge only one form of great cooking to-day – the French.

Cuisine has always been the most French of all arts, and Carême, like Brillat-Savarin, believed it to be also the oldest of the arts. Carême, who lived from 1784 to 1833, is considered the founder of *la grande cuisine*, which means classic French cooking in the great style. *La grande cuisine* was further developed by the great Georges Auguste Escoffier (1847–1935), who is remembered as *le Roi des Cuisiniers et le Cuisinier des Rois*. It was modernized by Prosper Montagné, who is remembered as the author of the *Larousse Gastronomique*, an encyclopaedic cook-book; and it was ultimately refined and perfected by Fernand Point (1897–1955), who was acknowledged as *le Roi* by his peers, the great chefs of France. French cuisine, which has always skilfully utilized the resources of all countries without being influenced by any other country's cooking, has itself had a lasting influence on the cooking and eating habits of all other countries. In fact, all over the world French cooking has become synonymous with good cooking.

In France, moreover, the philosophy of good eating is considered an abstract science, and good cooking a major art, not only by a minority of connoisseurs, as is true elsewhere, but by the population at large. A nation's eating standards are set not by its most expensive restaurant but by the quality of its home cooking, and French girls are still brought up in the tradition of their *grand'mères*, who wouldn't have dared marry without knowing how to make a good *omelette aux fines herbes* (not easy, because it must be made within a few seconds). The French working man loves his *bifteck* and *frites* as ardently as French epicures between the wars esteemed Fernand Point's *gratin de queues d'écrevisses*. France is the only country on earth that has a whole flock of institutes devoted to the serious

The Oyster Luncheon by the 18th century painter Jean-François de Troy

study of food and wine, with no commercial strings attached – an *Académie des Gastronomes*, for instance, and an *Académie du Vin de France*. It not only produces a different cheese for every day of the year – more, in fact, since there are now over four hundred different cheeses in France – but also has *maîtres fromagers* and *officiers de bouche du taste-fromage*. In France, the great chefs have never been considered servants – not even exalted servants – as they have always been in other countries (with the exception of ancient Rome and Greece, where they were men of some importance); rather, they have been considered artists, on a level with the country's great musicians, painters, and writers, and a good cut above politicians, generals and millionaires.

I am often asked when I first became interested in good food. I have no memories of early epicureanism; in fact, I didn't know what the word meant. In my homeland people liked to eat well and a lot but it certainly wasn't what the French call 'great cooking'. It meant thick soups, boiled beef and vegetables during the week, and a roast, *Wiener Schnitzel* or paprika chicken, on holidays. As a child I drove my poor mother crazy by refusing to touch any food except frankfurters and cocoa. In an earlier book I have admitted, 'I was kept alive on a diet of frankfurters and cocoa. I had to be tricked into swallowing frankfurters and cocoa in odd moments of mental bemusement . . .' I have nothing to add to this sad confession. Obviously I was not born to be an epicure. Later, I became fascinated by the store windows of a delicatessen; I still am. Whenever I am in Munich, a city devoted to gluttony, inhabited by ravenous eaters, I always spend an hour at Dallmayr's, one of the world's great delicatessens – just looking around and swallowing happily. I don't know what Brillat-Savarin would have said to that, but I like it.

During my formative years when I was an impecunious student and later a soldier, there were no opportunities for good eating. Before the Second World War, I had a couple of good years in Prague where portions were large, sauces were heavy and sausages were magnificent. But then I went to America where my diet consisted of Hamburgers and apple pie with cheese – excellent things, though perhaps not quite up to Brillat-Savarin's standards.

And so it was only after I was well past forty that I began to appreciate the noble art of *la grande cuisine*, which is as it should be. Didn't Brillat-Savarin say, 'No man under forty can be dignified with the title of gourmet'? It is one of life's cruel ironies that young people with healthy appetites rarely have enough money to satisfy the whims of their palate. When I was a bankrupt fiddler at the Moulin Rouge Music Hall in Paris

Training as a Gothic architect helped Viollet-le-Duc to reconstruct this Gargantuan banquet at the court of France in the 14th century

in the late 'twenties, I would often stop in front of the entrance of a famous restaurant to inhale wistfully the bewitching scent of a culinary creation whose price on the *carte de jour* equalled exactly my weekly salary. After a long gustatory daydream I pulled myself away and wound up at the familiar bistro which served a three-course meal with bread *à discrétion* – an expression I interpreted as permission to eat as much bread without being indiscreet and creating a public disturbance. A quarter-carafe of *vin ordinaire* was included in the price. I had never heard of vintages.

Over the following decades my economic position improved while my digestive situation deteriorated. The tantalizing blandishments of my palate were sabotaged by the nervous *putsches* of my stomach. At long last I could afford to pay for *foie gras* but I couldn't afford to eat much of it. I've learned that to eat well doesn't mean to eat much. I have no admiration for the late Curé de Bregnier who started out with soup and boiled beef, continued with a leg of mutton *à la Royale*, a whole capon and a big dish of potatoes and salad, and finished with a large white cheese 'into which he made an angular cut of ninety degrees'.

Gastronomy has gone through many changes in the past three hundred years. The development of the culinary art shows an unbroken trend from epicurean riches to dietary rags. After Gargantuan extravaganza there

96

came baroque opulence. The great eighteenth-century eaters were gluttons with an incredible capacity for putting away food. Their banquets were sumptuous orgies of intemperance, with no style. We read that Louis XV once was served a monster meal by Héliot, the Dauphine's *écuyer ordinaire de la bouche*, that consisted of dozens of beef dishes, nothing but beef, from beef-soup to brain fritters served with lemon juice. When Louis XVI was a prisoner at the Temple, he was served 'three soups, four entrées, three roast dishes, each consisting of three pieces; four sweet courses, a plate of fancy cakes, three compotes, three dishes of fruit, three loaves of bread with butter; one bottle of champagne, one small carafe of Bordeaux, one of Malvoisie, one of Madeira, and four cups of coffee'. That was just lunch. Dinner might be similar.

The great reformer was Carême, a man of imagination who was convinced that he had resurrected 'the ancient glory of French cooking'. But he was still obsessed with opulence and his ideas of gastronomy were synonymous with *gourmandise*. The Prince Regent of England once said to him, 'Carême, you will kill me with a surfeit of food. The temptation is really too great.' Carême replied that he was trying to stimulate the Prince Regent's appetite by a variety of dishes, not to curb it. Escoffier understood this well: 'Carême had grasped the essential truth that the richer the cooking, the more speedily the stomach and the palate tire of it.'

Escoffier reformed and refined *la grande cuisine*. After Carême's opulence Escoffier introduced elegance into the realm of gastronomy. By our standards his dinners were still lavish epicurean symphonies, but the movements were well balanced, and the nuances handled with subtlety. To celebrate the coronation of King George V, he designed a dinner at César Ritz's Carlton Hotel in London which began with caviar and fresh melon, was followed by a soup, a delicate mousseline of trout, a poularde fittingly named 'George V', and a saddle of lamb. After an intermission the guests stimulated their lagging appetite with duckling breast in port wine aspic, and then the symphony reached its climax with quails cooked in butter, accompanied by a magnificent sauce of the game liquor and white wine in a *cocotte* with freshly peeled grapes, and ended on a happy note with fresh peaches and strawberries.

The cult of gastronomy is a respected avocation in France, and sometimes a full-time profession. Members of gastronomic groups are men of knowledge and experience, who pursue their pleasurable researches with dedication, and who carefully avoid the spotlight, because for them great eating is a matter of art for art's sake. (The famous eating circles of past centuries, such as *Les Grands Estomacs*, which were devoted to Gargantuan

Alexis Soyer, the philanthropic
chef, whose cookery books
were best-sellers in
England in the 1850s.
From a drawing by his wife,
the painter Emma Jones

Brillat-Savarin, whose *Physiologie du Goût*
first formulated the philosophy of gastronomy

opulence, have been succeeded by fastidious connoisseurs such as the *Club des Cent*, an exclusive gathering of a hundred men, who consider themselves the supreme arbiters of French gastronomy. A great many enthusiastic eaters who have tried to get into either the *Club des Cent* or its offshoot, the *Club des Purs Cent*, must have been snubbed, since there exists for gastronomes a *Club des Sans-Club*, with its own yearbook.)

Nevertheless, gastronomy receives plenty of public attention in France, where prominent writers on the subject are universally respected. At one time or another, almost all great French writers have written about the art of good cooking and the joy of good eating, and, by the same token, almost all the classics of gastronomy and the culinary art were written by Frenchmen: Guillaume Tirel, known as Taillevent, was perhaps the first, *circa* 1380; and after him came La Varenne, Menon, Grimod de la Reynière (*Almanachs des Gourmands*, 1803–1812), Viard, Beauvilliers, Carême, Brillat-Savarin, Urbain Dubois, Gouffé, Baron Brisse, Philéas Gilbert, Tendret, Montagné and Escoffier, whose *Guide Culinaire* is a masterpiece.

Only in France could a manufacturer of motor-car tyres win fame

98

LEFT: Henri Soulé, proprietor
of *Le Pavillon* in New York City,
one of the best restaurants
in the western hemisphere

BELOW: Georges Auguste Escoffier,
*Le Roi des Cuisiniers
et le Cuisinier des Rois*

and fortune by publishing, at considerable expense and as a sort of glorified public service, a guidebook on his country's restaurants – the *Guide
Michelin*, which is regarded by all authorities as the best work of its kind
on earth, being honest, impartial, accurate, and fastidious. The editors
of the *Guide* have become the guardians of the national gastronomical
conscience. Almost every Frenchman knows his country's celebrated restaurants, just as an American knows his baseball teams and an Austrian
his opera singers. The *Guide Michelin*'s annual selection of three-star
restaurants is awaited in France with as much suspense as the outcome
of the World Series is in the United States.

In Vienna, a popular myth notwithstanding, only one inhabitant out
of nine has ever attended the State Opera, but even those who have never
been near the place have considered themselves its co-owners. It is doubtful
whether one Frenchman out of nine has ever stepped into one of his country's gastronomic shrines, since most Frenchmen cannot afford the meals
they offer, but everybody in France is familiar with their names: Fernand
Point's Restaurant de la Pyramide, in Vienne; Alexandre Dumaine's
Hôtel de la Côte-d'Or, in Saulieu; Lapérouse and Lasserre, in Paris; and

99

so on. The holy temples of *la grande cuisine* belong to the nation just like the Louvre or the Tomb of the Unknown Soldier. Good eating is simply a way of life in France, and the men who provide good food are widely known and deeply revered.

Thus, it is common knowledge that eleven restaurants out of the forty to fifty thousand that exist in France (no one knows exactly how many there are at any given moment, because their number is constantly fluctuating) were allowed three stars – the top rating – by the 1964 *Guide Michelin*, and also that the Restaurant de la Pyramide, in the rather dreary town of Vienne, in the Departement d'Isère, seventeen miles south of Lyon, is still considered the greatest of the great temples of French gastronomy.

Full-time gastronomes, epicures of long standing, anonymous *inspecteurs* of the *Guide Michelin*, and even competitors in the restaurant business sigh wistfully at the memory of a meal at the Pyramide. The *Guide Michelin* has never awarded anything less than three stars to the Pyramide, and recently one of its senior editors confided to me in a very, very weak moment, 'If we should ever consider awarding a fourth star to any restaurant – at the risk of starting another French Revolution – the Pyramide would get it.'

Last December, the respected *Guide de l'Auto-Journal*, which now ranks second in importance to the *Michelin*, declared of the Pyramide that it *'demeure sans conteste la première table de France'*. In the same issue, the *Auto-Journal*'s editor-in-chief, a nationally known gastronome, wrote, after a meal there, 'In the euphoria following my *déjeuner* at the Pyramide, I've classified the great restaurants of the world. First: Point's. Second: None. Third: None. Fourth: Select one from among the three other stopovers of my gastronomic pilgrimage.'

These would be extraordinary tributes under any circumstances, but, as it happens, one circumstance renders them totally unprecedented, and that is that they were paid to a woman – Mme Marie-Louise (Mado) Point, Fernand Point's widow, who for the past nine years has managed the Pyramide single-handed and faithfully served *la première table de France*.

In France, *la grande cuisine* has always been considered strictly a man's business. Women have their place in the kitchen as long as they practise *bourgeois*, or home, cooking – and no French connoisseur lightly dismisses the value of a woman's home cooking – but where the exalted creations of *la grande cuisine* are concerned, Frenchmen agree with Louis XIV, who liked to have women at his table but preferred men in his kitchen.

100

The celebrated chefs of the past two hundred years have all been men. There have been some well-known women cooks in the last fifty years, particularly in Lyon, the region of culinary momism, where elderly epicures still talk about Mère Guy, Mère Fillioux, and Mère Bigot. But all these mothers practised very good home-cooking rather than *la grande cuisine*. Even Mme Brazier, whose restaurant, the *Mère Brazier*, on the Col de la Luère – a hill not far from Lyon – was again awarded three stars by the 1963 *Michelin*, has never competed with her famous male colleagues. Instead, she served her customers, many of them bankers and silk-manufacturers from Lyon with a well-developed epicurean mother-fixation, the favourite dishes of their youth – *quenelles de brochet* and *poularde demi-deuil* –which she prepared very well indeed.

The art of the restaurateur – as distinct from that of the chef – has also traditionally been practised by men in France – ever since, according to Brillat-Savarin,

around 1770 . . . Finally there came along the first intelligent fellow who decided for himself that . . . if he should cut off a fowl wing to please the first comer, there would not fail to be another arrival who would gladly accept the leg: that the carving of a choice slice in the obscurity of the kitchen would not ruin the rest of the joint; that nobody minded a slight increase in cost when he had been served well, and promptly, and properly . . . this intelligent fellow became the first *restaurateur*, and created a profession which is always a successful one if he who practises it possesses sincerity, a sense of order, and skill.

Aux Trois Frères Provençaux, one of the earliest 'Restaurants'. From a 19th century print

Among the first of these intelligent fellows was a certain Boulanger, who in 1765 began to sell soups on the Rue Bailleul as *restaurants* (i.e., restoratives), hanging out a sign that read, 'Boulanger sells magical restoratives'. Evidently he knew his business, and so did Messrs Bathélemy, Maneille, and Simon, who in 1786 opened near the Palais-Royal, a restaurant that they named *Aux Trois Frères Provençaux*, though they were neither brothers nor Provençal. Brillat-Savarin praised their cod-with-garlic. Over the next twenty years or so, the Véry Brothers offered delicious truffled entrées; a restaurateur named Badeleine took great care with his fish dishes; and a certain Henneveu offered both good food and, according to Brillat-Savarin, 'mysterious private little rooms on his fourth floor'. All of them were men — not one woman among them.

When Fernand Point, the greatest practitioner of *la grande cuisine* in our time, died, in Vienne, on March 5, 1955, Frenchmen everywhere mourned the death not only of a great Frenchman but of a great restaurant; among gastronomes the regretful consensus was that Point's Pyra-

'Only the perfect harmony of all the senses can make possible the supreme enjoyment of food and drink.' *Taste* by Abraham Bosse, from a set of engravings of the Five Senses

mide was *finie*. The French consider cooking an art, partly an imitative art and partly a creative one. Although in the past fifty years very few chefs have invented new dishes, most of them have been satisfied with the existing ones — they identify a particular variety of cooking with a certain artist, as they do when they think of painting or composing or playing the violin. Unlike disciples in some of the other branches of art, the pupils of celebrated chefs, who often perform admirably, under their master's guidance, seldom do well when they are on their own. As for a chef's widow, she is in the same position as the widow of a poet or composer, since creating a gastronomic meal is like writing a poem or composing a symphony, she cannot attempt to carry on her husband's work. Fernand Point's genius had created the Pyramide, and Frenchmen agreed that while Mme Point *veuve* might continue the Pyramide for a time, as a reverent tribute to her husband, no restaurant can live on the glory of the past, and sooner or later the end would come.

Yet in the March, 1962, issue of the influential monthly *Cuisine et Vins de France*, the well-known gastronomic writer, Michel Lemonnier wrote:

Fernand Point was a sovereign and at the same time the praiseworthy servant of an art and of a refinement to a degree which some perhaps would deem excessive, but in so doing would be signing their own death warrant since it is unquestionably also a matter of our entire culture ... Mme Point renders to him the greatest homage possible: she is devoted to the tradition, and continues it in such a manner that *la maison* remains at the peak of its perfection.

Fernand Point's peers, the great chefs and restaurateurs of France, agree. Alexandre Dumaine, who until his retirement a year ago was generally considered to have succeeded to the title of greatest living chef in France, remarked to me once, 'Mme Point was always her husband's fully-fledged partner. Together they developed that special blend of exalted hospitality in which everything is just perfect — the service, the food, the wines, the *ambiance*, the sense of enjoyment before, during and after the meal. Today the Pyramide is the greatest restaurant in France, as it was a quarter of a century ago, and Mme Point is incontestably *la grande dame de la gastronomie française*.'

Fernand Point developed a new concept in epicurean philosophy. This concept, his lasting contribution to the development of gastronomy, is that *la grande cuisine* must please all our senses — not only the palate and the taste-buds but also the eyes and ears and nostrils, and even the sense of touch. To Point, the after-taste of a great wine was incomplete without the melodious clink of fine crystal, and the sight of a dish was enhanced by the pleasant smell of the fresh napkin on the knees. Only the perfect harmony of all the senses made possible the supreme enjoyment of food and drink. Point was well aware that our eyes are always greedier than our stomachs, and he also recognized that the human appetite has declined steadily over the centuries.

All that Point was interested in was the pursuit of gastronomic happiness. He knew that the number of fastidious connoisseurs truly able to appreciate his cooking was necessarily limited. Self-appointed 'gourmets' who like to boast of finding an 'excellent bistro around the corner where the owner does the cooking himself' could scarcely do justice to Point's delicate sauces. And people who had just spent a week in Provence, eating such robust foods as *ailloli* (a mayonnaise with a garlic *purée*) could hardly appreciate the finesse of Point's *truite saumonée* or *caneton glacé*.

Yet Point was never discouraged by such considerations. He spent weeks designing and executing the *presentation* of a dish, because to him this was no mere effect but was essential to the full enjoyment of that dish. His *barquette de moules sur un lit d'épinards* — mussels cooked in white wine, embedded in a buttery pastry in the form of very tiny boats, and covered with a rose-coloured sauce whose ingredients could only be sensed, not guessed, the whole resting on a bed of delicate spinach — looked like an Impressionist still-life. And his crayfish *au gratin* was a lovely painting in orange, red, and brown. Point used to say that the crayfish *au gratin* should be treated like an old claret: one should look at its colour, inhale its fragrance, taste its delicate flavour.

At the Pyramide, the pâté of pheasant is served stuffed inside a pheasant. Conversely, its garnish is not only for the eye but also for the palate; the aspic is made from the finest ingredients, and flavoured with vintage *brut champagne* or old port wine. Sometimes Point would create one or another of the three most famous pâtés of *la grande cuisine* — *l'Oreiller de la Belle Aurore*, *le Chapeau de Monseigneur Gabriel Cortois de Quinsey*, and *la Toque du Président Adolphe Clerk* — which are superb productions made with whole saddles of hare, whole ducks, quails, chickens, partridges, woodcocks and so on. One such pâté would serve fifty people, and when the waiters brought it in, on an enormous silver platter, and began to cut it into thick slices, a hush would descend upon the dining room.

The best cooking at the Pyramide, however, was done on Tuesdays, when the restaurant was closed. Then Point would dream up new creations and try them out on his family and some close friends. Mme Point still remembers a Tuesday when he served her a *rôti de veau* with what seemed to be a simple *purée* of very young spinach. 'His eyes were twinkling with excitement as he watched me taste the *purée*', she says. 'It was the most delicate spinach I'd ever eaten — it had a very special, very delicious flavour.

The bill of fare from the *Restaurant de la Pyramide*. The creation of a gastronomic meal is like writing a poem or composing a symphony

Restaurant de la Pyramide

FERNAND POINT
VIENNE (ISÈRE)

30 Juin 1963

Brioche de Foie gras
Pâté de Volaille en gelée
œufs pochés Sydney

Turbot au Champagne
ou
Quenelle de Brochet Nantua

(2 couverts) Pintadeau poêlé aux Chanterelles
Chateaubriand grillé Béarnaise
gratin Dauphinois
ou
Caneton Nantais glacé
Salade Délice

Choix à la carte   Fromages
Caviar Extra
Melon de Cavaillon   Glace et Sorbet
Terrine de Foie gras   Gâteaux Succès
Terrine de Grives   Entremets variés
gratin d'Écrevisses   Corbeilles de fruits
Écrevisses en Buisson
Jambon et Saucisson
de Campagne   45 Francs sans vin

Fernand was as happy as a child – his surprise had come off. It wasn't spinach. At dawn that day, he'd gone down to his kitchen and started to pluck the tiny leaves of watercress off the tiny stems. He'd worked for hours, cleaning thirty bunches of watercress, and then he'd made the *purée* out of the leaves. He always asked me to guess the ingredients of a new sauce, and was always glad when I didn't guess correctly. I remember a sauce he once made of underdone roast duck – the duck's liquor with port, cream, truffles and a few drops of *fine champagne*. I guessed everything correctly except the *fine*. Fernand was delighted.'

The first time I was a guest at the Pyramide – it seems ages ago now – I was awakened from a sound sleep at half past five. Fernand Point was standing by my bedside, pink and smiling, and he asked me sweetly, 'What would you like to have for *déjeuner, mon petit?*' I got mad, and said, 'A *bouillabaisse* from Toulon'. I knew, of course, that that was one dish Fernand never made. He used to say that a *bouillabaisse* should be cooked and eaten only in a place from which you could look at the Mediterranean, and, of course, he was right. But I hadn't counted on Fernand's magnificence. That morning, he'd gone down and 'phoned to Toulon. Around nine o'clock a truck drove up with large tanks containing a huge collection of Mediterranean fish. Alive. There were all the fish you use to make a *bouillabaisse* in Toulon, in a place from which you can see the ocean – whiting, *roucou*, Saint-Pierre, gurnard, conger eel, chapon, dory, *rascasse*, weever, *baudroie*, crabs. There were also *langouste* and *loup de mer*, the most expensive ingredients.

The *bouillabaisse* was marvellous. We remembered it again the other day when I made my annual pilgrimage to the Pyramide and sat alone with Mme Point after a wonderful meal. This time we had only tasted some of Fernand's great creations. Nowadays we don't eat any more; we taste; we've learned that if you want to live well for a while you must eat wisely.

'I don't know which was the most beautiful thing about the *bouillabaisse*,' I said, and I inhaled deeply and reverently at the memory as if the dish were on the table in front of us at the moment. 'The fragrance? The flavour? The aftertaste? I've never had such a succulent *bouillabaisse* in Toulon itself!'

Mme Point nodded. 'But Fernand modestly claimed that it wasn't a real *bouillabaisse* because it wasn't made within sight of the sea.'

'He called it *crème de mer*,' I said.

'Yes. "A very simple dish", he said.'

We sat in silence for a minute, thinking of Fernand.

'The bouillabaisse was about as simple as his *pot-au-feu*,' Mme Point said. 'He made that for Jos one day. You remember Jos?'

I nodded. Joseph Niego, a Frenchman of Turkish descent, a successful theatre manager in Paris, had been one of Point's closest friends. Right up to his death, a few years ago, Jos had come to Vienne every summer to spend a week with them. When I'd asked how he could eat all the wonderful things for days on end, he'd said, 'I don't eat. I just taste a little of everything. And I don't eat bread and butter, as you do.'

'The *pot-au-feu* was a fairy tale,' Mme Point went on. 'It was served on our largest silver platter, which is about a yard long. Fernand arranged on it a whole side of boiled beef, a large boiled ham, two *poulardes de Bresse*, boiled *saucisson de Lyon*, and several other things. First he'd cooked the beef, which needed the most time, and then the ham, then the *poulardes*, and so on – all in a bouillon with vegetables. Then he'd thrown away the vegetables, and cooked fresh ones, to be served with the meat. Yet Fernand insisted on calling it *"un tout petit pot-au-feu"*.'

I'll never forget my last meal with Fernand Point. It was the ninth of January, 1955. Little did I know that he would be gone a few weeks later. There were four of us for lunch – Fernand and Mado Point, his old friend Louis Couchoud, a physician, philosopher and poet who was born in Vienne and had returned to spend his last years there, and I. It was a memorable *déjeuner* – really *une petite merveille*, as Point tried to make every meal – and while we sipped the wonderful Château Ausone 1929, a perfect bottle, with Point's favourite cheese, a Saint-Marcellin made in the nearby countryside, Couchoud said that such a meal should not be paid for with hard cash – it just didn't seem right. Fernand Point ought to place a top hat in the entrance hall, so that the grateful guests could put offerings there before leaving – the women their bracelets and rings, the men their watches and wallets – and then deferentially tiptoe away.

Point considered the suggestion in silence for a minute, and then he replied, in his slow, musing way, 'Yes – and then somebody leaves and takes the top hat along with all the offerings in it.'

The Blessings
of Conversation

I'M AFRAID a generation is growing up which never heard of the blessings of conversation; they don't even know what it means. My young friends tell me that conversation is dated, *passé* – an anachronism like the hansom cab, the player piano, a girl dancing the can-can. But both conversation and can-can had their hidden charms. Emerson called conversation 'an art in which a man has all mankind for his competitor'. The art is almost as forgotten as Emerson in certain circles.

Even our generation, which is no longer young but refuses to be old, has a feeling of nostalgia at the mention of 'conversation'. It reminds me of my maternal grandmother, a formidable Victorian figure in my Moravian hometown who went through life dressed in austere black and fortified by austere principles. Unkind people in town compared her to the Austrian Empress Maria Theresia who had borne sixteen children and efficiently managed her children, her husband and her empire. My grandmother had only thirteen children and no duties of state but her husband had died shortly before the birth of her youngest child and she brought them up all by herself, with dignity and authority.

She had managed to marry off two of her daughters to the last two available sons of Grandfather Wechsberg, a legendary character who had arrived in town many years ago, a frightened boy sitting on a hay-cart, and had become the local Rothschild winding up with real estate, a mill, factories and a private bank. When I asked him how he had amassed his wealth, he didn't give me the customary prescription of thrift and hard work. He tapped his right temple and said, 'I used my head'.

No wonder my maternal grandmother was envied by all other matrons with marriageable daughters in town who considered her coup highly unfair. My mother, one of the two lucky girls to 'get a Wechsberg' al-

109

In Paris-the older generation still knows
the blessings of conversation

ways liked to recall the story of what had happened the day after her marriage. It seems that Grandfather Wechsberg, an enterprising Edwardian patriarch, with *boutonnière*, beard and genuine gusto for the best things in life — I owe him a lot, really — was seen walking up and down in front of my grandmother's house, playing with his elegant ivory stick, chuckling, enjoying himself enormously. This was duly reported to my grandmother who couldn't resist the temptation and appeared in the entrance door, where she greeted the *boulevardier* and asked him why he was so happy. 'Because, dear Madame, you still have two unmarried daughters and I have no more sons', Grandfather Wechsberg said. He doffed his derby and turned around, departing jauntily and feeling like the Roman emperor who had done his good deed for the day.

This bit of repartee always struck me as a fine conversational opening, although on that day, I regret to report, it became a sort of closing remark. My grandmother was so angry that she didn't talk to Grandfather Wechsberg until the birth of their common progeny — myself. I'm pleased at the thought of having brought these two good people together again simply by appearing in this strange and wonderful world.

Every Sunday morning at half past eleven my grandmother had her *jour*. That meant she was at home for friend and foe, receiving them all in her large drawing room, a gloomy chamber which remained locked up all week, smelling of dust, with slipcovers screening the contours of all chairs. On Sunday morning the dark curtains were drawn, the windows opened, the slipcovers removed, the Biedermeier chests dusted off. Small Meissen *bonbonnières* filled with delicious Swiss chocolates were strategically placed on small tables all over the room. The stage was set for an hour of conversation —the pleasure of civilized verbal intercourse.

It was an artistic performance which didn't always come off. Stage people will understand; improvised comedy is one of the hardest things to perform. Grandmother's drawing room reminded me of the typical set then fashionable in the 'conversational comedies' that were quite popular with the subscribers at our local theatre though not with the critics who used the term disapprovingly to pan a play that lived on its wits instead of on solid dramatic structure. Some Sundays were flops, but when all went well, my grandmother's *jour* was a smash hit.

There were unwritten, but carefully respected, ground-rules. Everything could be said provided you knew how to say it. There were no outright taboos in my grandmother's drawing room — perhaps she was more Moravian than Victorian after all — but certain subjets might be on the forbidden list for the time being; for instance, the precarious situation of Uncle Hugo's finances, who was always on the verge of bank-

Samuel Taylor Coleridge, a great table-talker, was not a master of the Art of Conversation; a drawing from Max Beerbohm's *Poet's Corner*

ruptcy and sometimes over the verge, or the difficulty of finding a husband for Aunt Grete 'who should have been married long ago'.

Apart from such temporarily undesirable topics, anything went. One could skilfully minimize important matters or add some glamour to a trivial occurence. Always the conversation was performed for its own sake, as a study in tact, an exercise in eloquence, a test of self-discipline, a demonstration of *esprit*, an experiment in diplomacy-at-home.

It was not easy to define exactly what conversation was; it was easier to explain what it was not. Conversation was not an argument, nor a discussion, nor a dialogue. Conversation was always practised in a sphere of the semi-abstract, the untopical, the general rather than the specific. As in a morality play judgements were pronounced and conclusions drawn; a touch of lofty sophistication and healthy self-mocking was always apparent. Masters of the game never took notice of themselves, avoided coming close to reality, shunned 'issues'. More than once they reminded me of actors in a play.

I was always surprised at the latitude of their topics. Economics, history, the Monarchy, Aunt Berta's reports from the Vienna scene, social problems (the local miners were dissatisfied), community questions, religion, the drama, Paris fashions, reports from Monte Carlo. Even sex was permissible though the subject was artfully paraphrased and no one would utter it in three letters. People had more leisure in those days and talked around a subject rather than about it. Today they are more direct and less tactful.

Conversation never degraded into mere gossip. Conversation might be compared to a brilliant *coloratura* aria, with *virtuoso staccato* runs and glittering high Cs, while gossip was like a vulgar beer song whose silly refrain is repeated *ad nauseam*.

The masters of the art of conversation played with words as jugglers played with balls. They would throw the words high up in the air and let them orbit in space (and mind) for a while before they caught them again with an imperceptible twist of the wrist. They were not raconteurs – people fascinated by the sound of their own voice. We know these only too well from parties and dinner-tables and casual meetings in railway compartments; many of them are specialists in jokes or travel talk, literary chitchat or in first-person stories, all of them boring.

Conversation was communication, a two-way street. Its reason was give-and-take, back-and-forth, action-and-reaction. It was followed by the listeners as the ball is followed by the spectators in the centre court at Wimbledon. The referees saw to it that the rules were not violated. Rule No 1 was to give all participants in the conversational game an equal break. The company was not divided into people who spoke and others who listened. To be sure, there were star players who spoke up more often than others, but it was a conversational democracy and everybody had the right to speak up if he had something to say.

This meant that somebody had to listen. It sounds incredible now, but people were actually willing to listen in those days. Women particularly were wonderful listeners. My grandmother could give a man the impression that she was all ears, that nothing mattered while he was talking, and this raised his self-confidence and for a short, unforgettable moment made him hold the centre of the stage. (Grandmother was less charitable to women; when certain ladies spoke up she might even break a rule by offering around chocolates just as the lady was coming to her point). These were my early Voltaire and Goethe days. Looking at my grandmother's guests I imagined that this must have been the sophisticated atmosphere in the literary and political salons of the Marquise du Chatelet or Madame de Staël.

Conversation is doomed because people no longer listen. They just wait for a chance to cut in and start their own monologue. Life has become a succession of endless monologues that no one wants to hear. Instead of conversations we have cocktail-parties – orgies of soliloquy. Some people have become master craftsmen in the technique of non-listening. I know a man

The Moorish Coffee-House by Vasily Kandinsky

who pretends to listen to A, while he talks to B, and looks at C, yet somehow he conveys the impression to all three people that they fascinate him. This takes years of hard training and an overzealous practitioner sometimes winds up in a schizophrenic ward. It's a dangerous game, but it has its attractions. While you stare fixedly at the mouth of the soliloquist you are really waiting for him to run out of logic, syntax or breath. As soon as he makes the slightest involuntary pause, you fill the conversational vacuum with your own words. It doesn't matter what you say as long as you say it quickly. Don't wait too long. Somebody else may get in there and you'll have lost your last chance of speaking during that evening.

When three or more people take part in the game, the contest can be quite exciting. The rules of talkmanship demand that no matter how tense you are, you must look outwardly relaxed, holding your glass, sipping your drink. But all the time you watch the soliloquist. Talkmanship forbids you to interrupt him or her in the middle of a sentence. Be alert: sooner or later there comes a moment when even the most experienced monologuist may have to swallow, moisten his lips or inhale. Quick, grab the conversational ball before someone else gets it and run with it — as long as you can talk.

In the jungle of our society the man with the fastest reflexes and strongest vocal chords will survive. It's no longer a question of having something to say but of being able to say it. Once a man has the word and runs away with it, nothing will make him give it up. He carries on his monologue triumphantly, well aware of the aura of animosity that is rapidly building up around him. The others stare fixedly at his lips, wishing he would bite his own tongue, run out of breath, or drop dead. No one listens. Everybody thinks of what he was going to, and couldn't, say. They unsaid sentences are one of the great frustration of our civilization.

Compared to this interlocutory rat-race the unhurried, pleasant Sunday morning conversations in my grandmother's drawing room were truly an exercise in civilization. Today's cocktail-parties are full of bores and bored people; but my grandmother's guests were never bored. They had a wonderful time. They looked as if they'd been drinking champagne, which was remarkable since champagne was served only at weddings or whenever Uncle Max, the Wechsberg family's black sheep, came home from Vienna to intervene with his father on behalf of his creditors who asked for prompt payment of his debts. Uncle Max, a master conversationalist with a fascinating supply of topics on hand, was my grandmother's great weakness. He was permitted to come up any day, any time for an hour of conversation. Uncle Max could make an entertainment out of insurance statistics.

His sardonic innuendo was as sharp and infallible as the stiletto of an Italian *bravo*. Long after he'd left, my grandmother would be smiling to herself, enjoying the echo of her conversational *divertissement*.

The art of conversation was a little like the technique of fencing. You tried to hit your adversary without being hit yourself, but if you were hit, you were expected to keep your bearing and poise. Talkmanship dictated that you must at all times talk directly to each other. Today people talk *past* each other; there are no points of direct conversational contact. After such tangential talk has gone on for some time the players have moved apart so far that they suddenly stop to look at each other in embarrassment; neither of them knows what they started out to say in the first place. Each has stubbornly followed his one-way track of soliloquy and now they find themselves stranded in a conversational traffic jam with no policeman to disentangle the confusion.

At an informal gathering or a cocktail-party the abysmal moment of truth is quickly bridged over by fetching fresh drinks. After the third drink nothing matters: the accumulation of noise and nonsense makes it hard for a man to listen to the sound of his own voice, which automatically terminates any attempt at conversation. A man no longer cares to talk when he can't hear himself. The antagonists deeply inhale and separate.

Conversation came easy to the people in my grandmother's drawing room. This was the era of brilliant dialoguists – G. B. Shaw, Henry James, Hugo von Hofmannsthal, Ferenc Molnar, Arthur Schnitzler. All over Europe spirited *feulletonistes* carried on dialogues with themselves when they had no one else to talk to.

Geographically, the centres of conversation were western and central Europe, the boulevards of Paris and the coffee-houses of Vienna. Conversation reached out as far south as Spain and Italy and east all the way to the Balkans and the bazaars of the Middle East, but it thinned out toward the north, where the people, depressed by fog and cold and darkness, tended toward silence. Perhaps the greatest breeding ground of conversation was the Viennese coffee-house, a unique institution which was seventy per cent atmosphere and thirty per cent matter. Its dark wood-panelled walls, stained by generations of smokers, its marble tables covered with mountains of newspapers, its chandeliers with soft lights and well-upholstered benches were designed to create a sense of tranquillity and a feeling of privacy that was conducive to the delights of conversation.

There were seven hundred coffee-houses in Vienna around the turn of the century, some patronized by artists and actors, and others by politicians and lawyers, but conversation flourished in all of them, and its great masters, Peter Altenberg and Egon Friedell, were as famous in the city

The *Kaffee Griensteidl*, one of Vienna's seven hundred coffee-houses, which was famous as the meeting-place of the literary world in the 1890s

as opera singers and composers. London had club-life and pub-life; Vienna had coffee-house-life. The last war and the Nazi occupation have destroyed the atmosphere of Vienna's coffee-houses and a coffee-house without atmosphere is as worthless as a bank without its depositors' confidence. Nowadays the coffee-house has to compete with Italian-style *espresso* bars that are furnished in avant-garde style, with garish lights and plastic trays, chromium counters and bright colours. A jukebox is going *fortissimo*, and the coffee is made with the help of hissing steam. Conversation is as impossible there as in New York's Times Square subway station. People at the *espresso* don't converse. They monologize.

We live under the dreadful dictatorship of implacable monologists. Our novelists, politicians, head-waiters, economists, educators, hairdressers, scientists, housewives, lawyers and gangsters carry on endless, boring monologues. Painters soliloquize about modern art instead of producing it, and composers develop atonal theories instead of writing music. No one wants to converse; everybody wants to convince. Everybody wants to persuade everybody else that he is right and all the others are wrong. This is no climate for the planting of tender conversational flowers. In its extreme form the mania of the monologue leads into the underbrush of dialectics whose practitioners are able to turn white into black — or any colour into red — at the drop of a cliché. Or one winds up in the no-man's land of empty oratory when words are uttered, without any sense, in order

115

'We live under the dreadful dictatorship of implacable monologists. No one wants to converse, everybody wants to convince.' An orator at Speakers' Corner in Hyde Park

to keep everybody else present from uttering equally senseless words. Master dialectitians and marathon orators have become the heroes of our anticonversational epoch.

Conversational purists claim that conversation must always remain disinterested, *ars gratia artis*. You cannot converse in order to sell something. Conversation is never a business talk. The purpose of conversation is to experience intellectual enjoyment, not to make a profit. It is said that the hectic tempo of our time, with radio, jukebox and television, has killed off conversation. This is not true. Conversation was finished long before television gave it the *coup de grace*, because people no longer had something to say to each other, and because of their refusal to listen. 'Inject a few raisins of conversation into the tasteless dough of existence', says O. Henry. The dough is very dry and the raisins have become rare.

All year long I get letters from people who write me that we must meet on my next trip to America. 'There is so much to talk about.' When I meet them at last, they are as delighted as I am. For a few minutes there is some genuine, though somewhat abrupt, conversation; this is the rocket age and people switch with bewildering rapidity from one topic to the next. The presidential election. How are the kids? You must see the show at the Museum of Modern Art. Is it true what they say about Mac? Bill? Joe? Jim? The new season at the Met. The old season on Capitol Hill. Subjects are checked off like items on a shopping list.

After a number of staccato sentences I am forced into an armchair, a glass is put into my hand and I face a television screen where the forbidding shape of a famous soliloquist appears. Someone utters the conventional phrase, 'hope-you-won't-mind-we've-got-to-listen-to-this-one', and that is the end of our conversational efforts. The monologists have the field to

116

themselves. The slim thread of mutual understanding is broken, the sequence of sentences shattered. I know that we'll never have that long, good talk. So we will have to resort to letters again. And what are letters? Written monologues.

Even young couples who ought to be in love no longer listen to each other. They sit in dimly lit joints where the noise relieves them of the necessity of telling each other something true and tender — something that is so very hard to say. Bus passengers are warned not to talk to the driver, but no one dares anyway. The driver is a congenital misanthrope suffering from ulcers who soliloquizes about those bastards in the bus who make him sick. In the streets of our big cities one frequently sees people who talk to themselves because they have no one else to talk to. The human race increases at a frightening rate but the people get lonelier all the time.

Perhaps the renaissance of conversation will come from the children. Small children unknowingly practise the pleasure of conversation, talking about the colours of the flowers, the beauty of a pebble, the wonder of a pool of dirty water. Little girls tell secrets to each other, never straying off the subject, never trying to sell each other; they converse in their own childish, charming, true way. I listened to them the other day as they talked about a lovely bluebird near the lake in the park. The bluebird was a genuine symbol of conversation, part fact and part legend, full of the unfathomable romanticism of life that is the distilled essence of conversational understanding.

The pleasure of conversation might be rediscovered after a considerable part of the world's population has wilfully eliminated itself, and the survivors may live in caves and ruins without the blessings of television, motor-cars and jukeboxes. Conversation will become a necessity, perhaps even an art. People will remember the good old days when they were too busy to talk to each other. God knows, they may have real conversations again as in my grandmother's drawing room — but I hope I won't be there any more.

117

The Empress Maria Theresia with her husband and thirteen of her
sixteen children. The author's grandmother also brought up a very large
family, and was consequently often likened to the Austrian monarch

Nostalgia

AS LONG AS I can remember, Marie, our cook, 'belonged to the family'. In the Moravian town where I grew up, Marie had moved into my parents' home the day after they got married. My mother's mother, a sensible woman, had hired and trained Marie and sent her over as part of the dowry. Grandmother knew that an experienced cook is more valuable in a new household than a set of old Meissen china.

My first memories of Marie go back to my pre-school days when I came home from a long walk, cold and hungry. I would run into the warm kitchen without taking off my coat. Marie would cut off a thick slice of fresh, dark bread and put butter and salt on it. It was wonderful. Every Tuesday and Friday Marie would bake fresh bread for us. I can still smell the sourish scent of yeast in the large kitchen. The sour dough would remain standing there overnight, and the next morning Marie would knead the dough and shove the round form into the oven. Later – I always tried to be in the kitchen at that time – she would open the oven and take out a crusty, round loaf of warm, dark bread, 'Polish' bread they called it at home. The transformation from dark-grey dough into dark-brown bread was one of the early miracles of my childhood. Marie would always cut off the *Scherzl*, the end, for me. I thought there was no greater delicacy on earth.

Marie seemed ageless. I couldn't imagine that she had ever been young; perhaps, I thought, she had been born grown-up and old. In my cruel moments, when she refused to divulge what we were going to have for dinner, I tried to make her mad and said, 'Marie, you are *old*'. Far from being angry, Marie would smile and say, 'If you don't want to get old, you will have to hang yourself on the next tree while you are young.'

In our home Marie was known as 'the cook' but guests from the outside

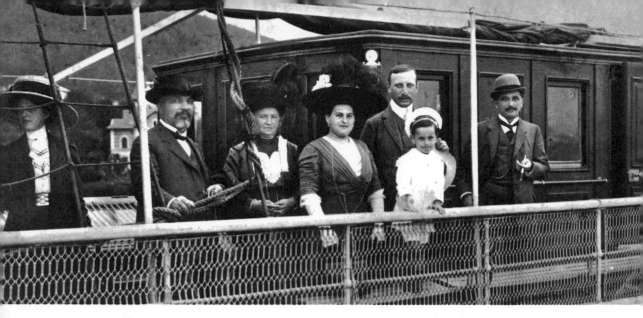

The Wechsberg family on holiday at the Adriatic port of Opatije when the author was just three years old. Marie is standing behind Mrs Wechsberg

world who came to the house called her respectfully 'the Moravian cook'. In Vienna my aunt Berta, a rich woman, was envied by her friends because she too had a Moravian cook. The fame of these cooks — all of them were women — had spread all over the Habsburg Monarchy, from the Carpathian Mountains to the shores of the Adriatic. In Vienna, the 'best people' had a Moravian cook, or perhaps one from Bohemia or Hungary; I was convinced that the Emperor Franz Josef I also had a Moravian cook, though for the sake of his reputation — an emperor is an emperor — he may have been forced to hire a French male chef, or at least a Viennese chef.

The fame of the Moravian cooks was based on sound instinct and solid performance. Among our acquaintances Marie was celebrated for her 'false' (thick) soups and 'warm' desserts. Prominent visitors who came from gastronomic wonderlands — France, Hungary, Belgium — were delighted with Marie's cream soups, and with her *Dalken* and *Kolatschen* and *Streuselkuchen* (a poem of short dough spread with a crumbly Streusel and fresh blueberries), her *Butterteig* (puff paste) that 'melted on the tongue', *Topfenpalatschinken* (pancakes filled with curdled sweet cream), her *Schinkenfleckerl* and noodles. Marie's *Marillenknödel* (sweet dumplings filled with fresh apricots) once delighted Franz Schalk, then the director of the Vienna State Opera, who came to our town to conduct some concerts of the Vienna Philharmonic. My mother had succeeded in 'getting him', much to the chagrin of the wife of the local brewery owner, and of the general manager of the Vitkovice Iron Works who had also tried to invite him.

Schalk disillusioned me bitterly. He talked with great warmth about

Marie's dumplings but ignored my questions about Beethoven's Pastoral Symphony which he had conducted the night before. He said his teacher Gustav Mahler, another great Moravian, had always raved about such dumplings.

'I now understand what Mahler meant,' Schalk said and took another dumpling, the eighth. I'd kept count. My mother was overjoyed. She would always urge her guests 'to have more' and was personally offended when they declined. For years after that historic meal Schalk remained her favourite conductor. I remember asking him something about Gustav Mahler whom I revered. Schalk stroked his grey goatee and said, 'Young man, I think it's more amusing to talk about Frau Marie's *Marillenknödel*.' I still admired Schalk as a musician but was disappointed about him as a human being. (Other celebrated conductors have affected me likewise.) I regretted that Schalk had been invited.

Personally I was never a connoisseur of Marie's warm *Mehlspeisen*, but I loved her roasts which were basted with love and finished with compassion. And her vegetables were sensational — to use an expression I learned many years later in Hollywood. Marie managed to marry off peas and carrots, gastronomically incompatible partners which do not belong together; under Marie's blessings they made a perfect ménage. When I came to New York as a hungry emigrant in the late 'thirties I ate the absurd mixture again in a cafeteria on West Fifty-seventh Street. There the peas and the carrots, thrown together without affection by an indifferent member of the Chefs, Cooks, Pastry Cooks and Assistants Union of New York, Local 89, were not married. They weren't even betrothed.

Marie's mushroom sauce had the heavy fragrance of our Moravian woods where we children spent happy summer afternoons collecting big *Steinpilze*, delicious mushrooms with dark-brown caps and white stems that hide under moss and near the roots of the fir trees. And I never got tired of watching her as she made mashed potatoes. Marie would mash the potatoes 'with warmth', bearing down on them with vertical thrusts, and then she would add butter and cream. Years later Alexandre Dumaine, then the greatest master of *la grande cuisine* in France and thus the world's champion, explained to me that one must never, never stir the potatoes with rotary movements. Yes, Marie was a cook by intuition. She never learned to pronounce the word *cuisine* — she spoke only Czech and Czech-accented German — but she knew its deeper meaning.

Marie was born to cook as other blessed people are born to write poetry or compose symphonies. I'm now convinced that she was a cooking prodigy; perhaps she had cooked for her dolls — if she ever had any dolls. I never saw her read a cookery-book. Once my mother showed her a recipe for a special cherry cake, part of a legacy left her by an old aunt with a tiny gold ring and some worthless war bonds. For two days Marie didn't speak to my mother. 'What's wrong with *my* cherry cake?', she said at last, when diplomatic relations had been re-established. 'Isn't it good enough for you?' My mother remembered her lesson and never gave her any recipe again. And when friends asked her for the recipe of Marie's *Streuselkuchen*, she wouldn't even dare pass on the request. Marie never let anyone have her own recipes. She said they couldn't be written, they were only 'in her head'.

Marie was often bad-tempered, but that is the privilege of people who spend a considerable part of their lives near a hot range. In our family there existed a theory (not known to medical science) that 'the heat from the kitchen range raises one's blood pressure'. Marie was particularly highly-strung on days when we had guests for dinner. When we were alone, she would cook the midday meal on the big, black coal range, and use the small gas stove for dinner. But for dinner guests she had to build a fire for the second time that day in the big range, and that was hard labour.

We lived on the fifth and highest floor of the family house. Grandfather Wechsberg, a man of Solomonic judgement, had allocated the bottom two floors to the family bank, and the third and fourth floors to my father's older brothers. 'The younger they are, the more steps they should mount,' he said. We mounted exactly one hundred and thirty four steps. I remember the number better than my age. The steps didn't bother me, and they kept elderly aunts from visiting us. The aunts usually collapsed on the lower floors. My cousins Kurt and Hans envied my brother Max and me because we were splendidly protected on the top floor against boring relatives.

The house had no lift. A primitive windlass had been built on the backside of the house, facing the court. Baskets filled with anthracite — we lived in a 'black coal' town — were hoisted up from the cellar to the upper storeys. One person had to turn the windlass downstairs while Marie, up on the small kitchen balcony, would shout 'Hüh!' or 'Hoh!', like a coachman to his horse, to indicate whether the handle should be turned clockwise or counter-clockwise. I didn't mind doing the dirty work with the handle until my younger brother, Marie's protégé, who was up with her, discovered that he could throw pieces of coal down on my head with impunity while I was unable to retaliate eye for eye, tooth for tooth.

When the windlass broke down, which happened frequently, Marie had to carry up the heavy baskets all the way from the cellar to the fifth floor. One hundred and thirty-four steps and she must have been over fifty and suffered from cramps in her legs. Other people have become revolutionaries

A distant view of the author's home town

for much less reason. When she had reached the top floor at last, she would store the coals in a large box on the balcony. She would split her own matchwood and put it with an old newspaper into the stove, and placed larger logs on top. I remember that she was always looking for old newspapers. There was never enough paper around the house. After my father's death, very early in the First World War – he'd led his Austrian infantry company in a heroic, hopeless charge against the Russian machine-guns somewhere in Poland – my mother said she wanted no more newspapers in the house.

Marie subscribed to a church newspaper but refused to burn it in the stove. She would look around grumbling until she found some paper. At last the fragile structure of paper and wood was inside the large, white-tiled range, and Marie would put a match to it. When the logs were burning, she would add selected pieces of shining-black coal. Half an hour

123

later a soft, pleasant warmth would emanate from the kitchen stove — the sort of warmth no gas or electric range will ever give. But for Marie it wasn't pleasant. It was just hot.

She had a small room behind the kitchen with just enough space for her bed and a chest, but not for a table and a chair; if she wanted to read the Bible, after work, she would sit down at the kitchen table. A tiny window in her room looked out on a light-shaft which was just a black, dark wall with very little light. The room was grey and when Marie sat down on her bed — where else could she sit down? — her face looked almost as grey as the wall outside.

Nowadays people advertise for a 'housekeeper' (the word 'cook' is considered undignified) offering a big room with bath, radio and television, short working hours and long week-ends, no children and no dogs, no guests and no fuss, the pay of a junior executive and a share in the employer's enterprise. And still they cannot get anybody. Reading these ads, I have a strong feeling of guilt, as I remember Marie in her terrible, tiny room, with no time off, and long, long hours. She almost never stopped working.

Marie always had one foot in heaven — or, more exactly, in the church around the corner. During the month of May she attended *Maiandacht* every evening; that was a tacit agreement with my mother. I still associate May with cold cuts for dinner. Marie was a deeply devout person and went to Mass every morning before breakfast. The Old Church — it called itself with becoming Christian modesty 'the old one', without resorting to the exalted patronage of one of the Saints — was just a block away. When the church bells rang at a quarter to six in the morning, Marie would start on her slow descent and arrive in church just in time, and when she returned to make breakfast, she was always quietly happy, at peace with herself.

She must have been a very lonely woman. Once in a while an old, shrivelled lady, dressed all in black, with a black handkerchief, came to visit Marie in her kitchen. Marie addressed her as *Vy*, the Czech plural form used as a mark of respect. I was surprised to hear that the old woman was her mother. I called my mother *du*, singular, like 'thou'. I asked Marie why her mother was always dressed in black. She said, 'My mother has worn black since my father died thirty-three years ago, and that's the way it ought to be.'

Sometimes on Sunday afternoon a heavy-built man with a black moustache would come up, sit at the kitchen table, and get some coffee 'from the morning' and a couple of *Kolatschen*. When he was there, Marie was always bad-tempered even though she didn't have to cook dinner for her guest. He was a widower who couldn't make up his mind whether or not to ask Marie to marry him. He never made up his mind, unfortunately. His name was Výborný, which is Czech for 'excellent', an eminently suitable name for a locomotive engineer.

Pan Výborný was one of my childhood heroes. In my dreams I saw him behind the controls of the Orient Express, taking his train through dense fogs, raging blizzards and incredibly high snow drifts. My illusions were only slightly shattered when Marie told me that Vyborny was the engineer on a small, dirty coal-train in the iron-works.

He owned a big, heavy, round engineer's watch and let me play with it, while he took another *Kolatschen*, the fourth or fifth one ('don't mind if I do, no one else makes them as well as you'), and then he would leave, taking his watch along, and Marie would be in a worse temper than ever. My mother never went near the kitchen on Sunday night.

I rarely saw Marie after I left my home-town and came back there only for short visits. She no longer worked at home. I believe the hundred and thirty-four steps had become too much, after all. When my mother moved into a smaller apartment, on the second floor of a modern building, she was alone and did not need a cook. Sometimes Marie came up for a visit. She would sit in the small, modern kitchen and look suspiciously at the modern gas range.

'Don't like it,' she said. 'Gives no warmth at all.'

She didn't trust the lift and walked up the stairs although her feet bothered her badly. After a while she came no more. My mother said Marie had gone to live with another old woman in an old house near the Old Church, and that she still went to Mass every morning, and to *Mai-andacht* every evening in May.

She was buried in the small cemetery behind the Old Church. I'm sure she feels peaceful and happy there.

125

A tailor's workshop in 1618. Even then they would
sit cross-legged on the table to do their sewing

Quality

THE BOHEMIAN TAILOR is a symbol of quality. He's known all over the world like the Italian tenor, the Russian ballerina, the Swiss watchmaker, the Hungarian gipsy primas, the French chef. As always in such cases, imitations show up that are a long way from the original article. Italianized tenors, with a double chin but without *bel canto* training; 'French' chefs from Sicily or Bucharest; Russian ballerinas born in Nebraska and Idaho. And, naturally, 'Bohemian' tailors who never saw Bohemia.

Vienna's telephone directory lists among *Herrenschneider*, gentlemen's tailors, dozen of honourable guild members with Bohemian names – Bousa, Dvořák, Hantak, Hovorka, Humhal, Hurban, Jirinek, Kapounek, Karasek, Kníže, Kohout, Kolar, Kopriwa, Kotyza, Lesak, Marousek, Masarik Mejstrik, Minarik, Nerada, Pival, Ruzicka, Sedlak, Simak, Soucek, Splinar, Sprtka, Tlapa, Vesely, Vitovec, Zdrazil and many others whose names can be found in the telephone directory of Prague, Bohemia, as well as those of Chicago, Cleveland, New York, Sao Paolo, Sidney, Munich and Marseilles. There is even a tailor named Krejčí in Vienna who couldn't be anything else. *Krejčí* is the Czech word for 'tailor'.

Sometimes the Czech names were Germanized, Frenchified or Anglicized without the typical Czech accentuation, so that Růžička becomes Ruschitschka, but that fools no one and when the Bohemian tailors start to open their mouth they show their true colours. Like Americans they are unable to pronounce *Umlaute* – no Bohemian tailor could say, 'Deutschland *über* Alles', and it is doubtful that he would even try – and no matter what language they converse in, they always use the double negative of their ancestral homeland. ·

In Czechoslovakia the species of the gentlemen's tailor is dying out fast, and there are grave doubts about his ability to survive elsewhere. Mass

A tailor in London's Savile Row, monument to Victorian dignity

production and mechanization have caused the disappearance of the skilled artisan who can no longer compete with the big factories. And in the Communist countries he is doomed as one of the last relics of banned private enterprise.

The Bohemian tailors are different from their peers in England, Italy and China, who are also justly famous for their skill. The Bohemian tailor always looks his part — like the tailor in fairy tales and Wilhelm Busch drawings. The first tailor of my memory, a skilled artisan named Sehnal, was a thin, tuberculous-looking man with a cadaverous face and thick glasses which he wore way down his nose, looking distrustfully at his customer across the rim of his glasses. He sat with crossed legs in the middle of his large cutting table, though there were two or three empty chairs around. While he talked to you, he made incredibly quick stitches with a long needle. And he was always shabbily dressed.

By contrast, the distinguished tailor in Savile Row in London, whom I patronized during a period of unexpected affluence, was far better dressed than most of his customers. Wearing a conservative dark suit, standing between dark shelves with dark material of the highest quality, he was a monument to Victorian dignity. *He* decided what I was going to wear, highest judge in a sartorial court of no appeal. Once, in a foolish moment of mutiny, I asked him to somewhat 'Americanize' the contours of my jacket, and was told that 'that sort of thing' could be purchased in 'one of those shops' —and he made a vague movement with his hand pointing in the general direction of Oxford Street — but 'was not done here'. And he placed his hand on an old, dog-eared ledger whose first entry may go back, for all I know, to the reign of Henry VIII. There was never a hint of familiarity about him, even when I stood before him in my underwear, and he was trying to elucidate the doubtful shape of my hipbone.

The Savile Row tailor was the member of a powerful oligarchy. Pan Sehnal, the Bohemian tailor, represented democracy. He worked in mediaeval surroundings under the pale glow of a yellow lamp that made you think of Edison's early experiments. He talked the language of his ancestors, a hard *lingua franca* with many open *e*'s and an abundance of consonants. Certain Czech words consist entirely of consonants: *krk*, for instance, means throat, and *prst* means finger. *Strč prst skrz krk* is not a code telegram but means, 'Put the finger through the throat'. The English were hardened by their climate. The Bohemian tailors were toughened by their consonants. Italian tenors try to neglect the consonants; Bohemian tailors ignore the vowels whenever possible.

Sehnal, a virtuoso of the double negative, often confused his customers from abroad. My friend Franzl who had come to my home-town from the more melodious linguistic climate of Upper Austria, after the first fitting with Sehnal came to me in confusion. 'I haven't the slightest idea what he was talking about', Franzl said. 'He said to me, "If I make you under-collar, I won't have no material for upper-collar, and if you insist on upper-collar, you cannot have no collar at all, unless you want waistcoat too and then I have no material absolutely in no case." I told him I didn't understand, and he got mad and said he'd learned good *deitsch* in school.'

But though Sehnal's language may have been perplexing, there was no uncertainty about his technique of 'turning over' a heavily worn suit with shiny elbows into one that was 'as good as new', or to rejuvenate a shabby, double-breasted suit into an 'almost elegant' single-breasted one. No Savile Row denizen would have bothered. The lowliest Italian tailor would have thrown suit and customer out of his shop. And the Chinese magicians in Hongkong, whose specialty is to make twenty-four-hour suits without a fitting, only work with new material.

True, there are a few ex-Bohemian tailors who became emancipated and acquired a coat-of-arms, elegant manners and scandalous prices. They advertise in smart magazines and sell their own perfume for the gentleman who thinks he needs some. These tailors are always impeccably dressed. This alone makes them *déclassé*. The genuine Bohemian tailor's slogan was, 'Everything for my customers, nothing for me!' The better he worked, the worse he looked. The setting of a Bohemian tailor was old-fashioned as of an old diamond ring, but the stone was genuine.

If you look long enough, you will find a Bohemian tailor nearly everywhere. I found one in Berlin, in Bordeaux, in Saigon, in Hiroshima (that was before It Happened and I hope he's still alive and stitching), and of course in Hollywood where they have everything. After a cross-examination the Bohemian tailor in Hollywood turned out to be Vienna-born and Chicago-raised, but his consonants were authentic and he started every sentence with the verb. 'Am I no Czech, definitely not, am I American citizen,' he said proudly.

He was a genius who could spot the built-in mistakes of a ready-made suit and made the suit look like a custom-made one. In those days the American garment industry hadn't reached today's high standards and many ready-made suits would fit only the tall, elegant dapper dream figures printed in the pages of *Esquire*, of whom there are about four-and-a-half men among a hundred. The others suffer from minor anatomic deviations that remain mercifully camouflaged to everybody but a Bohemian tailor with his penetrating eye.

Hovorka, our man in Hollywood, looked me over the way a sculptor looks at an unhewn stone. He had his problems with idiomatic English, but none with the lamentable anatomical secrets of the male body. And he was a master of practical psychology. He could give his customers an euphoric sense of having a perfect figure while they stood in front of his mirror, wearing one of his creations. The transformation usually lasted only while you were there, and he performed the astonishing metamorphosis from a second-hand body into a de-luxe chassis. But the best thing about his new suits was that they didn't *look* new. You were never self-conscious when you first wore one, as you were after a new, bad hair-cut.

Hovorka had an exclusive clientele which included several film stars who secretly brought him their new, expensive, custom-made suits for alterations. They parked their big Cadillacs in a sidestreet – this was the era before Ghia and Bentley – and came in through the back door to avoid rumours of being broke. Once Hovorka took me into the backroom and showed me the suits hanging there. In the inside pockets I saw the labels of three Savile Row aristocrats, two internationally famous New York

'If you insist on upper-collar, you cannot have no collar at all, unless you want waistcoat too and then I have no material absolutely in no case.'
From a set of engravings by Chodowiecki

firms and an exorbitantly expensive gentlemen's tailor from Rome. All of them landed on the cutting table of humble Hovorka, a practising philosopher, like most Bohemian tailors. 'Come all here, sooner or later,' he said. It was his favourite expression which he'd read in the memoirs of a famous madam whose establishments were reputed from coast to coast. They all came to her, sooner or later.

The exiled Bohemian tailors have shown pride and dignity. They don't get assimilated. Their double negative infects the entire neighbourhood where the citizens soon speak with a sort of sing-song voice and are unable to pronounce *Umlaute*.

The syntax of the Bohemian tailor remains confusing, but their promises are kept. If you are told your suit will be ready on Friday, it will be ready even though the tailor will have to sit with crossed legs all night long on his large workshop table. From their forefathers who lived on the banks of the Moldau these men have inherited a sense of duty, restless energy, diligence and the dexterity of their *prst*, or finger. To be a tailor was always an honour in the country of Good King Wenceslas.

Currently my Bohemian tailor in Vienna is Adalbert Šilhavý (please note the accents), professor of masculine anatomy, designer of narrow lapels, master of the slim line, and creator of virile illusions. He knows more than my doctor about my sloping left shoulder. During the Nazi era in Vienna he was in trouble because he refused to divest himself from the two accents over his name and to have his name Aryanized. 'Wouldn't think of it never,' Šilhavý said. The Aryanizers departed.

He was one of six sons of a farmer in Klatový in Southern Bohemia, who knew his duty to Good King Wenceslas. Four of his boys became tailors. Šilhavý's only son is also a tailor and his father's partner; and *his* son, aged four, will also be a tailor, if the grandfather and father have their way. As long as there are dynasties like the Šilhavýs, there is no real danger for western civilization.

Adventure is
the Spice of Life

I ALWAYS HAD a romantic interest in long, dark tunnels, and once I spent eight hours walking through the Arlberg Tunnel, between St Anton and Langen in Austria, one of the longest tunnels in the world, and surely the darkest. Six miles and nineteen hundred feet, and not a single light in it.

I must have travelled by train over fifty times through the Arlberg Tunnel before I got the idea of walking through. I often go from Vienna to Zurich and Paris, headed west on one of the comfortable express trains that climb the spectacular slopes of the Inn Valley to St Anton where the ten-thousand-foot Arlberg massif blocks the way to the valley of the Rhine.

Always, the climatic ride through the tunnel has been a thrill to me. The westbound trains enter it at an elevation of 4,277 feet and then pick up speed rapidly. The thundering noise of the wheels is amplified as it reverberates against the great square stones lining the tunnel walls. They are dripping wet and in the light from the train's window look so close that you think you could reach out and touch them but the sight is soon blotted out by the mist that forms on the train windows. Passengers are warned to keep the windows closed, because the air in the tunnel is bad, and to keep away from the compartment doors, which might be thrown open by a powerful gust of wind.

I once rode through the tunnel when the lights in my compartment had gone out, leaving me in absolute darkness. I had started thinking about what could happen, and how terrible it would be if anything did happen, and then I was startled by what sounded like a cannon shot. A sharp blast rattled the windows and a train shot by going the other way. For a few seconds, while brightly lit coaches hurtled past, there was a deafening noise. Suppose a man were standing out there in the tunnel at such a moment, I had wondered — where would he hide?

A workman on the track at the entrance to the St Gotthard tunnel

At last, after what seemed like an eternity — but was really only nine or ten minutes — the brakes were being applied, there was the acrid smell of hot metal, and the darkness outside gave way to a pale dawn. The mist on the windows cleared up, the texture of the walls came into focus again. Then there was suddenly bright, almost blinding sunshine, and the train stopped at Langen, at the western end of the tunnel.

I kept thinking about it. Tunnels are proof of man's ingenuity and man's endurance. I remember the day I drove from Switzerland to Chamonix through the pass called the Col des Montets, and suddenly saw in front of me the towering granite-and-ice massif out of which rises Europe's highest mountain. On the left was the rock pinnacle called the Aiguille du Midi, ('Needle of the South'); next to it were Les Monts Maudits, truly Cursed Mountains that have caused the death of many climbers; and then came the Mont Blanc itself, 15,781 feet of monumental whiteness. And men had bored the world's longest highway tunnel, through almost eight miles of granite, gneiss and darkness.

Tunnellers are a very special breed of modern pioneers, *va-banque* players who love the glorious uncertainty of tunnelling. There is always high adventure in a tunnel. André Pierre Gervais, who headed the task force that built the French section of the Mont Blanc Tunnel, calls tunnelling *un voyage à l'inconnu*. You know as little about what you're going to find in the next ten feet as tunnellers did a hundred years ago. A tunneller needs instinct, a certain sixth sense, if he is to survive. He never lets himself be taken by surprise, is always prepared for the worst. He feels about the mountain as the seaman feels about the sea: he loves the mountain but he knows it's an implacable, unpredictable enemy that will kill you if you don't watch out.

When the blasts of the excavation shake the equilibrium of rock strata that have been relatively quiet for millions of years, the enormous weight presses down and trouble starts. No geologist can say what will happen inside the mountain; he can only tell what the mountain will be like, what sort of rock the tunnellers will encounter. But he cannot predict exactly where small air pockets will be in the rocks, or where the men will come up against decomposed granite — granite made so brittle by water that it became soft as kaolin, and the tunnel may cave in.

Tunnelling is a very old branch of engineering science. Two thousand years before the beginning of the Christian era, the Assyrians built a tube under the Euphrates River in Babylon to connect the royal palace with a temple across the way. Expert tunnellers today admit they couldn't do it much better. At the time of the Emperor Claudius, the Romans constructed a tunnel under Monte Salviano, in the province of Aquila, for the drainage of Lake Fucino — an enterprise that Pliny referred to as the greatest public work of his time. Some of the basic tunnelling techniques developed by the Romans were still as useful under Mont Blanc as they were under Monte Salviano. When the Italian tunnellers encountered a *zona tormentata* of decomposed granite, they had to use the 'Roman' method, drilling a tiny opening and cautiously widening it by manual methods. After the fall of Rome the old techniques were all but forgotten and the tunneller's art languished until the late nineteenth century, when the great Alpine tunnels were built.

I've ridden through all of them: the eight-mile Mont Cenis, completed in 1871 after work had gone on for fourteen years, during the first four of which the workers progressed an average of nine inches a day (as against a twenty-six-foot average for the Mont Blanc crews); the nine-and-a-third miles long St Gotthard in Switzerland, nine years in the building, from 1872 to 1880, during which time two out of every three workers were incapacitated by rock dust, high temperatures and the fumes from oil lamps; the twelve-and-a-third-mile Simplon connecting Switzerland and Italy, completed in 1905, the world's longest railway tunnel; and the nine-mile long Loetschberg Tunnel in Switzerland. I've been through the eleven-and-a-half-mile Apennine Tunnel between Bologna and Florence (1930); the Cascade Tunnel, in the State of Washington, just under eight miles and the longest in America; and the new Mont Blanc Tunnel which beats many records. It is the world's longest vehicular tunnel, and for over a mile-and-a-third lies a mile-and-a-third below the top of the mountain.

It had never occurred to me to *walk* through a dark tunnel until one day a few years when I happened to be in St Anton am Arlberg. I stood near the eastern portal of the Arlberg Tunnel, with its inscription 'Franz Josef I', the Imperial Habsburg coat-of-arms, and the date 1884. It was pitch-dark inside and quite mysterious. It seemed an inferno, though quite different from the inferno George Orwell had envisaged for the centenary of the tunnel, in 1984. I decided then to walk through the tunnel. I don't really know why I did. Perhaps I sensed that the journey through darkness would involve three things I've always been fascinated by mountains, railways and long tunnels.

In St Anton the following day I met an old man who had been there the day in 1880 when they had started to build the Arlberg Tunnel. He was Alois Kessler, an eighty-three-year-old retired railway man with a ruddy face and a goatee, and he still took a paternalistic interest in the Arlberg Tunnel.

'I spent thirty-five years in there,' he said to me. 'The darkest years of my life. First I was with the building force, and then I was foreman of the tunnel repair gang. I remember that day in 1880 as if it were yesterday. Kaplan Stocker read Mass at the foot of the mountain, where the entrance is now, and I was chosen to act as ministrant and carry the cross. Everybody in St Anton was there. An old sheepherder came down on the pass road — not the one the motorists use now, but the narrow lane on the other side of that — and when he was told that they were going to bore a hole straight through the mountain, he crossed himself and said, " Go home, you crazy people, and don't make the good Lord angry." '

St Anton and Langen became real gold-rush towns. People came from everywhere to work, and especially from Italy. There were more than four thousand foreigners in St Anton. Before drilling started, tracks leading up to the tunnel had to be laid, which required a lot of supporting walls and columns. They even set up a dynamite factory, where a hundred men made the dynamite that made the tunnel. Unfortunately, it finally blew up, but that doesn't mean that these old-timers didn't know their job. They

Miners at work during the final stages of the construction of the Simplon tunnel. A photograph from the early years of the century

started digging at each end, and when they met in the middle after three years, they were only a few inches out of line.

Those were the Middle Ages of tunnelling, when the men were blasting their way through solid quartz, which is almost pure silica. After a few years of inhaling quartz dust many men came down with silicosis, a dreadful, incurable disease in which microscopic dust particles cause a fibrosis of the lung tissue. Only in 1947 was wet-drilling introduced in tunnel work. Now the tunnellers use a hollow drill through which a continuous stream of water is passed. Water, one of the greatest threats to tunnellers, became one of their greatest benefactors, though it is still an enemy in many ways. Great progress has also been made in the ventilating techniques. But drilling a long tunnel is still a hazardous venture and no one can say how it will end.

It wasn't easy to get permission to walk through the Arlberg. I had to sign some forms, and pay for the insurance policy which the railway had taken out on my life, just to be on the safe side. The premium was seven Austrian schillings, less than thirty cents. It didn't seem tactful to inquire how much I had been insured for, but evidently the railway didn't put a high value on my life.

I walked through the tunnel with Johann Raffeiner, a thin, pale, soft-spoken, blond man, who is the *Streckenbegeher*, the man-who-walks-the-tracks. He has been walking through the tunnel for over fifteen years, six times a week. Carrying a rucksack, a carbide lamp and a heavy monkey wrench, he starts either in St Anton or Langen, stepping from one sleeper to the next, looking for breaks in the rails. There are sixteen thousand sleepers, and he's got to watch carefully. Some of the fissures are tiny, hardly ten millimetres long, but they can be very dangerous, and if anything happens to a train going over them, it's his responsibility. As many as eighty trains go through the tunnel every day at the height of the summer season.

Raffeiner told me that in the early days of the tunnel when the locomotives burned coal, smoke was the worst hazard. Whenever the wind came from the west, thick clouds of smoke would choke the tunnel for days, and it was hell to ride through. Sometimes the engineer and the fireman had to lie down on the floor of their locomotive when the train was going through; when repair-crews were inside, an engine and a coach were kept ready at each end to get the men out quickly in case they were overcome.

Now the tunnel's worst enemy is water. It seeps through the rocks and washes the sand ballast from under the sleepers, and new ballast must be packed under them, or else the rails will break. All the ballasting inside the

A page from *L'Illustration* commemorating the inauguration of the railway from Paris to Vienna via the Arlberg tunnel, 20th September, 1884

tunnel is done by hand — a carefully measured amount of sand packed under each sleeper. Water bothered the people who built the tunnel, and it will always bother everybody who has to keep it in shape. They'd tried out everything to stop the flow: they had filled up fissures with cement and covered sections of the roof with copper, but it was no use. The water always finds its way through, and if it doesn't wash out the ballast, its corrosive elements, sulphur and so on, go to work on the rails and make them brittle, and then the rails break under the weight of the trains.

A cold, raw wind was sweeping across the rails as Raffeiner and I walked into the western tunnel-entrance, each wearing an old-fashioned carbide lamp that had proved more reliable than a flashlight. The tracks curved slightly for a short distance just inside the entrance and then ran on straight ahead as far as the eye could see in the dim light. Raffeiner walked in the center of Track One, on the left side the tunnel, the track used by trains coming from Langen to St Anton. He said he always walked facing

139

the oncoming traffic – naturally, since he didn't want to be surprised by a train sneaking up on him from behind. But sometimes they had to switch the trains to Track Two. A sudden defect in the overhead wires could make such a switch necessary, and it was up to the dispatcher to let him know.

He walked ahead of me, keeping his eyes on rails and sleepers, and I walked closely behind him, hoping there would be no sudden switch today, and that the trains would not sneak up on us from behind. Gradually, the darkness grew thicker, and soon the circles which our lamps illuminated ahead of us were all that we could see. A telegraph cable ran along the left wall, and a coaxial cable for television along the right one. There was just enough space for two trains to pass – at its widest the tunnel was thirty-one feet – and between the tracks was a narrow drainage channel, with its top boarded over. Raffeiner walked slowly, methodically, stepping from one sleeper to the next with the steady beat of a metronome, never looking up. I did my best to keep the same gait. Every hundred metres a little niche was cut into the wall, and every kilometre there would be a big chamber, with a telephone.

Shortly after we passed the first chamber, I heard dripping sounds and then water splashed down from the roof onto my hat and coat. The sleepers and rails glistened with dampness in the lamplight. Continuous moisture wouldn't hurt the sleepers, Raffeiner explained to me, but the change from dry to wet was dangerous, and in some places the change was almost constant. The surface of one rail was pitted with small concavities that looked as if they'd been made with a hammer. When the wheels of the train went over these uneven spots they would hop up and down.

I asked him what he would do if he discovered a break in the rails. 'That depends on the break. If it were bad and a train were due, I would run ahead as far as I had time to go, and put three torpedoes on the rails, eighty metres apart. I always carry some in my rucksack. As soon as the first explodes, the engineer puts on the brakes. If there is no time for the caps, I've got to stop the train by signalling with my lamp.'

We walked on into the darkness. After a while I turned around. The St Anton entrance was a tiny speck of greyish daylight. I was becoming aware that the air had a foul, dead smell. A mouse scuttled across the tracks, its eyes glittering in the lamplight. Raffeiner said he ran across animals in the tunnel now and then again, mostly mice but sometimes a fox had wandered in and occasionally a deer would come in and go into a niche, and he would shoo it out to safety again.

A few moments later, Raffeiner asked, 'Did you notice anything just now?' He kept on walking, with his head down.

'No'.

'A train is behind us'.

We stopped. I turned around. Where the small grey hole had been, I saw the three headlights of an engine. I listened carefully, but all was quiet. There wasn't a sound in the tunnel. I asked Raffeiner how he'd heard the train.

'I didn't hear it', he said. 'When you hear a train in the tunnel, it's usually too late to do anything about it. There's no need to go to a niche because this train is going by on the other track, but you'd better step back to the wall now and hold on to your hat. It will be here pretty soon.'

The train had looked very far away only half-a-minute ago, but now it was approaching with what seemed incredible speed. Suddenly, I was hit by a strong draught – the air the train was pushing ahead of it. Then the headlights were very close, there was a rapidly increasing thunder, and the train seemed to leap out of the darkness and flash past us. The noise was tremendous. A strong current of air, smelling of hot metal, pushed me back against the wall, and my feet were almost pulled out from under me. I had a short, nightmarish vision of lighted windows and of people behind them. Then the train was gone and my eyes were full of dust and tears. After a moment, I could see the red tail-light dwindling in the darkness, and now the draught pulled me forward.

'The morning express from Vienna', Raffeiner said in a matter-of-fact way, and walked on. I was glad he didn't turn around and look at me. I think my knees were a little shaky.

'How did you know the train was coming?', I asked.

'It's a very slight change of pressure in my ears that tells me. It takes a while to get the feel of it, but the air is the safest indicator. You can't trust your hearing and on smoky days you can't trust your eyes either. And I certainly wouldn't want to trust the timetable. But I do trust the air inside the tunnel. It makes me think of a long sausage. It stands quite still until a train enters, and that pushes the sausage forward. After the train has passed, it draws the sausage behind it. Even on the coldest days, I never wear the flaps of my cap down over my ears, because I've got to notice each draught. The tunnel is no place for careless people. Some of my predecessors have been killed in here because they were careless for a moment. . . . There, did you feel anything?'

The draught in the wake of the train had stopped, and the air seemed quite still.

I said, 'The train has left the tunnel'.

'On the contrary, it has another five minutes in the tunnel. But now a *second* train has entered, from Langen, and it is pushing the air toward us. That neutralizes the draught of the train that has already passed. When

The festive reception of the ladies of Iselle by the ladies of Brigue, a photograph of the ceremonial opening of the Simplon tunnel in April, 1905

the air stands still in the tunnel, it means that there is no train inside — or that there are *two* trains, going in opposite directions.'

I thought of the train coming toward us out of the darkness on the track we were walking on, and asked Raffeiner if we hadn't better get into a niche.

'There's plenty of time,' he said. 'Before it gets anywhere near us, we'll see the reflection of the headlights on the overhead wires.'

After a few minutes, the wires began to shine softly, as if they had been filled with liquid red light. Raffeiner said the train was pretty close now but we couldn't see its headlights because there was a sort of hill a little farther on. The tunnel slopes towards either end; it was designed that way so that the water would drain off. It rises 24 feet from the St Anton portal to Kilometre 104, the summit, and then drops 290 feet to the Langen portal. We wouldn't see the headlights until the train reached the crest at Kilometre 104.

'There it is now,' Raffeiner said, and motioned me to follow him to a niche.

Some seconds after we reached it, the train came by, a long, slow freight train, its wheels banging hard against the rails. It seemed to have no end. The wind it made was so strong that I had to keep a tight hold on my hat, and the niche was neither deep nor comfortable. It was said to have space for eight men but I wondered how they could get in. The train went by at last and we walked on.

A little farther ahead I saw a small black plaque, bearing the inscription, 'H. KATHREINER – 10. 6. 1931'.

'One of my predecessors,' Raffeiner said. 'He'd been told in the morning that the early express would use the wrong track because of repairs in the tunnel. The dispatcher in St Anton wrote it in his book but Kathreiner must have forgotten. When he felt the express coming from behind, he didn't even turn around, he was so sure it was on the other track as usual. The engineer tried to stop, but it was to late. At eighty kilometres an hour, it takes seven hundred metres to bring a train to a standstill. The headlights shine only four hundred metres ahead, so the engineer no matter how hard he tries, can never stop the train if he sees someone on the track. You've got to watch out for yourself every step of the way. Before the last war, two men were doing my job, walking together through the tunnel. There was also a time when two men would start from opposite ends, meet in the middle, sign each other's book, and go on. Frankly, I wouldn't want to walk through with another man. When there are two of you, you're apt to talk and not pay proper attention to what you're doing and then something happens. Some days, I get busy with my thoughts – you can't help thinking when you are all alone here in the darkness – but I always try to snap out of it. I had a close shave last winter, and don't want it to happen again.'

Raffeiner stopped and lit another cigarette, his fifth or sixth that morning. He smoked a lot.

'It was a bad day, with a cold wind and a heavy fog. I had started from Langen, and there was snow piled up around the entrance and a lot of icicles. I felt miserable and wished I were at home. The sleepers were covered with ice, and I knew they would be for the first two or three kilometres. I was wearing shoes with thick rubber soles and had my ice-axe, but even so I had to be careful. You can't walk fast on a day like that. I had gone about six hundred metres when I saw the lights of the morning express from Vienna – the one we saw a while ago – coming down towards me. There was a niche next to me, but I didn't go in. The lights were still far away, at least three kilometres – or so I thought. Well, I walked on, and then I had that funny feeling in my ears – the air stood still, you know.

143

I turned around and saw that a train had entered the tunnel behind me from Langen. Then I remembered that the dispatcher in Langen had told me a special freight train would leave Langen at that time. I'd forgotten about it because I felt so cold and low that morning. The niche ahead of me wasn't very far, and I began to walk faster, but the ice made it hard. It was like in a nightmare, when you want to walk faster, and your feet are tied to the ground, with heavy weights hanging on them. I wasn't really frightened though. True, the train behind me was close, but the express in front of me was still a comfortable distance away, to judge by the size of the headlights.'

Raffeiner was silent for a while and drew on his cigarette. 'And then, suddenly, both trains seemed to rush at me. This was no nightmare; it was true. In a fraction of a second, I knew what had happened. The engineer of the express train had forgotten to switch on the large headlights. He was using the small lights. When I'd thought the train was at least three kilometres away, it was actually within nine hundred metres.'

'There was no time to rush to the niche. There wasn't even time to try to reach the side wall. I acted by instinct. I snatched off my rucksack, dropped my ice-axe and the wrench, and threw myself down alongside the drainage channel between the two tracks. It must have taken less than a second — a reflex action. The good Lord was with me. In many spots, there are shoulders of rock there, and if I'd hit a place like that, it would have been the end. But where I threw myself down, it was sort of hollowed out. There wasn't much space — I wouldn't advise you to try it. I had my head between my hands, trying to hug the icy ground, and then both trains seemed to race over me . . .'

It was very quiet in the tunnel, and a long while before Raffeiner spoke again.

'I must have stayed there quite a while. When I got up I could see nothing of either train — not even the tail-lights. I picked up my things and went right back to Langen. I didn't walk through the tunnel that day.'

The air was getting staler and warmer as we walked on, and I opened my overcoat. I smelled smoke. Raffeiner said the electric trains gave off a variety of fumes, and so did the Wagons-Lits cars heated by old-fashioned coal stoves.

'Today is not bad at all though,' he said. 'One day a few years ago, an avalanche blocked the Langen entrance, and they called for a snow-plough from St Anton. The snow at the Langen portal piled up until it touched the overhead wires, so the current was cut off, and they had to push the snow-plough in with a steam engine. The snow-plough worked for more than an hour but couldn't get through. All the time, the locomotive was puffing out clouds of heavy smoke inside the tunnel. I had walked in at St Anton that morning, and it was really bad. I could hardly see at times and I had to hold a water-soaked handkerchief in front of my mouth.

'The smoke seemed to get denser every minute. The station-master started in on a diesel switch-engine to see what had happened to the snow-plough, but he fainted before they got to me, and had to be taken out right away. I dragged myself to the nearest chamber – the one we passed a few minutes ago, at Kilometre 103 – and had to lie down. I was just able to call them on the 'phone to come and get me. I couldn't stay in the chamber because it was too full of smoke, so I opened the cover of the drainage channel between the tracks and stuck my head in there, hoping the air would be better. When they came to pick me up I had lost consciousness, and I didn't wake up until they put me on the diesel and gave me something to drink.'

As we neared Kilometre 104, the highest point in the tunnel, Raffeiner told me that this section and the section on the other side of the summit were the most dangerous, because trains could be seen only at the very moment they came over the crest – sometimes too close for comfort. A white line painted on the wall, rising gradually from the foot of the nearest niche, reaching the top halfway between the niche and the next one and then going down to the foot of the next niche, showed you at a glance the quickest way to safety. A few minutes later we crossed the summit, and now I could see a pinpoint of light far ahead of us: the Langen entrance, six kilometres away.

There was another small black plaque on the wall, 'SCHARNAGL – 12. 2. 1940'.

'He was a nice man, quiet and reliable, but one day he waited a minute too long to step off the track, and he was gone,' Raffeiner said.

I felt a slight pressure in my ears – the same sort of feeling, only much milder, that you get in an aeroplane as it comes down. I turned round but saw no train. Raffeiner said a train was coming behind us, on the other side of the summit. After a while, the pressure in my ears stopped, and the air became still. I looked into the darkness in front of us. The pinpoint of light was gone. I kept thinking of the two trains rushing toward us, and I was glad when Raffeiner stepped into the next niche. We waited there until both trains had passed.

At Kilometre 105, near the centre of the tunnel, we came to a niche where Raffeiner kept a supply of carbide and a candle in an old can of Dole Hawaiian Pineapple Spears. In a corner, water was dripping from the roof.

145

'The water supply never shuts off here,' he said, lighting the candle and blowing out both lamps. 'You have to be careful not to put too much water into the lamps or it will drown the carbide, and then halfway to Langen the lamp goes out. That has happened to me a few times. I had to feel my way along like a blind man, letting the monkey wrench glide along the inside of the rails as a guide. It's really dark out there. Take a look. There's plenty of time but the Arlberg-Orient Express will be along soon.'

I stepped out into the tunnel and looked back toward St Anton. The darkness was so compact that I felt as though I could hold it in my hands. There was nothing but dead, quiet, black space all around me; there had been darkness here for millions and millions of years.

Darkness can be frightening; in a strange place where you don't know your way around, or in a big city, when the lights suddenly go out, or when all noises are muted and all lights extinguished by a sudden fog, as in London. The sort of fog that John Galsworthy described in *The Man of Property*, as 'a vast, muffled blackness, where a man could not see six paces before him; where, all around, voices or whistles mocked the senses of direction, and suddenly shapes came rolling slow . . . and now and then a light showed like a dim island in an infinite dark sea'. The darkness that oppresses the mind and spirit, that made a Victorian writer exclaim, 'Oh, the desolation, the despair that overcame me!'

I once walked through utter darkness and suddenly heard steps behind me; it gave me a strange sensation of *déjà vu* – I must have gone through such an experience seeing a film, probably a Hitchcock murder picture – and yet I couldn't get rid of the steps. As soon as I stopped, the steps behind me stopped too, and when I walked, they were again behind me. The explanation came later and was an innocent one, as I made shorter steps and let my pursuer, whoever it was, catch up with me. He was a respectable man and he'd had a similar sensation; after a while he didn't know whether I was walking in front or behind him, or somewhere on his side. We decided to walk together until we came to some lights . . .

Now the darkness was different; not sinister and full of hidden threats, but soft and warm, like a dress made of heavy, dark velvet. It was a rare and precious moment; I had a sense of being alone with myself; it was like being on top of a very high mountain from where one could look all around and see no human being, hear no voice. There was no one around me; only the soft sound of running water far in the distance, a pleasant, eternal lullaby. I began to understand why Raffeiner kept his responsible, badly paid, hard job walking through the dark tunnel. It is not often nowadays that a man has the luxury of being completely alone with himself.

A sound startled me, and then I saw Raffeiner come out of the niche with the newly lighted carbide lamps. I had forgotten all about him. He handed me one lamp, and I held it tight, with almost loving care. I had never suspected that I would ever grow fond of a carbide lamp.

We crossed the tracks and opened the door into the chamber. It was hewn out of the rock, and looked like a prison cell without bars. After the deadness and stillness of the tunnel it seemed almost homelike and comfortable, as we sat on a crude bench and put our lamps on a wooden table. There was a closet containing several lamps like ours and some tools, and a telephone on the wall, its receiver and mouthpiece heavily insulated against the eternal moisture.

Raffeiner took off his rucksack and unpacked his lunch — a piece of dry bread and a few slices of bacon. He offered to share it with me, but I thanked him; I seemed to have no appetite.

Raffeiner looked at the walls around us. 'This is the middle of the mountain,' he said. 'The peak of the Arlberg is just above us. I believe the

The triumphant meeting of both parties of tunnellers
after the breakthrough in the St Gotthard tunnel

tunnel passes 1594 feet below the Arlberg Pass. Right over our heads is the Hospiz of St Christoph, where Hannes Schneider founded the Arlberg Ski Club. This chamber is 4250 feet above sea level. How do you like the healthy, bracing mountain air?'

He laughed and started on his lunch. He was quite relaxed as he munched his bread and bacon. I asked him what on earth had made him take this job. He said it had been the other way around — the job had taken him. He wasn't a local Tyrolian; he was born in Algund, a village in the South Tyrol, near the beautiful town of Merano, in a region that was once Austrian and is now Italian. He had come to St Anton in the 'thirties to work at the Hotel Post and in 1938 he'd started working for the railway. 'I've always felt the romance of the railway', he said. 'I can think of no prettier sight than a train with a steam-engine going through a valley at dusk, the white smoke curling along the blue slopes.'

I said I had already realized that he was something of a romantic.

'You've got to be if you work for the railway . . . I did a little of everything. In 1948, when the tunnel track-walker was to be pensioned, they were looking for a new man. No one wanted the job, as you can imagine. Everybody said it was dark and lonely and cold in wintertime. The pay isn't much higher than for outside jobs where the air is better and there is less danger. I decided to take it. I don't mind being alone . . . Strange, isn't it?'

I said it wasn't strange at all.

'I don't really get lonely in here,' he said. 'And now I've become fond of the tunnel. It's my baby. I have more responsibility than if I were a member of a track-gang. I am on my own. There is so much to think about while I walk through. And it's never dull. Most people in this world have dull jobs, and they get desperate and do all sorts of foolish things. There are not two days alike. There's always some adventure in the tunnel and you know you've got to be on your toes all the time or you're licked. It's a challenge and I like it. And I like the darkness around me.'

He was silent for a while.

'Sometimes when I change the carbide in the lamp, I don't light the candle and sit out there in the darkness for a while. I feel the darkness, and it gives me a sense of — of infinity.' He was groping for some words. 'Perhaps that's the way these astronauts feel up there, though in a different way.' Raffeiner gave a shrug. 'But what I like best about this job is the joy of rediscovery.'

I looked at him questioningly.

'When you've been in the tunnel all day long, you rediscover every evening the trees and the flowers and the mountains and the meadows around you. You don't take them for granted, the way people do when they are always out in the open.'

The telephone rang and I jumped, but Raffeiner paid no attention to it. He said it was an automatic signal, ringing all telephones in the tunnel, to let repair crews know a train was coming.

'That's the Arlberg Express now,' Raffeiner told me. He pointed at the carbide lamps on the table and said, 'Watch'.

Suddenly the flames in both lamps flickered, as if someone had blown on them. After a couple of seconds, they burned steadily again. Here we were inside a stone chamber in the middle of the mountain, five kilometres away from the Langen entrance, and the door was closed, but even here the draught showed that a train had entered the tunnel. It seemed absurd that in a few minutes the Arlberg Express, well heated, well lighted, with fine sleeping cars and a cozy dining-car, would be coming through on its way from Paris, through this blackness and deadness. Paris seemed very, very far away. How long had it been since I'd entered the tunnel? In this eerie world one lost all sense of time and space.

Raffeiner picked up his lamp and wrench, and stepped out into the gleam of light. I could tell that the train was approaching, but there was no sound. The train seemed to be a ghost train, a Flying Dutchman on wheels. After a while, the overhead wires began to glimmer and the rails began to hum softly. All at once there was a roaring noise, the head-lights became blindingly bright, and then the Arlberg Express went by, a great mass of steel, white smoke, sparks flying from the wheels, and dust. I saw sleepers and coaches and the brightly lit windows of the dining-car — it seemed to me that I could almost see the white table cloths and inhale the aroma of fresh coffee — and then it was gone, and there was only the red tail-light.

A few hundred yards further on, there was a large marble plaque on the right-hand wall. I read:

UNDER THE GLORIOUS REIGN
OF H. M. EMPEROR FRANZ JOSEF I
IN THE PRESENCE OF HIS EXCELLENCY,
FELIX FREIHERR VON PINO FRIEDENTHAL,
MINISTER OF TRADE, AT THIS SPOT THE
WALL BETWEEN THE PROVINCES OF TYROL
AND VORARLBERG WAS BROKEN THROUGH
ON NOVEMBER 19, 1883

149

This was where the two drilling crews had met. 'It must have been an exciting moment,' Raffeiner said. 'I wish I could have been here.'

Showers were pouring down from the roof now, and small rivulets ran under the tracks and into the drainage channel. The downhill walk had gone swiftly, and by this time we were so near to the Langen portal that I could see the station building and the sidings. Greyish daylight seeping into the tunnel accentuated the rough texture of the walls. There were dark spots where the lining appeared to have been repaired. Raffeiner told me that towards the end of the Second World War Langen and the tunnel entrance were occupied by a detachment of the SS. They drilled holes into the sides of the tunnel, filled them with explosives and were all set to blow it up, but were argued out of it by the old stationmaster at Langen. When the French moved in, they got the explosives out quickly. They also found a whole ammunition train parked inside the tunnel on Track One.

Raffeiner still kept his eyes on the rails, but I was magically attracted by the lovely picture of blue skies and white clouds, of mountains and trees and colours, framed by the tunnel portal, and once I stared so hard out there that I stumbled and almost fell.

Then at last we were outside, and deeply and gratefully I inhaled the brisk air, the scent of trees and mushrooms and resin and wet earth. Langen, often a greyish sort of place, looked marvellous to me that afternoon. The colours of the trees and meadows and houses were brilliant, and the air was as wonderful as a bouquet of old claret.

It was five minutes past three – almost exactly eight hours after we had entered the tunnel.

At the station I bought a ticket for the ride back to St Anton. The sun was warm and I suddenly felt sleepy. After a while the train came and we got on. It was an uneventful trip. The people in the coach seemed bored and no one looked out into the darkness of the tunnel. A man opposite me had been reading a paper, but the electric light was dim, and he seemed impatient to get through the mountain. It took us exactly nine minutes and twelve seconds to return through the Arlberg Tunnel.

A few weeks later, I happened to ride through the tunnel again, on a trip from Vienna to Switzerland. It was shortly before dinner time, and I sat in the warm, pleasant dining car of the Arlberg Express, having a drink. As we approached the tunnel, I looked out into the darkness and thought of Raffeiner, and then I had a sudden impulse. I called the waiter and asked for an envelope and a piece of paper. He brought them just as the train rumbled into the tunnel entrance.

I quickly scribbled a note, addressed the envelope to 'Johann Raf-feiner, Arlberg Tunnel', opened the window, and dropped it out. The draught caught it, and when I last saw it, the wheels of the coach behind the dining car seemed to be passing over it, and that was the end of it, I thought.

When I returned to Vienna, several days later, I received a picture postcard from St Anton. It showed the tunnel-entrance and was signed by Raffeiner. He had found my note in the dark tunnel the next day.

The Happy Dilettante

I AM an amateur, a dilettante — a man who does a thing because he loves doing it. The amateur's lot is not an easy one in a world run by non-amateurs and anti-amateurs — condescending experts, arrogant specialists, slick perfectionists. They call us dabblers and dilettantes because we can't do a thing well. They shrug their shoulders. What can you expect from a bunch of dilettantes whose enthusiasm outstrips their ability? At best, they call us 'gifted dilettantes' — which is like being a tenor who can sing anything except the high C.

They are wrong. The truth is that we are so crazy about doing a thing that we don't mind doing it badly. We have no fame — we gladly leave that to the experts — but we certainly have more fun.

It takes a lot of *Zivilcourage* to admit to being an amateur. We are suspect to anaemic anti-amateurs and true-blood non-amateurs because in this era of brutal materialism we practise a particular pursuit of happiness without hope of financial reward. There is something odd these days about a man who doesn't care about making money. A twentieth-century beachcomber, eh? A neo-nihilist, a super-radical. Even the Marxists love the comforts that money will buy though they may not always admit it. And here is a man who spends many happy hours doing something that will bring him neither status nor a promotion. An individualist, a nonconformist. Better watch that fellow. Universality is unpopular; nonconformism is suspect; individualism is dangerous. The amateur, a man of catholic tastes, an individualist and nonconformist to boot, must not be taken seriously.

We dilettantes don't want to improve our standard of living. We want to improve our lives. Some of us are not merely amateurs but card-carrying amateurs — members of chamber music or model railway groups, of

Welcome every dread delight by Ralph Kitaj.
His paintings have an immediacy which
appeals to experts and art-lovers alike

bird-watching or chess clubs, of singing and hiking societies, do-it-your-self outfits and similar cliques.

Fellow dilettantes, don't despair. History is on our side. Throughout the ages, gifted amateurs have pioneered new thought and stimulated dis-covery. Amateurs have changed the course of the world more often than the experts. Leonardo da Vinci was a noted amateur physicist and amateur builder. Goethe's universal mind was attracted by the mysteries of alchemy and chemistry, medicine and mineralogy, mathematics and statesmanship; he was an extremely gifted dilettante in zoology, botany, all the natural sciences; he was fascinated by the science of colours and philosophy. Voltaire, von Humboldt, Thoreau, Edison and Ford were fellow-amateurs with brilliant ideas, men of universal rather than special-ized thinking. They would have a hard time in this age of absurd special-ization. Today stage-hands may carry a chair but not a spotlight. Den-tists are not identical with dental surgeons. Sooner or later we are bound to have dental specialists for the right and left side of the mouth. Soup cooks will be divided into clear-soup cooks and thick-soup cooks. And meanwhile our soup is getting cold.

The expert has an answer for everything that happens within the narrow confines of his territory. Experts tell us everything down the line – what to eat, and especially what not to eat, what to think and why we dream, what to desire subconsciously and what to excavate from the deep dark abysses of our minds, where to go and how to get adjusted. Our sexual behaviour and unformed thoughts are pried into. Some of these experts seem to have a direct line to the Almighty. They predict how many people will get killed on the highways next weekend. They know next year's colours in fashion and trends in politics.

The expert is a product of the new American civilization. He was created in the retort of a super-Homunculus, somewhat like the secret formula of a popular soft drink. He has become an indispensable element of the new ruling class. Washington these days is made up of experts who, according to *Time*, 'can reel off facts and figures about complex problems without consulting a note'. The experts spend so much time memorizing their facts and figures that they can't afford to think of the people who are mostly concerned by these facts and figures. (There are expert conductors who conduct all scores by heart without being able to bring alive the spirit of the music. They are called *Maestro* – which is a little like being called *Herr Professor* in Vienna because one wears glasses.)

Under the hard stare of the Sub-Committee for the Investigation of Amateurish Activities courageous amateurs have admitted that they

Mr Churchill painting on the Riviera in 1930

want to get away from the pressures of the competitive rat-race and the hazards of professional pyramid-climbing at least for a few hours each week. There are other ways of escape. Some people literally retire from the world and go to an island. Others get drunk. Some become misanthropes and spend their leisure time writing anonymous letters to their newspaper. Some talk in a reclining position, at twenty-five dollars an hour, while others beat up their wives.

The dilettantes should take comfort from the fact that the pursuit of dilettantism is even more suspect in the un-free world than in ours. Behind the Iron Curtain dilettantes are accused of wasting time, which is a 'crime against the state' — because time, like everything else there, is state-owned. The Eastern-style dilettante is called a destructive element, a cosmopolitan rotter. He'd better look out if he knows what's good for him.

The lack of the competitive element is a distinctive feature of the

genuine amateur. We don't want to outpaint, outperform or outcook anyone; we just have a wonderful time painting, playing or cooking. Today
many 'amateurs' in sports play because they want to win. They don't
have the carefree, disinterested attitude that ennobles the genuine amateur. They carry the pressures of their daily professional life into their
leisure activities. Poor fellows, caught by the cogs of the wheel, unable to
get out of it even on Sunday morning. Admittedly there are some people
who play tennis or golf because they love to play, not to win at the risk
of a heart attack. Are you one of them? Are you happy and exhilarated
even after a lost game? Then, brother, you are one of us.

Our *Who's Who* in Dilettantism is quite a volume. For some reason,
generals prefer bridge and chess in their amateurish hours. Physicians
play music. Musicians like to tinker and build (Jascha Heifetz is an
expert boat-builder). Lawyers and teachers are gardeners and bird-
watchers. Hollywood residents go in for expensive collecting. Bernard
Gimbel, the department store tycoon, used to spar in his private gym-
nasium with ex-heavyweight champ Gene Tunney, who is an amateur
of cooking and tasting wines.

Let's not forget, fellow amateurs, that without our boundless enthusiasm a lot of experts would be out of business. Where would Mr Heifetz
be without that hard core of the amateurish fanatics — or fanatical
amateurs — who buy his records and come to his concerts, without being
dragged there by their *Kultur*-conscious wives? Where would the professional politicos be without the amateurs who do all the work and put
up all the money? Where would Mr Eastman and Mr Kodak be?

When I was a boy and learned to play the violin, I had juvenile dreams
of becoming a great fiddler. My dreams were temporarily shattered when
I happened to listen to a great fiddler, and came home in a depressed state
of mind. I knew I could never do half so well, so why waste my time?
I went home heartbroken, firmly resolved never to touch my fiddle
again. But the next morning I would be back practising Ševčík's scales
and the Kreutzer *études*.

My teacher told me, 'If you really love music, earn your money
by something else and make music for the love of it.' I wrote off his
advice to the inscrutable whims of adults. So I went ahead and became a
professional musician. I didn't quite make the Heifetz grade or the one
below, but I certainly played a lot of music, long and short, difficult and
easy, hot and cold. I played in large symphony orchestras and in small
jazz bands, in disreputable joints and in famous halls. I played mornings,
afternoons, nights. I played so much that it almost ruined my love-affair

155

with my fiddle. I knew, finally, that my teacher had been right. Today I understand why many professional musicians don't really love music. House-painters rarely paint still-lifes.

The professionals are tired of their art. We amateurs treat the object of our enthusiasm with the passion of a young lover. The professionals treat theirs with a detachment that is the result of a long and boring marriage. Routine is the mortal enemy of passion. We are enthused; they are, at best, interested. Professional musicians rarely talk about music. They talk of unpaid bills and priceless blondes; how much that horse paid in the third at Del Mar, a royal flush, and the social injustice that leaves conductors overpaid and musicians underpaid. One musician I know has three separate sets of wives, children and alimonies; no wonder he hates music. It's all work and no money to him.

In summer time we amateurs get together to play trios under the trees while the professionals run away from the very sound of music. After producing millions of notes the professional musician doesn't enjoy music any more. He must play a programme he dislikes under a conductor he hates for an audience he despises. Not long ago the members of

CONINGSBY;

OR, THE

NEW GENERATION.

BY

B. DISRAELI, ESQ. M.P.

AUTHOR OF "CONTARINI FLEMING."

IN THREE VOLS.

VOL. I.

LONDON:
HENRY COLBURN, PUBLISHER,
GREAT MARLBOROUGH STREET.
1844.

Benjamin Disraeli,
twice Prime Minister of England,
was one of Queen Victoria's
favourite novelists

THE

ODES OF HORACE

TRANSLATED INTO ENGLISH

BY THE RT. HON.

W. E. GLADSTONE, M.P.

LONDON
JOHN MURRAY, ALBEMARLE STREET
1894

William Ewart Gladstone, Disraeli's
political rival, was four times Prime
Minister, but nevertheless found
time to translate from the Latin

an orchestra in Copenhagen put cotton wads into their ears because they couldn't bear to hear the music — an agonizingly ugly, modern work — which they were performing. How well I understand them! I've often wished I could close my ears while I was listening to one of these atrocities of logarithmic anti-music.

While the second violinist sits there delivering his evening quota of sharps and flats, he thinks wistfully of the backyard of his home where he would like to build a flagstone terrace or of the basement which he wants to turn into a game-room. On the music in front of him it says *molto espressivo,* but can he play with much expressiveness when he sees that damn woman in the second row jingling her bracelets, with the bald, yawning man on her side? Now it says *dolce con moto,* but it's hard to be sweet and full of feeling while the precocious gnome in the fourth row is bored and making grimaces. Everybody wishes it were over.

During the interval the musician has an argument with his concertmaster. At home he will have another argument with his wife who complains that she hardly sees him any more. It's getting quite late and tomorrow morning he's got to get up early to practise and rehearse some

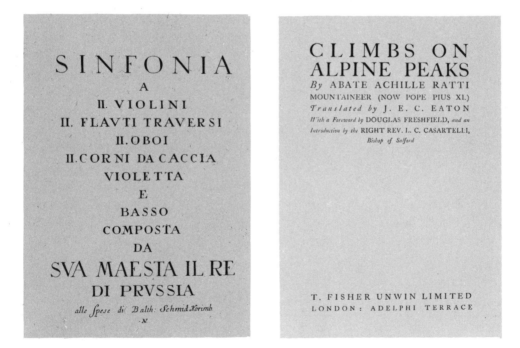

Frederick the Great of Prussia
was an amateur flautist and composer.
He infuriated his *Kapellmeister* Emanuel
Bach, because he never played in time

The English translation of a gem
of mountaineering literature

more, to give lessons to small would-be murderers who entertain visions of throwing their fiddles as well as their teachers out of their windows. And later there will be recording dates, concert dates, all sorts of dates except a date with that priceless blonde. Bores the hell out of you. And if you happen to play the trumpet or the piccolo flute, your family will seek convenient excuses to escape from home while you practise.

Consider now the happy lot of the musical dilettante. We play for the love of music. We care passionately about good music. Wherever I am, in America, or in Europe, or in between, I get together with fellow dilettantes whose 'enthusiasm surpasses their skill' and we play 'for amusement or gratification as opposed to professional pursuit' (Webster). We keep playing without hope of ever playing as well as we would want to, because we enjoy it so much.

In my days as a performer I was often bothered by people in the audience who followed the performance reading their scores. As I looked at these people down there who checked up on our fingering, bowing, phrasing, on syncopated demi-semi-quavers dropped in the heat of the performance, I suspected strongly that some of these 'amateurs' knew more about the music than we did.

Today I am one of the amateurs in the audience (I no longer use quotation marks in my thoughts when I think of the word) who follow the performance out of their score. I find my earlier suspicions well founded. We score-readers sometimes know more about the music than the 'professionals' up there who produce the notes without understanding what is really behind them. (Now I sometimes use the quotation marks in connection with the word 'professional'). In this age of radio and television, and owing to the high standards of well polished, nearly perfect recordings, it must be difficult for any artist, who isn't absolutely first rate, to impress even the inhabitants of a hick town.

In fact, there are hopeful signs that the twilight of the experts has already begun. The truth is becoming known at last that the experts have made an awful mess of things. The 'expert' statesmen have brought the world to the brink of disaster more than once. The 'expert' spies of the various intelligence outfits have slipped up so often that a healthy balance of betrayed state secrets has resulted. I had the highest admiration for the major intelligence services of the warring nations during the Second World War until I was assigned to a top-secret outfit whose members prided themselves on knowing more than anyone else. Since then I've changed my opinion about the professional intelligence people. In point of fact, I am convinced that our side won the war only because the experts on the other side were even worse.

159

Professor Albert Einstein, one of the great minds of
the century and a devotee of Johann Sebastian Bach

The expert city-builders and architects have made such a mess of our big cities that the inhabitants move out of them as quickly as possible. People go to the suburbs where they start having a wonderful time as dilettante builders and amateur architects. These pseudo-craftsmen tell their wives 'it's cheaper to do it yourself than to have it done', but they don't believe it. It's much more expensive but also much more fun. It gives them an outlet for their creative impulses; at least that is the highbrow explanation. The simple truth is that they love doing it.

Naturally, the experts take a dim view of such amateurs. They still prefer the expert statesman to the dilettante armchair strategist, the expert spy to the amateur snooper, the expert builder to the dilettante carpenter. They predict that the amateur strategist will cause a crisis, that the amateur spy plays with the nation's security, that the amateur builder's basement has crooked walls and will cave in. Just wait and see what the flagstone terrace will be in a couple of years. The poor experts just don't know the exhilarating sense of achievement a man gets out of a basement with crooked walls, or the badly done flagstone terrace.

Socially, the dilettante has also come into his own. It is no longer a secret that the expert is a conversational dud. He is unable to get away from The Only Thing He Knows. After ten minutes of boring, technical conversation he has lost all listeners, and finds himself talking to no one. But the amateur who knows something about everything (though not everything about anything) is less instructive and more entertaining. If he is a multiple amateur, one thing leads to another. I know a man who started out with amateur-photography in black-and-white, turned to colour photography, branched out into coloured movies, became interested in sound, installed highfidelity equipment and amplifiers with high frequency speakers and has now reached postgraduate status with something called 'presence' which sounds louder in the living room than three major American orchestras playing simultaneously in Philharmonic Hall. Such super-amateurs know more than the experts. Colour photography was invented by two ex-musicians, Leopold Godowsky and Leopold Mannes, who overtook the highly expert staff of the great Eastman Kodak Company.

My predilection for making music made me study the fiddle and musical theory which led to my becoming an opera fan and a member of the opera's claque, and finally I wound up on the stage. When I couldn't afford a ticket in the gallery, I would apply for a job as an extra which gave me a chance to hear the performance and get paid for it. I became an experienced Egyptian soldier in *Aida*, a member of the enraged crowd in *Carmen*, and an anonymous citizen of Nuremberg on the festival meadow in *Meistersinger*. I would be willing to perform once in a while but opera managers think I'm too old for these parts.

Dilettantism does strange things to people. A famous surgeon, whose speciality is the delicate cleaning of calcified arteries, rarely talks about his widely admired skill but gets quite excited about the uncalcified arteries of his Mercedes 220 which he often takes apart, for no reason at all. An eminent scholar of the law escapes from the dark labyrinth of legal interpretation into his sun-filled study where he happily paints atrocious water-colours. He does not consider himself a poor man's Picasso, never embarrasses his friends by offering them his works of non-art, is convinced the critics would hate his stuff.

I told him what Richard Strauss, an expert tone-painter if there ever was one, wrote to his expert word-painter, Hugo von Hofmannsthal: 'The plain people in the audience have the right instincts. Only the critics are wrong.'

And the twenty-six-year-old Mozart, already an experts' expert, wrote to his father in the autumn of 1782, about his piano concertos K. 413, 414, 415, 'These three concertos will please the experts. The non-experts will also like them, though they may not know exactly why.'

Benjamin Franklin,
one of the gifted amateurs
who pioneered new thought
and stimulated discovery

The Young Bacchus by Caravaggio

The Joy of Wine

TO WRITE ABOUT wine is as hazardous as to write about women. Both are surrounded by legends, and the facts are often obscured by fiction. Can one trust a wine's (and a wife's) vintage? Are their colours true? Are they honest? Do they have enough body and balance? For every rule about wine (and women) there is at least one exception.

Men fall in love continuously with wines and women, but I believe they are more faithful to their wines. Once they've fallen for a certain wine, it's usually love for life. Most men have learned by bitter experience that they'll never know the last secrets of wines and women. They can only marvel at both — nature's wonders for which man must render thanks to God.

Nothing is certain about the early history of wine. 'Wine', known as 'the fermented juice of the grape', comes from the Latin *vinum*, akin to the Greek οἶνος. The Greek word should come first. While Greek poets praised the sweet secret of wine, the rude Romans were still beating their womenfolk who had tried to taste the good stuff.

The pleasure of wine is almost as old as the pleasure of life. Archaeological researches prove that viticulture was known ten thousand years before the Christian era. Noah was not the first wine-lover though he has remained one of the best known; wine undoubtedly was already served in the Garden of Eden. Homer's nectar was just a very great year of a very great wine. Fellow wine-lovers will agree with this statement although professors of philology may dispute it.

The art of wine-making probably originated in Armenia, south of the Caucasus, and was well known in Mesopotamia and Egypt 3000 years BC. In Egypt Osiris was venerated as the first vintner, in China Poh-Hi, in India Siwa. The Greeks had Dionysus and the Romans had Bacchus. This infatuation with the tutelary deity is not accidental. The wine-maker needs God's help as much as a thorough knowledge of his exacting science. In ancient Egypt tax-inspectors checked the wines for quality as strictly as the French authorities have checked French wines since *Appellation Contrôlée* was created in the early 1930's.

Inscriptions have been deciphered on the clay stoppers of Egyptian pottery jars giving specific vintage details. But Egyptian authors didn't think highly of their wines which were too sweet. Furthermore, the Egyptians diluted their wine with water, a bad habit which is still widespread in all Mediterranean countries where people drink wine to quench their thirst. The French, Germans and English drink wine for enjoyment. When a Frenchman is thirsty he drinks beer or Vichy — but certainly not water. He knows from his *grandmère* that water is useful only for washing and cooking.

The experts now agree that Greece is the homeland of the wine. We'll never be able to pay off our debts to the Greeks: after Homer and Euripides, Aeschylus and Aristophanes, Socrates and Plato, the Acropolis and the Hermes of Praxiteles we now owe them the wonder of wine too. The art of making wine came to the Aegean Sea before the fall of Troy. Theophrastus in 287 BC wrote instructions to wine-growers who made good wines which were exported and exchanged for goods in the Black Sea and Western Mediterranean. From Greece viticulture travelled as far east as China (where wine-drinking was adopted only a few hundred years later, in the reign of the Emperor T'ai Tsung) and west to Rome, Gaul and Spain. Plato praises the vintners of Gaul and Pliny the Elder praises the Gaulish wines. As early as 600 BC real connoisseurs preferred 'Bordeaux' which I find easy to believe, having been a Bordeaux man since I learned the first thing about wine.

The Roman Emperor Domitian in 92 AD decreed that half the vineyards in Gaul must be cut down. But quality cannot be regulated by imperial decrees; and in the early centuries of the Christian era the regions of Bordeaux, along the Rhône and the Moselle, were famous as centres of viticulture. The roman Emperor Probus (232-282) abolished the anti-Gaulish wine-laws and is now revered as an early promoter of viticulture in France and Germany. Poor Probus; when he suggested to his victorious legionaries that they should give up the monotonous business of killing and retire to their peaceful vineyards for a truly fascinating life, they promptly slayed him. But to this day good Probus is remembered by millions of vintners while his colleagues who preferred the soldier's sword to the vintner's hoe are mercifully forgotten.

There exists an earnest belief among French wine-growers that the true purpose of the crusades was to bring back to France new varieties of vines. In all France the history of wine is connected with the history of the Church: wherever pious monks built a monastery they would plant a vineyard nearby. Some of the greatest vineyards of France were planted by monks. The Clos Vougeot which produces such a great Burgundy that French regiments marching by traditionally salute the vines, was planted by the Cistercians. Today the promotional though harmless organization of the Chevaliers du Tastevin eat and drink there, shouting out between sips of wine and swallows of food, 'Never in vain, always in wine!' In French it sounds even better.

When Henry Platagenet, later King Henry II of England, married Eleanor of Aquitaine in 1152, large shipments of Gascon *clairette* were sent to English ports. The English never gave up their love of clarets. In 1350 the equivalent of one million cases was exported from the port of Bordeaux. Four hundred years later six million cases were shipped.

In France, the paradise of wine, almost two million people, one French-man out of seven, earn their living by making wine, and they make some of the greatest wines ever made. No matter how low you may rate the century we live in, we wine-lovers call it the golden age of wine.

In 1905 the French passed a law that said, 'No drink may be kept . . . or sold under the name of *vin* that is not exclusively produced from the fermentation of fresh grapes or the juice of fresh grapes.' The emphasis is on 'fresh'. An Italian law of 1925 calls *vino* 'the product of the alcoholic fermentation of the juice of grapes, either fresh or slightly dried', while the German wine-law of 1930 follows the strict French definition. Conse-quently, next to the French, it's the Germans who make the best wines.

We wine-lovers do not like the prosaic definitions of the law-makers, although we admit their necessity. Pleasant experience has taught us that

The Emperor Probus, a martyr to the cause of Wine, who is remembered with gratitude by all who love the wines of France and Germany

165

In every country where wine is grown the wine-harvest has always been a great event. An early 19th century Italian engraving

one sip of a wine tells us more about it than all the books written on the subject. The best wine-library consists of dusty bottles, not of dusty volumes. Wine-growers and wine-collectors call their finest treasures *la bibliothèque*. 'Real wine knowledge comes from drinking,' writes my friend Alexis Lichine, one of the world's great authorities on the subject. 'The more wines you taste, the more you will enjoy them.'

Wine people are hospitable, always happy to open a bottle for you, but you should observe certain unwritten rules. In the house of a hanged man one doesn't mention the rope, and in a Burgundian wine-cellar one doesn't talk about Bordeaux. And *vice versa*. There are people in Burgundy who deny the existence of Bordeaux wines altogether or call them 'very light Burgundies' such as the wines of St-Emilion and Pomerol, 'the Burgundies of Bordeaux'. In Chassagne where they make the world-famous Montrachet, it wouldn't be polite to mention some of the excellent wines from the Rhine and the Moselle. And when you drink a bottle of 1953 Niersteiner Brudersberg, Riesling, Trockenbeerenauslese, it would be tactless to talk about the sweet, great wines of Château d'Yquem – especially when somebody else offered you the bottle.

Talking about wine is the next best thing to drinking it. We wine-lovers know that wine is not only to be drunk, but to be enjoyed. King

Edward VII of Great Britain, a real connoisseur, said, 'Not only does one drink wine, but one inhales it, one looks at it, one tastes it, one swallows it . . . and one talks about it.'

Much wine-talk, however, is pure nonsense. As more people learn to drink wine, there is a belief in some circles that wine drinking must be surrounded with pretentious ritual. As a status symbol the wine-cellar now outranks the kidney-shaped swimming pool and the cabin cruiser. The owner of the cellar serves a young Beaujolais in an old basket, offers sweet candies with a dry Moselle, and believes that a château in Bordeaux is a castle. He talks knowingly about 'the Forty-Niners that need time to mature', and imitates the dialect of the experts without mastering its meaning.

Such people must be punished. When they start discussing *finesse* and 'acquired bouquet', or even 'a well-developed acquired bouquet with balance', one interrupts them, with a thoughtful expression, sipping the wine they've just poured. 'Not bad, but really no comparison to yesterday's sensation. A souple body, with capricious *fraîcheur*, pleasant to the tongue, perfumed and generous, without any *goût de terroir*. Plenty of tears, with a *tendre* after-taste, that gives you a delicate sensation of roundness in the right spots. Full in character. Harmonious!'

'What wine was that?', the wine-snob asks. He is so surprised that he almost drops his expensive baccarat glass.

'No wine. I was talking about Brigitte Bardot in her new picture.'

The wine ritualist is as wrong as the man who claims that all wine rules are hokum thought up by high-pressure wine-salesmen. Most of the rules have a sound basis in fact. White wines are best when they are slightly chilled and most red ones should be chambered; try the contrary and you'll see how bad the wines taste. Dry white wines go best with fish and sea food, and red wines with meat and game. But rules are here to be broken. If you enjoy an old Chambertin with a young herring, or a well-aged *poulet* with a very young Montrachet, by all means go ahead. *Chacun à son goût.*

Wine is a product of the soil — which the French call *le terroir* — and of the sun. The juice of the grape is liquid sunshine. The sun is every-where, but the soil is different and gives the wine its distinguishing character.

Wine is also a work of art, made by man. Erudite judgement is needed as to the time when the grapes should be harvested, how long the wine should ferment, remain in the barrel, how to treat it when it gets sick, when it should be bottled. Wine is as capricious as a woman, and changes its taste constantly — even after it has been poured into the glass. Sound judgement is also necessary to know when wine should be bought and when it should be drunk. Every bottle is a journey into the unknown. Even a familiar wine suddenly plays tricks and creates surprises. One can never be sure of it before tasting a wine.

To learn to enjoy wines takes patient study and constant training. Man is not born with a knowledge of wine; he has to learn it as he learns to write or read. Money will buy the finest wines, but there ought to be a law against selling the truly great wines, supreme achievements of our civilization – of which there are never enough – to people not worthy of them. Madame Dumaine refused to sell the treasures of their cellar to people who had fortified themselves with a couple of cocktails before dinner. Fernand Point used to say that the greatest wines should be drunk *à genoux*, on your knees.

People who make wine will tell you that the way to learn about wine is to start with wines from their own district. Start with the lesser red table-wines, they say, and work your way up. Begin with young wines which are fresh and full and uncomplicated, and will teach you a few things about the *goût de terroir* where they come from. Such wines will explain to the beginner a few things: the bouquet of the wine, its first smell; the aroma, the taste in the mouth; and finally the lingering after-taste which is often quite distinct from the aroma. The pupil will learn to differentiate between light and full-bodied wines, between mild and fruity, acid and flat wines. He will recognize certain wines, perhaps remember them.

Such simple wines are found in many regions on earth. Every French wine-district has its *vins du pays* or *vins de carafe*, and they are always good when they are honest – when they were really grown in the soil they were supposed to be grown in. Franconia in Germany; the South Tyrol, Lombardy and Piedmont regions in Italy; wines that should be drunk *al fresco*, in plain sunshine, preferably in the company of a pretty woman, with the accompaniment of an Italian song. (They may taste quite different when you drink them alone at home on a gloomy November night.)

The advanced student now turns to the good wines (not yet the great ones) from Bordeaux and Burgundy, the genuine, fruity, young Beaujolais (which is so hard to find!), the wines from the Côte Rôtie, sturdy and sun-drenched, Hermitage and Châteauneuf-du-Pape, the good wines from the Loire, from the Jura, Alsace; he should try the gay Champagne, full of *joie de vivre*, and other sparkling wines. He will get acquainted with the good wines of Germany. The dry German wines aren't dry but fruity, and the sweet ones aren't sweet, but rich and elegant. Most of them have the characteristic, flowery taste of the Riesling grape.

If the student happens to be English, he will begin a serious study of the Sherries, the pride of Spain, and the Ports, the pride of Portugal. English taste has created the fame of Sherries and Ports, of the hocks (called after the town of Hochheim which isn't even on the Rhine but up the Main) and the clarets (*clairette* in ancient Gascony was a blend of red and white wines, but now denotes all red wines from Bordeaux).

By that time the student, after years of intelligent tasting and drinking, is able to distinguish a poor wine from a good one and to describe them in the wine-drinkers' peculiar jargon, a number of shorthand clichés for subtle but different taste sensations. The wine *argot* is as incomplete as the notations of the composer of music, and often it is necessary to search between and behind the meaning of the words to describe exactly the taste of a certain wine. In Burgundy they have eighty-nine different epithets for identifying a wine which may be flavoury, full-bodied, clean, sound, sweet, dry, elegant, firm, oily, harmonious, ripe deep-coloured, velvety, light, silky, generous, and so on and on. They say that a bottle is 'serious', or that 'it lacks insight'. I've heard one of them say, 'An excellent Corton 1899 – still full of charm and enthusiasm.' And another expert knowingly shook his head and said, 'Yes – like a wise, old man who has had plenty of

'The best wine-library consists in dusty bottles.' The cellar of Château Mouton Rothschild

'Wine is a tranquillizer, good for your body, beneficial for your
soul, the ideal medicine for every sickness.' A Paris *bistro*

fun in life, yet never got blase.' And they looked at each other and nodded, and sipped a little of the wine, and their faces had the transfigured expression of the saints on paintings by Andrea del Sarto, Giotto or Goya.

To the wine lovers the wine is a baby, a pretty girl, a wise old man, a beautiful woman, a robust peasant or a fragile, old lady. By the time they talk that way they are ready for the great, Dionysian test — a difficult, mysterious examination. Much knowledge and patience, experience and discrimination, memory and instinct are needed. Some people fail the test; others get afraid and quit.

The man who passes the test is at last permitted to approach the great wines of this world. There are perhaps not more than two dozen of them — nature's wonders and masterpieces of man's art. Thanks should be rendered to the Lord — and to the men who brought up these wines with loving care, as a mother brings up her babies.

I compare these wines to a Schubert song, a poem by Heine, a painting by Renoir. About half a dozen of these liquid miracles are white wines: the great Le Montrachet from Burgundy, the incomparable, sweet Château d'Yquem from Sauternes, and certain *Kabinett* pieces from Germany — the celebrated Johannisberger Kabinett, from the Rheingau, or the great Wehlener Sonnenuhr, pride of the Mosel.

Most of the great wines are red. The finest clarets belong to this noble group (Château Lafite, Château Margaux, Château Latour, Château Haut Brion, Château Mouton Rothschild, and in the same class are Château Cheval Blanc, Château Ausone and Château Pétrus), and the greatest Burgundies (Richebourg, La Tâche, Chambertin, Musigny, Romanée Conti, Clos Vougeot, Grands Échézeaux). These wines should be drunk with reverence and gratitude, in small sips, happily and devoutly — and not very often. Such a wine should always celebrate a very special event — it must never become a matter of routine.

Years ago, when I was in my salad days, green in my judgement and vinegarish in my conclusions, I considered everybody a barbarian who didn't like 'my' wines. Since then I've learned that there is not only *in vino veritas*, but also tolerance. Today I won't say that a certain wine is bad — except when it is dishonest, badly made, musty and maderized and otherwise generally undrinkable. Instead I say, 'This wine is not for me'. The old saying *de gustibus non est disputandum* has never been truer than about wine and women. One man likes blondes and Bernkasteler Doktor, the other prefers brunettes and Château Pétrus. Bad women and bad wines cause headaches that last longer than the morning after.

To find a woman who shares one's wine taste is as rare as to find the

best vintage of one's favourite wine. Often he likes a pheasant *en cocotte* with a Château Cheval Blanc and she prefers Sole Meunière(she's dieting) with a Mosel. If they love each other, they'll compromise on steak and Beaujolais.

Wine is a tranquillizer, good for your body, beneficial for your soul. Many people call it the ideal medicine for every sickness. The French League against Cancer claims that wine protects you against cancer; their statistics prove that there is less cancer in the wine-regions of France than elsewhere, possibly owing to radioactive potassium carbonate and magnesium in red wines. That may be open to questioning but the beneficial effect of wine on heart and soul, on reason and emotion, is a fact. Wine discussions rarely degrade into vulgar brawls such as are common among beer-drinkers. Wine-lovers drink wine for many reasons, but never because they want to get drunk.

The inspiring influence of wine on poets, artists and other creative people is a matter of long-standing records. On others the influence is not always inspiring. When Maréchal Juin, several years ago, visited the cellar of Château Mouton Rothschild he asked for a wine made in 1866, 'a wine from undefeated France'. Less patriotism was shown by Bismarck who was once reprimanded by Kaiser Wilhelm II for drinking Champagne instead of German Sekt. 'Your Majesty', said Bismarck, 'I am the greatest patriot in your Reich but patriotism stops at the palate.'

The Prussians always had great love for Champagne. When they were about to attack Chalons in February, 1814, they fortified themselves for the task by bringing thousands of bottles out of the cellars and started to drink the bubbly stuff which some considered 'a sort of Weissbier'. In no time they were reeling and staggering as they began to march against the enemy. Chalons lost several thousand bottles of Champagne and General York lost two companies of drunk Prussian soldiers.

Drinking good wine is a refined pleasure. Wine-lovers, the aristocrats among hedonists, rarely discuss business over their glasses, as whisky-drinkers do, and avoid politics and economics, the favourite topics of *Stammtisch* beer-drinkers. Wine-lovers prefer to talk about their wine, and the better the wine, the more poetic their talk. Certain wines exclude the use of prose.

We wine-lovers are members of a world-wide secret organization which has no printed statutes but many unwritten laws. We don't drink wine to keep up with somebody who just 'laid in a cellar', or because we are thirsty, or because it's the thing to do. We drink wine with our meals, and not afterwards with the cigars, as some people do in Germany. The Italians say that a meal without wine is like a day without sun. The French who like metaphors with a feminine fragrance, compare a meal without wine to a woman without tenderness. But they all mean the same. We always hope to have another glass of wine as long as we are around.

Some time ago I accompanied my friend Alexis Lichine on a tasting trip through Burgundy, from where we went to one of his vineyards in Bordeaux — Château Lascombes in Margaux. Lichine, one of the greatest enthusiasts on the subject of wine, has dedicated himself to the proposition that a hundred million Americans should drink wine instead of coffee with their dinner. He has been obsessed with wine since the age when other children drink milk. He often dreams of wine and afterwards is able to recall exactly how his dream vintages tasted.

On this trip we had met in Lyons and started to go to Bordeaux by way of Burgundy, which is the most pleasant detour I can think of. Bordeaux is a wine oligarchy, run by firmly entrenched groups — influential brokers, wealthy shippers, proprietors of great châteaux who like to call themselves *l'aristocratie du bouchon*, the cork aristocrats. There is no such lofty feeling in the sun-drenched small villages of Burgundy, a wine democracy, where the people work hard and get little for it. The small growers are rugged individualists who have their own methods and swear by them. To them the wine is their baby and belongs in the family. They make the wine but often sell it to the rich shippers who make the big money. The shippers put indirect lights in their cellars and have stacks of promotion literature printed. I wouldn't go near their places.

On this trip we stopped at a group of grey, old stone buildings that were surrounded by rows of low-planted grapes. This was the village of Chassagne-Montrachet which makes knowledgeable wine-lovers as rapt as pilgrims approaching St Peter's in Rome.

A lovely place. Winding cobbled streets, a few lazy dogs sleeping in the shade, a couple of children and no one else around. We stopped near a house with a cobbled courtyard, in which the week's wash had been hung up to dry. Lichine said I was going to meet Claude Ramonet, the owner of a vineyard called Les Ruchottes, one of the greatest white wine makers in the world. 'I've known him and his brother Pierre for twenty years. They never once slipped up. Their wines are consistently great, but there is so little of it that they don't want to sell. Claude will tell me he's got almost nothing, but the difference between almost nothing and nothing can be considerable. There will be some tremendous haggling. He will sell me some wine, and afterwards he will be terribly unhappy. To him selling some of his wine is like seeing the children leave home.'

In the courtyard, Lichine patted a furiously barking dog, and shook hands with a woman who had come out of the house wiping her hands on her apron. I thought I detected the aroma of *tomates provençales* in the air. He introduced her as Mme Claude Ramonet and inquired about her health, her husband's health and their son's health. (*'Ah, Monsieur, c'est triste, il est toujours au régiment.'*) Madame inquired about the health of Lichine's children. Just then, a high Loisseau tractor, specially designed to straddle the rows in a vineyard, with enough space for the vines between the wheels, rolled into the courtyard. Madame's husband, a slim, blond, sunburned man in dark-blue overalls and blue beret, jumped down from its high seat. He shook hands unenthusiastically with Lichine but brightened up somewhat when he learned that the children were doing nicely.

Lichine started things off by saying, 'The air is humid, but with all this sunshine the grapes seem to have been growing fantastically. *Il paraît que c'est superbe chez vous.*'

Ramonet merely shrugged, and said that he couldn't sell Monsieur a single barrel more than they had already agreed on. People were after him all the time, he went on, some of them even calling him from his vineyard in the middle of the morning. *'C'est idiot!* No, no, Monsieur, not one barrel more!'

174

The wine-harvest in a village in Burgundy. The small growers there are rugged individualists who have their own methods and swear by them

Lichine, far from disheartened, suggested amiably that Ramonet show
us his cellar. This request is never refused. Without further protest the
grower led us up the street to an ancient stone building and, when he
had unlocked the door, down into a damp, cold, dusty chamber, its air
heavy with wine fumes and distrust. I shivered. Lichine said that if I
thought this was cold, I ought to go along with him on a tasting trip in
winter, when the dampness cut like a knife and there was no escaping it
until a hundred wines had been tasted. Ramonet dipped a *pipette* into a
barrel of white wine, filled two glasses for us and a *tastevin* — a shallow,
dimpled, silver saucer — for himself.

'This wine is still fermenting,' Lichine told me, in English, when he
had taken a sip, 'so in judging it you've got to read between the lines.
In my opinion, it's going to turn out to be excellent. I'm going to get
some of it.' Then, switching to French, he said, 'It has the unmistakable
flavour of Les Ruchottes. Dry — soft, rather than hard. Flowery, with a
certain expansiveness and a very clean finish, but no sweet aftertaste.'

Ramonet looked pleased. When Lichine, plunging ahead, asked if he
wouldn't reconsider and sell him some of this superior wine, he said, 'Oh,
well, maybe one barrel, but not at the old price.'

175

Lichine straightened up like a Soviet diplomat about to say *Nyet*.

'And why should I pay more for this?' he asked, belligerently.

'*Parce que . . .*'

'*Parce que quoi?*'

'Everything's gone up,' Ramonet replied, but his resistance was plainly crumbling and he gave a meek shrug. 'Cost-of-living. Taxes. Everything.'

Lichine put down his glass and delivered a stern homily on inflation as one of the major afflictions besetting France, after which the two men engaged in a bargaining duel that would have drawn a crowd even in the bazaars of Beirut. At one point Lichine, in the true *nyet* spirit, actually walked out. But he was soon back, and in the end all was well. Ramonet had unhappily consented to part with three barrels of his treasure, and Lichine had agreed to pay slightly more than the old price.

'That's the kind of fellow I'm fighting for,' Lichine said when we were back in the car. 'A straight and honest grower. The people around here are so thrifty they don't even drink their own good wine — they make a *petit vin*, unbalanced and slightly acid, for themselves. But they've got the courage of a gambler who puts every cent he has on one horse.'

For centuries wine-lovers have argued whether Bordeaux wines are preferable to the Burgundies, and what about the great hocks? A meaningless argument: it always depends on a special bottle. But at least one world-famous expert admitted to me in a very weak moment that the drinking of a great Bordeaux is most probably 'the highest achievement of the pleasure of wine', and another world authority admitted that his last wish in life would be 'a beautifully preserved, fully matured bottle of a great [Bordeaux] château'. All of us agree with the Venerable Archdeacon Cawnthrope who said, 'Sweet women always, sweet words sometimes, sweet wines never'.

Beginners usually start out with the Burgundies which have more body, and a stronger bouquet, and then they gradually move to the more delicate, more elusive company of the great Bordeaux wines. Some people love all good wines and many women, and some find happiness with a single wine and a single woman. 'Your wine has become a necessity to me', Voltaire wrote to the owner of the Le Corton vineyard near Beaune. 'I give a good Beaujolais to my guests from Geneva but in secret I drink your Corton.' Smart man, Voltaire. Every wine lover is saddened to see his favourite wine being washed down by people who don't appreciate it.

Personally I consider the Burgundies feminine wines, with their flowery, fruity taste and round body, while the great Bordeaux reds have on elegant leanness and masculine physique; however, there are respected

1934, one of the great years
of Château Cheval Blanc

wine-men who feel exactly the opposite. Until ten years ago my idea of
the perfect bottle was a great year of Château Margaux, a wine famous
for finesse and elegance, balance and bouquet. Today I have moved south
to the more fullbodied wines of St Emilion ('the Burgundies of Bordeaux')
which are big and soft and fat and velvety. I always think of velvet
when I drink these wines; never a trace of hardness or fullness that comes
from too much acidity or tannin. These wines taste best with simple foods
– roast or grilled meat – which I like best. Today my perfect bottle of
wine is a great year of the great Château Cheval Blanc, the greatest of
the St Emilions.

St Emilion is one of the loveliest wine-towns on earth – very old, with
traces of Romanesque architecture, once a stopover for Breton pilgrims
on their way to Spain. It took its name from St Emilion, a pious hermit
who lived in a cavern underneath the ruins of a small chapel. There is
still the block of stone where he slept, and when you sit down on it, lean
back and close your eyes; you may make a wish and it will come true.
I sat down, leaned back, closed my eyes, and wished for another great
bottle of Château Cheval Blanc. Nearby there is a shallow well filled
with hairpins. If a girl throws in two hairpins and they fall down on the
bottom in the form of a cross, she will be married within a year. If she
has no hairpins, the guide assures her she may throw in bobby pins.

There are no international standards of taste. The only way to find
out about wine is to taste it. Professional wine-tasting is a tough business
in a competitive world, in which a man is only as good as his taste-buds.
He tastes raw, green wines with the idea of buying them when they are

177

young and cheap, holding them until they age, and selling them at a profit. These experts always ask themselves, 'How will this wine taste five or six years from now?', which is like going into a maternity ward and picking out the baby who is going to be the biggest success in life. There are men who taste wines all day long, and the wonder is that they are still able to enjoy a glass of wine with their dinner.

People who really love wine may become exhilarated by wine but they will never get drunk on a great wine. A man who loves love will never make love when he is drunk; he wants to enjoy love with all his senses awake. To drink a great wine when one no longer knows what one is drinking is a sacrilege.

Winemanship is not synonymous with the pretentious ritual often performed by promotional wine-societies. Such ritual amuses the insiders but frightens away the uninitiated. The true wine-lover is unimpressed by the pretence that is created around wine. He knows the great history of wine but doesn't abuse it to show off. He knows what wine he wants and tries to get it with a minimum of fuss. He makes no fetish of vintages but knows when a wine should be drunk. Every year countless bottles of good wines are spoiled by being opened before they have properly matured, or too late when they are past their prime.

Winemanship includes a solid knowledge of wine and a fastidious sense of discrimination. The wineman doesn't buy a wine because it happens to be a bargain; he knows that good wines are never inexpensive. The only 'bargains' are good wines bought so early that their qualities are not yet apparent; it takes the talent of a true expert, and the wineman doesn't pretend to be an expert.

In a restaurant winemanship calls for presence of mind and steadfastness of purpose. Bad wine-waiters in pretentious restaurants try to push the wines that need to be sold, or they like to sell their expensive wines. Winemanship calls for quiet authority. The wineman orders the wine that he wants to drink and not the wine that the *sommelier* wants to get rid of. A good restaurant always has a good and inexpensive *vin du patron*. It also has a list of carefully selected, fine wines which are sold only to deserving customers.

The wineman remains unimpressed by baskets and towels wound around bottles, by fuss and pomp. He pours his wine himself. Winewaiters pour too much wine too often into the glasses; naturally, since their job is to sell wine. They rarely watch for the sediment in old bottles which isn't pleasant to swallow.

The wineman unhesitatingly turns down a wine that is corky, maderized, clouded or bad. In a good restaurant the wine is tasted by the captain and will be replaced. In a bad one the price of the wine appears on the bill. Such restaurants should be avoided thenceforth.

In his own home the wineman doesn't make much fuss when he opens and pours the wine, a few drops of it first into his own glass so that bits of cork would remain there, not in somebody else's glass. He may taste or sniff the wine but he does it unobtrusively. The only rule in modern wine etiquette is that the woman never pours the wine in public when a man is present. A sensible rule, since women always pour too little or too much. The exception to the rule is Madame Mado Point in Vienne, who knows more about wine than any other woman, and most men, I know. Sometimes — when we eat in her little private dining-room — she pours the wine herself. No one minds and the wine is always very good.

A few years ago Madame Point had a disturbing experience which proves that wine will always remain a mystery even to those who know so much about it. In November, 1955, after the recent death of her husband, she made her annual trip to the Beaujolais country to taste the new wines. At the Restaurant de la Pyramide a special *cuvée* of Beaujolais is offered to the guests as *vin du patron* — always good and inexpensive. It was her first trip alone to the Beaujolais region and she was depressed. Early in the afternoon she arrived at the large cellar in Juliénas — a sun-drenched, old, picturesque wine village surrounded by vineyards, where everybody who works for a living works the wine. Women rarely come to buy wines there. For generations women were not allowed in the cellars of Beaujolais because they were said to bring bad luck to the wine.

Buying young wines is difficult. The wine has no pronounced taste yet and it takes knowledge, experience, instinct and perhaps also a little luck, to pick a winner. Madame Point tasted about forty different wines but always came back to a particular *cuvée* of Juliénas. She liked the wine. She thought it was going to develop, and she bought thirty barrels. The owner of the cellar smiled. Afterwards he told her this was his favourite *cuvée* too, and he was glad it went to his favourite restaurant.

Thirty barrels of wine is a lot; in the Beaujolais country a barrel contains 218 litres. The barrels were shipped to the cellars of the Pyramide in Vienne. The Beaujolais people say the new wine should spend the Easter holidays in its new home where it is going to be drunk and where a real expert will take good care of the wine. This is called *les vins font les Pâques*, but it may be more than a superstition.

A few weeks later the cellar-master came up with a worried face to inform Madame Point that something had gone wrong with the wine. It was very, very bad, as she soon noticed; it was, in fact, completely undrinkable. Having paid a great deal of money for her thirty barrels, Madame Point supposed that she might have made a mistake when she'd tasted the wine in her depressed state of mind. She telephoned the owner. He came to Vienne, tasted the wine, shook his head, advised her not to look at it for the next two months, and assured her that all would be well. Madame promised to forget about the wine, but being a woman she was understandably curious, and went down to the cellar every morning. The wine had become absolutely impossible; it seemed to be suffering from a mysterious malady, and it seemed impossible to her that it should ever be drinkable again. Instead of getting better it got worse all the time.

Madame Point had given up all hope when all of a sudden, late in January, shortly before the two months were up, the wine recovered miraculously. Six months later experts considered it the year's outstanding *cuvée* in the Beaujolais.

People who taste wines as a business behave quite differently when they taste an old wine for pleasure. They examine the colour and clarity of the wine, watch its 'tears' — droplets that form around the inside of the rim as the surface alcohol evaporates — and after that they inhale the aroma of the wine, while a remote, abstract look shows in their eyes. Then they take a sip, whirl it around the tongue, and having swallowed it, analyze the after-taste, moodily staring at a glass. Lichine tells me he's enjoying such a wine for what it is, not for what it will be. He leans back and tells the wine, 'Now go ahead, please me, speak up on your own behalf.' Old wines have an intellectual rather than an emotional attraction. Often he feels, 'Too bad really I didn't drink it five years ago when it must have been glorious.'

Connoisseurs are forever engaging in the pastime of guessing wines — their place of origin and year — which is an exclusive form of entertainment, as appealing to wine experts as scaling a peak in the Himalayas is to mountain climbers. You are in the inner sanctum of the true experts, knowing that outsiders will never reach even the outer courtyard.

Guessing wines is not the same as 'blind tasting', when the competitors try to guess a wine without looking at it. Real wine-lovers know that their enjoyment is a combination of all five senses, and seeing a wine is twenty per cent of it.

To guess a wine a man must have a fastidious sense of taste, a discerning palate, a thorough knowledge of wines, and above all, experience gained only after years and years of sipping, tasting and eliminating. It is easy to distinguish a heavy red Burgundy from a delicate, elegant

The cellar-master at Château Lafite examines the wine and watches its 'tears'

Médoc, or a dry Mosel from a sweet Sauternes, but when you get into the viticultural stratosphere of the great Médoc châteaux, which often resemble one another as closely as true-blue diamonds, the test becomes very difficult. Even great experts make mistakes, since it is easy to be deceived by a wine that has been prematurely bottled or freakishly fails to turn true to type, or is too young to possess the identifying characteristics that appear with age. At a blind tasting in Bordeaux a few years ago, several owners of celebrated châteaux did not recognize their own wines, which is like a mother who doesn't recognize her own children. Real experts have humility and know they are fallible; they know that you never learn about wines by reading books, only by using the corkscrew.

Lichine came through a few years ago with a memorable demonstration of guessing which he put on in Bordeaux at a wine-tasting arranged by the *Institut National des Appellations d'Origine des Vins et Eaux-de-Vie* in Paris. He was given an unlabelled bottle of wine to

guess. He was told only that it was true (having the characteristics of its particular soil), and that it was the product of one of the great years. 'You pinpoint your wine by a process of elimination, starting with the region and working down through the district to the commune,' he explained to a friend after the test was over. 'Usually it takes me about half-a-second to feel whether the wine is really true or is dishonest. In this case I didn't have to worry about that. I quickly identified the wine first as a Bordeaux, then as a Médoc, and then as a Saint-Estèphe. I had now eliminated region, district and commune. After that I put the geographical problem aside temporarily and turned to the question of the year.

'It wasn't one of the '40s or the '50s — that was elementary — and I knew it wasn't a '34 or a '37, the two great years of that decade. It just didn't have the right characteristics. And gradually I became convinced that it could only be from one of the great years of the '20s — a '24, a '26, a '28, or a '29. I eliminated '26 and '28, because the wines of these years have a pronounced hardness and this wine didn't. It might be a weak '24, or a soft '29. I tasted again. The wine was full and round and slowly dying out, which is typical of a '29, so I eliminated the '24. Now, then, where did it come from exactly? There are only three great châteaux in the commune of Saint-Estèphe — Château Calon-Ségur, Château Montrose and Château Cos d'Estournel. In a second, I eliminated Montrose. Thirty seconds more, and I eliminated Calon-Ségur. I can't really explain what goes on in my head at such times. My brain is filled with names and years, and the ones I eliminate just drop out, as if they were falling through a strainer, and in the end only one name and one year remain. So I said, "This is a Château Cos d'Estournel '29." And it was.'

Solitude or Companionship

I'M FOND OF the wonderful, English institution, the pub. Where else on earth can you get a drink, a glass of wine, a beer (cold or warm), a sandwich, and be surrounded by congenial people in a picturesque setting and civilized atmosphere? The voices are low, the wood panelling is dark, and you find either solitude or companionship — whichever you prefer. No bright colours, cold metals, garish lights. The spirit of Shakespeare and Dickens is well preserved in these pubs which are full of character, and of characters. An Englishman, S.P.B. Mais writes, 'The day the pub of England dies, England dies, for in the pub you will find the heart of England.'

Only born-and-bred Englishmen, and even not all of them, are able to decipher the mysterious code of the pubs. The hours are confusing, the licensing laws complex, the semantics bewildering. There are subtle differences between inns, taverns and public-houses. The Oxford Diction- ary defines a public-house as 'an inn or tavern providing food and lodg- ing, especially alcoholic liquors to be consumed on the premises'. A 'fully licensed' pub sells all kinds of drinks. A beer-house is not licensed for spirits.

The pubs of London are among the last bastions of individualism. Each of them has an inimitable, personal atmosphere. To the uninitiated alien they all look alike — quaint names, curious sign-boards, panelled rooms, hidden cupboards and secret spy-holes, dark wood and old lamps. But to the local resident they are as different as are triplets to their mother. A friend of mine lives in a street with four pubs, and a fifth is just around the corner. 'The first is our "local",' he says. 'A respectable, middle-class pub. The second is a slumming place where it is now chic to be seen. The third is a Scotland Yard hangout; there are always C.I.D.

Le Déjeuner by Auguste Renoir, one of the artist's café masterpieces

inspectors hanging around, talking shop — the place to go if you need a policeman in a hurry. The fourth is run-down because the publican drinks. And the fifth, around the corner, is a meeting place of underworld types who are unafraid of the Scotland Yard men nearby. There you are. No one could possibly make a mistake and go to the wrong pub.'

According to William Fitzstephen, the secretary of Bishop Thomas-à-Becket and author of a description of twelfth-century London, 'drinking and fires' were the plagues of London. Before 1550 anybody could open a pub. Forty years after the first licensing laws were passed there were more than a thousand taverns in London. All Lord Mayors tried to limit the amount of drinking, and all failed. At the time of Dickens there was 'one tavern to every sixty houses'. The gin shops had thousands of (satisfied) customers a day. Much of the city's crime and poverty could be traced to gin shops putting out signs that purchasers could get 'drunk for a penny and dead-drunk for two pence'. Some even supplied free straw for customers on which to sleep it off.

A popular feature was the 'Ordinary', a sort of *table-d'hôte*. For a fixed, small price you could have numerous helpings of various dishes. In the time of James I a complete meal consisting in beef and beans, capon and duck, cake and fruit cost one shilling. Those were the days. 'There is nothing,' Dr Johnson remarked once, 'which has yet been contrived by man by which so much happiness is produced as by a good tavern or inn.' The good doctor didn't know what he was talking about; his favourite stimulants were tea and coffee. Writers have always been fond of taverns (and still are); many plays and books were written, many newspapers partly edited, on London tavern tables.

The decline of the pub began early in the nineteenth century, when tavern groups with growing membership began to build their own premises. Clubland was born. Taverns became less respectable, were no longer meeting places of politicians, writers, artists. John Hawkins calls some of Dr Johnson's friends 'low ale-house associations'. I wish I had been one of them.

Gradually the taverns became pubs as we know them today. Let us hope they will be with us forever, like the British weather and the English girls with their lovely complexions.

The most important feature of the pub is the landlord. In *The Art and Practice of Inn-Keeping* Alexander Part describes the landlord: 'He must be genial, not easily discouraged, watchful over himself, his staff, his customers. He must be a ready speaker and a readier listener. He must be house-proud, a student of human nature, active, methodical, good-tempered under trying conditions; his character must be above reproach.

Detail of the door of a pub in Soho, London

His patience must be beyond that of an ass. He is expected to be a good accountant, a born caterer, an expert chef, a good housekeeper, a good buyer and seller, an encyclopaedia of general information. Yet the man who combines all these qualities will even then fail to be successful unless he really loves playing the part of the host. It is your welcome and your air that counts most.'

The crisis of the pubs reached its climax between the two World Wars when working men no longer went to the pub to spend the evening talking to their friends or playing darts. Middle-class men didn't want to take their wives there, and instead went to cafés and restaurants. Many pubs became shabby and dreary; some couldn't even earn their rent.

The big breweries are credited with the recent renaissance of the pub. They bought up the pubs and made the landlord the manager. He would get a basic salary and a percentage; the breweries would supply the beer, and also the wines and spirits.

Many pubs are family affairs, like the small French café, run by the landlord and his wife, with a couple of girls. The barmaids should be pleasant but not complaisant; pretty, patient, good-humoured. You would be surprised how many there are in England, working hard for little money.

The pub has several, strictly separated and voluntarily respected social strata. There is the working men's public bar, and the middle-class saloon-bar where prices are a little higher. Strangers will be delicately steered toward the saloon-bar. There is no hint of snobbishness, but the public-bar *habitués* prefer to be undisturbed by outsiders. In fact, the pubs are truly democratic, and no one feels out of place there. In the countryside the local squire drops in for a pint to talk with his labourer about weather and crops, shooting and poaching. A generation ago no lady would want to be seen in a pub but now it's all right for her to go there, and she does, late in the afternoon, when she is tired from her errands, and needs a gin-and-tonic, or a whisky. Drinks are cheap but infinitesimal; it's advisable to start off with a double whisky.

Nearly everybody in London goes to a pub once in a while — for a quick lunch, a snack, an afternoon beer with friends, a couple of drinks before dinner. The pubs go with the times. The influence of the Continent is getting stronger in English life (though the English don't like to admit this). Many pubs now serve good, strong coffee. There is even a London pub where the language, *cuisine* and atmosphere are strictly French, *The York Minster* in Dean Street, with photographs of *Tour de France* cyclists and famous boxers on the walls. The English like their beer and ale at room temperature but a good many pubs now keep bottled Lager on ice.

The Public Bar of a London pub. The pub has several voluntarily respected social strata. The public bar *habitués* prefer to be undisturbed by outsiders

The licensing hours are farcical. Everybody admits it and no one does anything about it. The pubs are always closed when a man badly needs a drink or congenial company. Generally the pubs open around noon and close at around three o'clock, and open again around five-thirty and close around ten. But there are pubs with unorthodox hours, near the railway stations and in the Covent Garden market district, and experts will tell you how to keep drinking in London around the clock, just by moving around.

The names and signs of the pubs seem to come out of *Alice in Wonderland*, and often keep even the English guessing. What is one to make of *The Salutation and Cat*, *The Queen's Head and Artichoke*, *The King's Head and Eight Bells*? Perhaps they go back to a merging of two licences. National events, religious meanings, mythology, folklore, sports, legends, monarchs and heroes are commemorated in these names. Disastrous political events are indicated when *The Crown* became *The Mourning Crown* or when *The King's Head*, after the untimely end of Charles I, altered its sign to *The Royal Martyr* which later became corrupted to *The Royal Mortar*. Royal badges — *The Red Lion, The White Hart, The Queen's*

Neuner's 'Silver' Coffeehouse in Vienna, where even the coat-hangers were of pure silver. The Waltz Kings Lanner and Strauss are standing to the right of the picture

Arms — were always popular. So were animal names: *The Greyhound, The Running Horse, The Fox and Hounds, The Coach and Horses*. More mysterious are *The Pig and Whistle*, and *The Cat and Fiddle*. Several taverns in London are called *Hole in the Wall*, perhaps to remind of the hole in a leper's cell through which a priest blessed a dying man. Innkeepers had more imagination in the old days.

There are legendary pubs in London. *The Anchor*, on the river-bank on Southwark Bridge Road, has such mysteries as a doorless room, and a staircase behind double-cupboard doors. *The Bull and Bush* in Hampstead, built in 1645, and famous in song and prose, was Hogarth's home, frequented by Garrick, Shelley, Keats, Dickens. *The Bunch of Grapes* on Lime Street overlooks the Thames, where generations of watermen have 'taken their pint'. *The Olde Cheshire Cheese* in Fleet Street is associated with Dr Johnson and Boswell. *The Hoop and Grapes* in High Street, Aldgate, claims to be the oldest licensed building in London. *The King's Head and Eight Bells* is in a quiet part of the Chelsea Embankment where Carlyle lived and wrote. *The Nag's Head* in Floral Street, Covent Garden, is a veritable museum of exhibits connected with the theatre, opera and ballet, and theatre bills are wrapped around the columns in the saloon-bar; this pub even has its own catalogue (printed by the brewing firm that owns it, to be sure). *The Printer's Devil* in Fetter Lane, off Fleet Street, has a history of printing, fine interiors and good cooking (a perfect combination). *Ye Olde Swiss Cottage* in Finchley Road was an old favourite of Dickens. It changed hands a few years ago for £176,000, the highest sum ever paid for a licensed property. If you ask me, it's worth every penny of it. As I said, I'm very fond of these pubs.

And I'm fond of the sidewalk cafés in France, Italy, Spain, everywhere. The word immediately has wistful associations for the returning American or English traveller. That afternoon on the Champs Elysées when you 'just sat there', watching the people go by . . . The lovely evening in Rome's Via Veneto . . . in Venice's Piazza San Marco . . . in Marseilles' Cannebière, where so much Gallic wit and humour originate . . . in Dubrovnik's *Gradska Cafana* . . . in St Tropez. What would the Riviera, the Adriatic be without sidewalk cafés? And what makes them such a pleasant memory?

The answer is that Europeans have learned that sidewalks are not only for walking. The Continent's sidewalk cafés are many things to many men — a place to meet, to rest one's sore feet, to chat and relax. They are ornamental embellishments and commercial enterprises. To people who appreciate the small, inexpensive pleasures of life these cafés are the symbol of a graceful, contemplative, unhurried way of living.

New Yorkers 'relax' in dim bars and noisy jukebox joints where the din of voices offers a convenient excuse for not having to listen to the other person. The air is heavy. The liquor is hard. It's a far cry from the bright, cheerful café, paradise of conversationalists who believe in companionship and communication. The sidewalk café grew out of the European coffee-house that will be three hundred years old in 1984, God willing. We owe it to a distinguished Serbian double-agent named Franz Kulczycki (or Kolschitzky) who worked for both sides during the Turkish siege of Vienna in 1683. After the Turks were beaten, Franz managed to cross the thin line between disgrace and glory. Instead of being shot as a spy he was rewarded as a patriot with several bags of tasteless, raw coffee-beans that the Turks had left behind. No one in Vienna knew what they were for, but man-about-world Kulczycki roasted and ground them, and opened the first coffee-house near St Stephen's Cathedral. Little did he know that he had conferred a major blessing on western civilization. By 1780 there were over a hundred coffee-houses in Vienna. Gents would remain inside, playing cards and billiards, smoking and telling each other tall stories. Ladies were served 'frozen cream' in the 'garden', a part of the pavement separated by a low barrier, symbolic protection of the guests' privacy, and there they were chatting happily. The sidewalk café was born.

In the more easy-going Latin latitudes no one cared about privacy. The pavement part of the café became larger, and sympathetic city builders put the houses back and designed wider boulevards to make more space for more cafés. In the Champs Elysées the canopied terraces are thirty feet deep; in St Tropez they are even deeper.

The sidewalk café has long emancipated itself. The Viennese coffee-house was the introvert's home. The guests were protected from the outside world by mountains of newspapers, trays with water glasses, and waiters with bodyguard training. Young men wrote their doctor's examinations there and old men their last wills. There were special coffee-houses for dramatists, soccer-players, artists, stamp collectors, politicians, complaisant ladies, real ladies, civil servants. One is not surprised to read that in Neuner's 'Silver' Coffeehouse even the coat-hangers were of pure silver. The most famous pre-war coffee-house was the 'Central', where a gloomy Russian sat around brooding and playing chess until the German General Staff smuggled him into Czarist Russia where he changed world history. His name was Lenin. By 1925 Vienna had 1,250 coffee-houses, leaving little room for anything except wine and opera. The coffee-house was cozy but never gregarious. The invisible barriers never broke down.

By contrast, its Latin offspring became a place for relaxed extroverts who wanted to see and be seen, loved air and sunshine, didn't mind rubbing elbows with the people at the next table, and easily made friends. A civilized institution with none of the special etiquette of the more dignified coffee-houses. A man stretching out his legs expected other people to step on his toes, with no apologies. In my more youthful, less inhibited days I patronized certain cafés in Montmartre where it was not unusual for a girl to arrive with one man and depart with another whose acquaintance she'd just made at the neighbouring table. That couldn't happen in a coffee-house where literature was created (Ferenc Molnar wrote his wonderful *Liliom* in the *Café New York* in Budapest to the accompaniment of a brass band), and revolutions were plotted in the back-room. The coffee-house stimulated anarchy. The sidewalk café created good cheer. People there have nothing to hide.

I have a theory, totally unconfirmed by scientific research, that the easy-going, slightly frivolous mood of the sidewalk café made it seem suspicious to Anglo-Saxon Puritans. The English claim they couldn't

A boulevard café in Paris, 'headquarters of the amused observer of human foibles, and a hangout of the oppressed who find solace from matrimonial or professional troubles'

have these pleasant establishments because of their odious climate. The climate is odious in London, to be sure. So it is in Copenhagen, Stockholm and Berlin, in Lille and Le Havre, where they have pleasant sidewalk cafés. But the absence of sidewalk cafés at home gives the English a good excuse for hopping over to Paris as often as possible. There they sit in the wicker chairs of a café on the Champs Elysées, holding hands, inhaling the sweet fragance of the forbidden fruit, comforted by the thought that back home everything is as it should be.

What the puritans never bothered to find out is that the café is as respectable as Sunday afternoon in a bourgeois French provincial town, where nothing happens because everybody is watching. Whatever thoughts of sin exist in a sidewalk café are immediately diluted into harmless gaiety by the light-hearted *ambiance* of the place. It's basically old-fashioned, with a slight touch of nostalgia, although it may have

chromium fixtures and modern furniture. In the sunny countries where *joie de vivre* is not an empty phrase, the café is the headquarters of the amused observer of human foibles, and the hangout of the oppressed who find peace and solace from matrimonial or professional troubles.

The old coffee-house encouraged meditation and conversation. The sidewalk café stimulates observation and conversation. No matter what happens you can always get away to the little corner *bistro* with its marble table-tops and wicker chairs under the striped awnings with the sign of an apéritif or brewing firm. I still remember my delight at first

seeing the sign BIÈRE SLAVIA on the awning of a café on the Grands Boulevards which reminded me of my favourite soccer club, back home in Prague. In those days the climate didn't bother us. On cold and rainy days the *garçons* would place small coal stoves between the tables. We sat there in our overcoats warmed mostly by companionship.

To the *habitué* the café is the magic carpet of his fanciful associations, compensation for the drudgery of daily life, an everchanging wide screen of the street scene. On a sad day there is always hope that a friend will show up for a glass of beer and an hour of talk. Or a pretty woman will walk by and smile back to you, and the day is no longer sad. The sidewalk café is one of the last bastions of conversation — talk for good talk's sake. It may be an inaudible dialogue, carried on with a good book, but it's still an exercise in communication. When the history of the café is

written, the long, impressive list of works of art stimulated by it will be led by Renoir's joyful masterpiece *Moulin de la Galette*, the apotheosis of the café. No one on a café terrace talks business or wants to close a deal. Commercial motives are conspicuously absent. Occasionally a pedlar walks by, carrying Oriental rugs and souvenirs, but the moment he sits down and becomes a guest, he stops selling. The civilizing influence of the establishment is impressive. It makes poets out of merchants and philanthropists out of crooks.

The café is no place for hard drinking. If you need a couple of very, very dry ones before catching the 5.25 to Westport, don't go there. In a French café small plates are placed on top of each other to indicate the number of drinks you've had. Drunkards would be immediately revealed by the height of the stack of plates. Café purists claim the table-tops should be of grey marble, preferably cracked, so they can hear the sweet click when the *garçon* puts down the small plate with the glass. Beer is served in a wine glass and called *bock*, wine is served *en carafe*. In Italy coffee is served in a *demi-demi-tasse*, always espresso. Checkered table-cloths are popular with Germans, many of whom have a checkered past, and white ones in Switzerland whose flag is a white cross in a red field. And one day, inevitably, somebody began to serve food.

Purists blanch at the idea. They said food should be served inside, away from exhaust fumes and falling leaves, dust and wind. The terrace should be for people who like to meet friends or discuss politics over coffee, soft drinks, an apéritif, beer — anything that doesn't interfere with the pleasure of looking, talking, listening. Genuine sidewalk cafés — not the super cafés for the well-heeled tourist — don't serve food because the waiters couldn't do it. In the establishments along the Riviera the *habitués* sit practically in each other's lap. The women wear slacks because their skirts would get caught by the legs of the chairs (and of the men). Frenchmen love sidewalk cafés facing a body of water — a lake, a river, a pond, or the sea. Looking at water is the only use the French have for it. Don't expect a French *garçon* to serve you a glass of water or ice-cubes.

Italians love their cafés facing a great, old church. Sitting in Venice's San Marco or Milan's Piazza del Duomo one always sees *habitués* get up from a table, step into the church, and come back after a while, looking at peace with God and themselves, and then they order another espresso.

The sidewalk cafés in West Berlin's Kurfürstendamm were there in the early post-war years even before the houses behind them were rebuilt. People needed companionship more than homes. Today the cafés are sturdy all-weather establishments, with glass walls and infra-red heat-ducts. Even on cold nights the clients sit there gobbling heaps of whipped

193

cream, drinking *Weisse mit Schuss*, a quaint mixture of a pale, flat beer with raspberry juice.

Jules Romains admired many things in America but he missed the sidewalk cafés in New York. In *Salsette Découvre L'Amérique* he wistfully and in vain looks for a quiet, nice spot in the city with a corner bistro and a terrace bordered by a couple of potted bay-trees, *une terrasse de bistrot parisien, avec ses douceurs et ses loisirs.* Yes, with its pleasures and leisures. But how can there be terraces since there are no real cafés? 'The café is a flower — when the flower opens, there is a terrace.' In his introspective moments Romains wondered what New York would look like today if history's travel schedule had been somewhat different, and the first waves of immigrants who gave their initial imprint and created the traditions would have come from the Latin countries, the Mediterranean, Southern Europe. Suppose the *Mayflower*, called *Fleur du Mai*, would have sailed from Marseilles, via Genoa or Palermo? 'Close your eyes ... Can't you see the arcades, the grand palazzi, large and straight, with many horizontal lines, along the avenues, the arcades in the cross-streets, not always at a right angle — a sort of Cannebière running from Rockefeller Center down to the Battery, with one café every two blocks ...'

Yachtsmanship

I SPENT some of the best years of my life on ocean liners, big and not so big ones, but until a while ago I'd never set foot on a private yacht. Proof (if such were needed) that I always moved in the wrong circles at the right time, or in the right circles at the wrong time, but never in the right circles at the right time. I now know what life on a 'boat' is like. I'm not surprised that hundreds of thousands of people who think they can afford one are mad about it.

By 'boat' I mean one of these small, luxurious pleasure craft which are called by their owners, often with more pride than truthfulness, cabin-cruisers or yachts. 'Boat' seems a safe definition for an avowed non-expert who keeps insulting his fellow yachtsmen by speaking of 'downstairs', 'in front', and 'behind', when such nautical expressions as 'below', 'fore', and 'stern' (or 'aft') are indicated.

My initiation into the sacred yachtsman's ritual took place one sunny summer afternoon in La Darse, the yacht harbour of Villefranche, on the French Riviera. By coincidence, at almost exactly the same minute, Sir Winston Churchill boarded Onassis' *Christina*, a few miles farther east in the harbour of Monaco. The event was properly covered by the press: 'As Sir Winston approached the gangway, he almost tripped over a small dog that belonged to a lady standing nearby,' a newspaper wrote. 'The lady apologized to Sir Winston. He smiled.'

By contrast, not a single reporter was present as I boarded the U.S.M.Y. (United States Motor Yacht) *Brittina*, an Italian-built, 58-foot, 700-h.p. twin-diesel motor yacht. Any boat over 48 feet is called a yacht. Its owner, Patrick Dolan, an Irish-American advertising tycoon from London, is an old friend with whom I shared pleasant secrets and memorable moments during the Second World War when we were engaged in various undercover activities.

The ritual of my initiation began with the skipper's stern admonition to remove my shoes *at once*. Such requests are made, much more politely, in any well-run Japanese house, where *ghetas* are provided for the innocent playboy of the Western world. No such courtesy was extended to me on the *Brittina*, and I had to walk across the deck in my stockinged feet. This indignity reduces a man's size and ego by more than the two inches he actually lost. The deck was made of teak, which is harder to clean than a camel-hair rug.

Taking off one's shoes is only the first step calculated to break down a man's healthy self-confidence and get him conditioned to the simple life aboard a seventy-thousand-dollar boat. At the end of my first afternoon I had removed my jacket and tie; on the second day I wore slacks and a T-shirt; on the third I was persuaded to purchase shorts and a pink shirt that was the prescribed attire for males and pseudo-males in the uninhibited sidewalk cafés of Saint-Tropez, pronounced 'Saint-Trop'; on the fourth I walked around barefooted, with no shirt at all; and on the fifth, as we anchored near the nudist colony on the island of Levant, I avoided the climax of this nautical striptease only by refusing to go ashore stark naked. So much for the sartorial problems of a yachtsman whose image, in the smart magazines, seemed always elegant, with white slacks, navy-blue jacket, fancy neckwear and a white admiral's cap. Obviously the elegant yachtsman exists only in my imagination.

There were moments during the first days when I wondered what my friends in conservatively dressed circles would say if they suddenly saw me. But as the days went by, the guilty feelings went overboard with the empty liquor bottles, and I began to enjoy myself thoroughly. The undressing of my body was followed by the disrobing of my soul. Away from civilization, I began to cast off inhibitions like so many pieces of clothing. I no longer cared about anything. Nothing mattered except the play of the light on the water, the everchanging pattern of the waves, the soft, silky breeze that seemed to caress my skin and my soul, and the pleasant motion from the (stainless) teak deck under my feet.

The gradual subversion of what is falsely known as the civilized life is the real reason for the popularity of boating. In 1904, there were fifteen thousand pleasure boats in the United States. Last year, I read, there were over eight million. Some of the new breed of Sunday skippers do terrible things. They buzz each other for fun, cut across bows, and swoosh through swimmers as if their boats were equipped with *filets de sole* instead of with razor-sharp, whirling propeller blades. They operate on the theory that what you don't see won't hurt you. I know a man who spent eighty thousand dollars on a splendid cruiser but refused to shell out one

The pattern of a ship's wake

more dollar for a proper chart, and eventually ran his $80,000 investment up on a reef.

There is a little of the Rousseau in each of us, but most people merely talk about going back to nature and never do anything about it. A boat is the perfect answer for the man who has everything, and wants to get away from everything. Any effort to do some writing, read or think is doomed from the start. It becomes difficult to keep one's eyes opened for any length of time. You sink into a wonderful euphoria which reduces the big and small problems of life to microscopic size so that they can be placed into a tiny sea-shell.

There is a radio-telephone aboard to keep in touch with the world, but who wants to? There is no television. The radio is turned off as soon as one has heard the all-important morning weather forecast. You get totally disinterested in political and economic crises; the only crisis you may have to face is a meteorological one. When Radio Grasse predicts *mer agitée*, or even *mer peu agitée*, you know you'd better be careful. The Mediteranean is a treacherous body of water.

I had brought some work along but never so much as opened my brief-case. A briefcase and a typewriter are incompatible with a yacht. But although you do nothing at all you are always very busy. You run up front ('forward') to catch the sun or back ('aft') to avoid it; you hold fenders alongside the hull during exciting parking ('mooring') operations; you run downstairs ('below') to put on a sweater because it has suddenly got cold; you get ready for a drink, climb down the ladder for a swim, sprinkle yourself with precious sweet-water, run below to take off the sweater because it has suddenly got hot again, look through your field-glass at landmarks, lighthouses and bikinis, get ready for another drink, try to find a good spot for the night, and do a hundred-and-one other things that are very important. Naturally there is no time to think of your work, the sad state of the world, or any other problem that seemed to occupy you in your pre-boat life, millions of years ago.

There is something about life in a boat that is quite unique. You are utterly and totally independent of your fellow-men though not of the sea; you never get rid of the mastery of the sea around you. No one will phone or drop in unannounced. You are more secluded than on a mountain top; you are physically, spiritually and emotionally on your own.

If the boat has enough elbow room and your fellow travellers are congenial, you have the sensation of being suspended in a wondrous vacuum where the hours don't count and the days have no names. There is nothing around you but the sea and the sky, but they change all the time and there is not a single monotonous moment. Far from being boring, as I

En bâteau à Argenteuil by Edouard Manet. River boating is
more peaceful, and there is no risk of a *mer très agitée*

The U.S.M.Y. *Brittina* which initiated the author into life on a 'boat'

always thought, life in a boat is full of excitement but it is the healthy excitement of man concerned with the basic, primeval needs — food, drink, sex, survival. You drift along the azure-blue coast with no purpose, no appointments, no plan. The cells of your mind relax with the muscles of your body. You find yourself staring into bluish space, and after a few days of this *dolcissima vita* you don't give a damn about anything. This, for all I know, may have been life in the Garden of Eden.

At midday you ride at anchor in a deep-blue bay surrounded by dark-green pine trees. The water is so clear that you need no goggles to see the sea-grass on the bottom. At night you prudently seek shelter behind the breakwater of a harbour. You are just the length of the gangway separated from the blessings of modern life — shops, banks, teleprinters, waiters, *spécialités de la maison* — but instead you sit on the aft deck and watch the goings-on over there with utter detachment. Having known the Riviera for many years from the land looking out on the sea I know today that it's very different to see it from the sea looking out on land. The narrow space between the *Brittina's* stern and the wall of the pier created an absolute sense of isolation, an invisible wall of privacy and protection. The robber knights of the Middle Ages may have felt that way when they returned from their pilfering forays to their castles and gave orders to have the drawbridge lifted, while their angry victims across the abyss looked on in bitter frustration.

I remember a lazy afternoon in Saint-Tropez when I sat on the aft

deck, watching the exhibitionists in the crowded sidewalk café. It was only a few steps from there but the short distance gave me a sense of seeing an old slapstick movie. Another time I sat on the aft deck watching the lights go on in Monte Carlo. There would be people in the Casino chasing the little roulette ball, and after a while they would get up and come out but I wondered whether they, too, would enjoy the lights as I did. One rarely does, after leaving the Casino.

For the people who own one of these floating castles life aboard is a healthy exercise in humility. One night we docked in the Ile de Porquerolles, a deceivingly sleepy island off Hyères with a lot of buildings and secret French Navy equipment that is strictly off-limits for the tourists, guarded by the French Navy. Among the small boats of the local fishermen our *Brittina* looked like a minor *Queen Mary*. And the next night we barely squeezed in next to a magnificent yacht in Cannes. It had more personnel than a small hotel and according to gossip had been chartered by a man from, naturally, Texas, for twenty-eight days for the sum of thirty-six thousand dollars. 'No matter how big your boat is you soon discover that somebody else's is a lot bigger,' Patrick said, wistfully gazing at the $1,300-*per-diem* yacht. A couple of seamen gazed right back at the ladies on our little boat. The seamen wore blue shirts with the name of their yacht in big white letters. They reminded me of the late Errol Flynn who had been a great yachtsman. They were tall, sunburned, handsome and apparently ready-for-anything. Our ladies were very pleased to be gazed at.

Yachtsmen are friendly people with a fine sense of yachtsmanship. No matter how crowded a port, there is always space for one more, even if one has to pull up alongside another boat whose deck one uses, with proper apologies, when one wants to go ashore. Naval etiquette demands that you wear your shoes in your hands and say 'good afternoon', without introducing yourself.

Boats are heavens of anonymity. Yachtsmen are forever visiting each other, looking at their sails and swapping improbable tales of rough seas and sudden gales but they are not interested in each others' social or financial standing. They may be great friends, drinking and talking boats, but they don't know what the visitor is doing away from the boat. The line of your deck interests them more than the size of your bank account.

When yachtsmen go for a stroll, they walk around the yacht harbour looking at boats as collectors look at paintings and men look at women. They take in the line, consider whether it's ship-shape, study the sails.

They admire a boat's sturdiness and guess correctly its hidden power. They dearly love their own boat but always look for a better one. They dream of making that trip around the world aboard a sturdy Norwegian trawler; they have exciting visions of setting sail for Macao, Mauritius, Tobago, Tristan da Cunha. They love the big sail-boats that look deceivingly bare but when you go downstairs — sorry, below — you discover a wood-panelled, Victorian library, a bathroom with a full-size tub, a fine galley and a small wine-cellar. Some are true yachtsmen who go out into sea and storm all alone. Rugged types who can do everything except swim — true sailors never swim because they know it's useless. Sometimes they are accompanied by attractive, tough-looking girls who can cook a *bouillabaisse*, stitch together a pair of shorts, carry on a conversation in four languages, handle a rope, and wash the deck. And that isn't all, brother.

The true yachtsman takes a dim view of the power-boatman who faces up to reality, knows that red sails at sunset belong in a movie, doesn't want to mess around with a big, beautiful sail-boat, and relies on the power of his diesels rather than on the shape of his sails to get him out of trouble. Among the power-boatmen some buy their boat by catalogue — the lowest rung in the social ladder. Some buy a boat and then change it until it can't be recognized any more. Some decide to design their own boat, turning down the expert advice of naval architects, retired admirals-of-the-fleet, and owners of ship-building yards, getting into wild fights

LEFT: The author aboard the *Brittina*. A quiet moment between running *forward*, *aft* or *below*, drinking or swimming
RIGHT: Patrick Dolan, owner of the *Brittina*, the author's partner in various undercover activities during the Second World War

with foremen and workers. And when their dream boat is launched, they are terrified. Is that what they wanted? They press their lips together grimly and vow that their next boat will be a better one.

Then there is the problem of registration and flags. The proper yachtsman flies several flags. The owner's national flag waves from the stern. In port you also fly the 'courtesy' flag of the country whose guest you are. Members of exclusive clubs fly the flag of their yacht club — there are subtle social shadings but let's not go into *that*. Smart millionaires fly the flag of Panama, Liberia or Monaco where their boat is registered, for obvious reasons. I never saw a Greek multi-millionaire flying the Greek flag; they all seemed to prefer the Panamanian flag.

To fly the English flag around the Mediterranean is considered pretty bad, unless the owner also flies the flag of the Royal Yacht Squadron, which seems to be the key to the English yachtsman's heaven. To fly the American flag is even worse and automatically makes the owner a sucker who is never given an even break. He pays twice as much for fuel and laundry, and when he clears 'for foreign' in a port, a transaction involving several rubber stamps, he is discriminated against by arrogant port-captains whose sympathies are *not* with the United States of America. The port-captain asks the American where he wants to go from here, and when he is told the destination, he shakes his head.

'Impossible, Monsieur. That's 610 miles. Your range is only 600 miles. You can't go there.'

So the American takes the port-captain down into the engine room and mumbles something about the carburettors being specially whipped up, and after a while the port captain relents, whereupon the American pays $240 for bonded diesel fuel which infuriates him because he knows that the Panama-registered millionaire over there paid only $60 for ex-bond fuel. The American drowns his disgust in bonded gin which is a dollar a bottle. In fact, gin is almost cheaper than tonic water, which explains the high percentage of happily intoxicated gentlemen crew-members. In order to save on the high cost of tonic water, they drink gin with gin.

An unwritten code governs the conduct of guests on a yacht. More beautiful friendships have been broken up on boats than anywhere else on earth. In fact, a week-long cruise is a strong test of an enduring friendship. A boat is not a hotel. Living in confined space calls for tact and tolerance, patience and pumping. The water supply in your toilet — called 'head' on a boat — doesn't come when you pull a handle or press a button; you have to pump. Guests are warned not to throw anything into the 'head'. No wonder some people develop a regular bathroom phobia.

'A boat is the perfect answer for the man who has everything and wants to get away from everything.' Aristotle Onassis' yacht at Monte Carlo

Guests are expected to keep their cabin 'ship-shape' — always ready for inspection. If you were a member of the armed forces, you will have no trouble in slipping back into the mercifully forgotten routine. Guests are also expected to be helpful during landing operations, holding fenders over the railing to protect the boat's hull. Fenders are rubber bags covered with plastic material; they would be useful for motor-cars in crowded parking-lots.

If you follow strictly the long list of don'ts and do's; if you will be patient when lunch is three hours late; cheerful although the boat rolls heavily in a bad storm; happy after pumping your 'head' for minutes; unperturbed by the all-night noises of the crew on the boat next to you, sinister Spaniards playing a dangerous card game; helpful to get drunks off the boat and get ladies without high heels on; if you will try to be all things to all men aboard and not send off long cables, you may be accepted.

I heard of a man from Wall Street on a cruise who felt 'cut off from the market' which he expected to go up shortly. During a bad storm he handed several urgent code messages to the crew and asked them to send them off at once via Radio Grasse. This means getting hold of Radio Grasse, which is difficult even in good weather and spelling out every word using the international alphabet, which is worse. The crew politely took the broker's messages, and when he wasn't looking, they threw them into the *mer très agitée*. When the Wall Streeter returned to New York, he was delighted to find out that his orders had never arrived since the market had gone down. Saved him a lot of money. He even sent some gifts to the crew members. I believe there is a moral in this story, although I don't think that Messrs Merrill Lynch, Pierce, Fenner & Smith will like it.

The guest who has comported himself in accordance with the un-written code, occasionally brings flowers to his hostess from ashore, and a bottle of honest wine to his host; who is able to cook a good meal in the tiny galley without messing it up; who keeps his friends alternately amused and intrigued by his unpredictably charming utterances — such a guest will know he has been given the seal of approval when he is asked again. It's easy to be invited the first time to join a yacht; but few people pull off the almost impossible feat of being asked a second time.

I'm not yet sure whether I made it, although Patrick has been talking lately of going to Tristan da Cunha in a Norwegian trawler. He first mentioned the forlorn island in the South Atlantic one evening shortly after we'd left the pleasant yacht harbour of Le Lavendou around seven o'clock, expecting to be by nine p.m. in nearby Saint-Tropez for the night. Half an hour later a strong Mistral started to blow astern — from the rear — which is especially dangerous. All owners of small power boats dread a stern sea. If the wind is blowing hard the boat can be lifted out of the water on top of the swells. The propellers could run free for a couple of seconds and break up the boat. The *Brittina*, instead of sliding smoothly through the water, was shuddering as she came to the top of the swells.

It had suddenly become very dark. The coastline, miles away, was a confused jumble of lights, with no recognizable shape. We must have overshot the big red light of the harbour of Saint-Tropez because we were already somewhere near Cannes when we discovered that we were off course. (On land one would say we were lost.) We turned round in the dark Mediterranean, which was very sinister that night, not at all like in the travel brochures. We finally managed to discover the red light of Saint-Tropez; I never thought I would come to like a red light so much. Fortunately we had plenty of fuel and plenty of power in our Diesels. (My question what would have happened if we'd run out of fuel in the middle of the storm, was not answered. The guest who wants to be re-invited should not ask such questions.)

There were reefs near the harbour entrance with a light-house between them, but the light had gone out that night. As we slid through the entrance into the calm waters of the yacht harbour of Saint-Trop, three hours later than anticipated, I understood what poets, sailors and yachts-men mean by 'riding out the storm' and 'making port'.

It was an interesting experience but I can't help worrying about Tristan da Cunha — *if* I should be asked again. What's going to happen if we overshoot the lonely, little island in the South Atlantic on a dark night? Where do we go from there?

Making Music

FEW OTHER WAYS of pursuing happiness are as stimulating and rewarding, exciting and relaxing, as playing string quartets with congenial fellow players. Chamber-music is more than a hobby: it is a lifelong passion.

Ever since chamber-music emerged in the sixteenth century, probably in Italy, it has been written primarily for amateurs, played mainly by amateurs, and kept alive mostly by amateurs. If it is often performed by people whose enthusiasm outstrips their technique, they sometimes reach a subtle psychological *rapport* and an inner harmony rarely attained by celebrated virtuosos, tempestuous prima donnas, or, for that matter, the frustrated second trombonist of a. major symphony orchestra. For them, music is ordinarily a competitive business, a race that goes to the fastest or to the loudest.

Not so chamber-music. It is based on give-and-take; it is civilized and egalitarian; it is a garden of musical fellowship from which the law of the jungle has been banished and in which egotism simply cannot thrive. But though chamber-music is non-competitive, it is far from being lukewarm, and nothing could be more wrong-headed than the view that chamber-music players are austere and bloodless esoterics, as anyone can attest who has watched a chamber-music group in action, soaring to the heights of happiness when a movement comes off and plummeting to the depths of despair when, as happens more often, it doesn't.

Chamber-music players are compelled to put up with imperfection but they do not tolerate the slightest lack of zeal. Watch four amateurs in action and you will instantly recognize them as musical throughbreds. In this status-seeking world of ours, chamber-music is perhaps the last stronghold of the uninhibited idealist and the uncorrupted amateur who

'The Music of Friends'. The Composer La Barre stands among his friends, who are about to play one of his trio sonatas; a French painting of about 1705

isn't trying to prove something — to himself or to anyone — but wants to make music for the sake of music.

I've seen it happen even with famous professionals who enjoy an evening of chamber-music as much as the lowly amateur. When Heifetz or Stern, Primrose or Casals, or the overworked second violist of a major symphony orchestra wants to put his chores of the day behind him and have real fun, he plays with a string quartet.

Chamber-music ensembles made up of celebrated soloists are seldom well integrated, because great soloists often cannot subdue their personalities and mannerisms. Each tries to overshadow the group, and sometimes wrecks it thereby. The great professional quartets are marvels of integration; the slightest *rubato* by one player is instinctively followed by the others; even their bow pressure seems synchronized; they seem to breathe in the same rhythm; yet although the four instrumental voices are perfectly blended, the individual work of the performers is always clearly discernible.

The audience of a chamber-music concert always contains a large percentage of slightly frustrated fiddlers, violists and cellists. Chamber-music amateurs, unlike other music lovers, are not satisfied merely to listen to recordings or broadcasts: no sooner have they heard a work than they want to sit down to perform it themselves.

Chamber-music has no hard-and-fast ground rules, but it does observe certain conventions. The number of players vary, but there have to be at least two and there should not be more than eight or, at the most, ten. Sonata teams are generally not considered to be chamber-music players; on the other hand, the lovely Mozart duos for violin and viola are certainly chamber-music, and very fine, too. Madrigal groups are often rejected ('not instrumental enough') while a small orchestra playing Bach or Handel often qualifies. (*Hausmusik*, a term often used for popular music played by small groups, is not considered chamber-music by the purists. A trio arrangement of Rossini's *William Tell* overture or of tunes from *My Fair Lady* may be fun, but it isn't strictly chamber-music.)

Pianists are welcome — though not pianists who insist on banging away like soloists and drowning out everybody else — and so are flautists, oboists, and clarinettists. Horn-players will be invited occasionally, and there exist woodwind and brass groups. Primarily, however, the instruments of chamber-music are the strings — violin, viola, cello — and the most popular combination is the string quartet, with the string quintet and string trio strong runners-up.

People who prefer their music flamboyant, with strong tone colours and dramatic effects, are usually happier with symphony orchestras and military

'The secret of chamber-music is to listen to your
fellow-players, while you yourself are playing.'
The title page of a book of French *Chansons*

bands. But if you like economy of means, a balanced ensemble, subtlety of texture and clarity of expression, chamber-music is your best bet. Playing in a string quartet is an exercise in democracy and a study in humility, a truly civilized pastime.

The secret of chamber-music is to listen to your fellow players while you yourself are playing. Some people never learn it; let them join amateur orchestras or play sonatas with their wealthy aunts. A good string quartet, somewhat like a good champagne, must be a blend. When four amateurs manage to play together softly yet clearly so that each instrument can be heard and the texture of the music becomes transparent, they've got something. The have created a string quartet, surely the most sensitive musical instrument of all, and one of the supreme achievements of western civilization.

I have been a passionate player of chamber-music since I began as a lowly second fiddler at the tender age of eleven, when my Uncle Bruno, the most enthusiastic organizer of string quartets in our home-town in Moravia, drafted me on the shortest notice to take over the second-violin part of Beethoven's *Opus* 18, No. 4, because his regular Second Fiddle, a noted surgeon, had had to hustle off to perform an operation. (In quartet lingo a fiddle is an instrument while a Fiddle is the person playing it. One of the mysterious gifts of chamber-music players is their ability to hear capital letters.)

I've remained an incurable addict for the past forty-five years and find myself in complete agreement with Henry Peacham, the seventeenth-century British essayist, who wrote in his book *The Compleat Gentleman,*

Infinite is the sweete varietie that the Theorique of Musicke exerciseth the mind withal, as the contemplation of proportions, of Concords and Discords, diversities of Moods and Tones, infiniteness of Invention, etc. But I dare affirme, there is no Science in the world, that so affecteth the free and generous spirit, with a more delightful and in-offensive recreation, or better disposeth the minde to what is commendable and vertuous.

What exactly is the object of our addiction? The term *Musica da Camera* indicates that this sort of music, unlike church music or opera, was intended to be performed in a chamber, and in the early days the chamber in question belonged to an aristocratic patron. Like so many great achievements, chamber-music began unobtrusively and its origins are obscure, but the experts agree that from the beginning its essential characteristic was the scoring of individual parts for several instruments, to be played at the same time. In at least one case the aristocratic patron was also the composer. Henry VIII of England, who acquired every

worthy instrument he could lay his hands on – lutes, virginals, organs, recorders, flutes, cornets, guitars and horns – wrote some chamber-music and liked to play it with his courtiers.

Perhaps the first mention of chamber-music in literature was provided by the Spanish writer Jorge de Montemayor, in his pastoral novel *Diana Enamorada*, published in 1559. The instruments involved were four wooden cornets and a sackbut, and the author gives such a vivid description of the playing of chamber-music that one must conclude that he was a devotee himself; actually he had studied music in his youth. During the second half of the sixteenth century, Claude Gervaise and Eustache du Caurroy, two gifted French musicians, wrote several suites for viols. But private music-making never developed in France, where musical tastes were influenced by the artistic dictatorship of Louis XIV who preferred the more spectacular arts of ballet and opera. Chamber-music has never appealed to the spectacular-minded.

Hearing, from Abraham Bosse's set of engravings of the Five Senses. One of the singers conducts and two others play an accompaniment on lute and *viola da gamba*

At Madrid's Prado there is Jan Brueghel's painting *El Oído* (Hearing), one of five pictures illustrating the senses. It shows a still life of musical instruments scattered on the floor; on the music stands are the parts for *Madrigals for Six Voices* by the English composer Peter Phillips, who lived in the Netherlands and published his music there between 1612 and 1630.

The phrase 'chamber-music' appeared in English for the first time in 1630, when the composer Martin Peerson published, *Mottects or Grave Chamber Musique. Containing songs of five parts of several sorts, some ful, and some verse and chorus. But all fit for voyces and Vials, with an organ part.* During that time English composers exercised much influence in Germany, teaching in Germany, and publishing chamber-music collections with German imprints. German musicians came to England for instruction, particularly to learn the *viola da gamba*. Two centuries later, German writers referred to England as *Land ohne Musik*. They may not have known how much their country owed to England, or they may have found it convenient to forget it.

For a time, the viol — a relatively large and clumsy instrument, which was held between the knees — was the central instrument of chamber music, and during the Renaissance the 'chest of viols', a set of six matched instruments — two treble, two tenor, two bass — became synonymous with chamber-music. By 1660, when the great instruments made by the Amatis in Cremona were widely admired, the violin assumed its regal place in chamber-music, in spite of the spirited opposition of diehards like Anthony Wood, an Oxford man, who claimed that gentlemen 'esteemed a violin to be an instrument only belonging to a common fiddler, and could not endure that it should come among them for fear of making their meetings vain and fiddling'. In London, John Jenkins (1592–1678) issued his *Twelve Sonatas for Two Violins and a Base with a Thorough Base for Organ or Theorbo*. In the diaries of John Evelyn and Samuel Pepys we read of the enthusiasm of London society for chamber-music which was played in clubs run by John Banister and Thomas Britton, or in private homes. 'There was also much music-making, on a rather lower social plane, in inns and taverns all over the country', writes the English musicologist A. Hyatt King, but this sort of music was mostly performed by professionals.

With the violin in the ascendant, a good deal of pioneering in chamber-music was done during the seventeenth and early-eighteenth centuries, by Vivaldi, Gabrielli, Frescobaldi, Vitali, Corelli, Purcell, Buxtehude, Dall'Abaco, Handel, Bach and others. All of them wrote music for several instruments, and many of them cultivated the trio sonata, usually for

'I dare affirme, there is no science in the world that better disposeth the minde to what is commendable and virtuous.' *A Concert* by Lorenzo Costa

strings. When the great Cremonese violin-makers wanted to try out their new instruments, they sat together in the evening hours and played the sonatas by Corelli whom Antonio Stradivari, Guarneri del Gesù, Bergonzi *et al.* much admired. But none of the great composers of that time hit upon the string quartet as we know it today. That astonishing invention was made by Joseph Haydn.

In 1755, when Haydn was twenty-three, he was invited to spend some time in a country house in Weinzierl, Austria, as the guest of a patrician music-lover named Karl von Fürnberg. There the young man played the

Joseph Haydn. His Opus 1, No. 1
is now generally regarded as
the world's first string quartet

The title page of Mozart's six 'Haydn'
quartets. The two composers played in quartets
together, Haydn first violin and Mozart viola

violin at chamber-music evenings, and there he composed his *Opus* 1,
No. 1 – now generally regarded as the world's first string quartet.

When Haydn left Weinzierl, early in 1756, he had written at least
six quartets, calling them *divertimenti, cassazioni,* or *notturni.* By modern
standards, they were rather naive and simple, being dominated, like most
chamber-music of the time, by the first violin. But Haydn's ideas were
developing, and in *Opus* 20, written in 1772, at the home of Haydn's
great aristocratic patron, Prince Nicholas Esterházy, he let the four voices
participate on equal terms, with the cello singing out the opening theme
– something that had never been done before.

From then on until his death in 1809, Haydn kept turning out masterpieces, each in a different mood but all rich in invention, vibrant with
feeling, full of beauty. His last works, the two great quartets of *Opus 77,*
which he wrote toward the end of his life when he was in his late sev-
enties, have the magic of vigorous youth, transparent charm and distilled
passion – reminding one of the miraculous achievements of Giuseppe
Verdi who was seventy-four when he finished *Otello* and as an octogenar-

Al mio caro Amico Haydn

Un Padre, avendo risolto di mandare i suoi figli nel gran
Mondo, stimò doverli affidare alla protezione, e condotta
d'un Uomo molto celebre in allora, il quale per buona sorte,
era di più il suo migliore Amico. — Eccoti dunque del pari,
Uom celebre, ed Amico mio carissimo i sei miei figli. — Essi sono,
è vero il frutto di una lunga, e laboriosa fatica, pur la speranza
fattami da più Amici di vederla almeno in parte compensata,
m'incoraggisce, e mi lusinga, che questi parti siano per essermi
un giorno di qualche consolazione. — Tu stesso Amico carissimo,
nell'ultimo tuo Soggiorno in questa Capitale, me ne dimostrasti
la tua soddisfazione. — Questo tuo suffragio mi anima sopra
tutto, perchè io te li raccommandi, e mi fa sperare, che non ti
sembreranno del tutto indegni del tuo favore. — Piacciati dunque
accoglierli benignamente, ed esser loro Padre, Guida, ed Amico!
Da questo momento, io ti cedo i miei diritti sopra di essi: ti
supplico però di guardare con indulgenza i difetti, che l'occhio
parziale di Padre mi può aver celati, e di continuar loro
malgrado, la generosa tua Amicizia a chi tanto l'apprezza,
mentre sono di tutto Cuore.

Amico Carissimo   il tuo Sincerissimo Amico
Vienna il p.mo Settembre 1785.
                                                    W. A. Mozart

Mozart's dedication of his quartets,
the 'fruits of long and arduous labour',
to his dearest friend Haydn

Wolfgang Amadeus Mozart,
'the greatest composer known to mankind'

ian wrote *Falstaff*, which combines the smiling wisdom of old age with
the warm beat of a young heart. Altogether, Haydn wrote eighty-four
quartets, in which he brought this noble art form — the finest, purest,
deepest kind of music — from birth to full maturity. It's an almost incredible accomplishment for one man.

With his first quartet, Haydn inaugurated what is now called the
classic period of chamber-music, which ended with the death of Beethoven in 1827. During those seventy-two magnificent years, Mozart
wrote his twenty-five quartets and Beethoven his seventeen, which, with
Haydn's eighty-four, form the permanent gold reserve of all good string-
quartet players. In dedicating six of his 'ten famous' quartets to his
admired older friend Haydn, the young Mozart wrote that they were
'the fruit of a long and arduous toil'. You would never think so. They
are divine music, seemingly written without any effort whatever, and a
splendid example of Mozart's genius.

Haydn, a genius himself, recognized genius. 'Before God and as an
honest man,' he told Mozart's father, 'I tell you that your son is the

215

'Chamber-music is the garden of musical fellowship.' From *The New Most Beautiful Garden of the Choicest Musical Flowers*, a song-book of 1605

greatest composer known to me . . . He has taste and a most profound knowledge of composition.' How right Haydn was! Mozart has remained the greatest composer known to mankind.

(The Irish singer Michael Kelly, who performed in Vienna in the seventeen-eighties, mentions in his *Reminiscences* a quartet evening at which 'the players were tolerable'. The players were Joseph Haydn, first violin; the composer Karl Ditters von Dittersdorf, second violin; Wolfgang Amadeus Mozart, viola; and the Viennese musician Jan Baptist Wanhal, cello.)

As for Beethoven, his 'early' quartets – the six of Opus 18 – occasionally betray the influence of his predecessors, but by Opus 59 ('the middle quartets') he was very much on his own, and his bold, new style gave rise to grave doubts in contemporary musical circles. The violinist Radicati, who, at Beethoven's request, worked out the fingering for Opus 59, wrote, 'I told him that surely he did not consider these works to be music? Beethoven replied, "Oh, they are not for you, but for a later age."' In 1824, Prince Nicolas Borissovitch Galitzin, a Russian amateur cellist who lived in Vienna and commissioned Beethoven to write three quartets, said in a letter to the composer, 'Your genius is centuries in advance.' The Galitzin quartets belong to the 'late' Beethovens, as we call them.

They are the most beautiful works in the whole chamber-music literature and among the greatest music ever written. Enormously difficult, deeply moving, superbly rewarding, they should be played only at the end of a quartet evening. Nothing can top them — although sometimes we follow up with a shorter Mozart, whose heavenly genius is the perfect antidote after Beethoven's earthbound suffering. I was past fifty before I approached the 'late' Beethovens, but I don't regret having waited so long.

These quartets must not be simply played; they should be approached with reverence, understanding and dedication. The greatness that lies between and behind the written notes cannot be grasped at once but must be gradually discovered. For me there is more modern music — or perhaps I should say, timeless, true, absolute music — in these late Beethoven quartets than in anything written since then.

We chamber-music players have forbidding tasks, but we are also very lucky. Some of the greatest composers have written some of their greatest works for us. No doubt they were intrigued by the subtlety and the refinement of this kind of music, and fascinated by the challenge of saying something deep and important with the bare essentials. Since the bare essentials quickly expose any shoddiness or trickery, what they produced had to be perfectly made and uncompromisingly honest to be succesful. There are plenty of phoney symphonies and phoney operas, and there is, of course, lots of phoney music anyway; but there are very few phoney string quartets, and those are simply ignored.

In addition to the quartets of Haydn, Mozart and Beethoven, there are about a hundred and fifty important trios and quartets and quintets by Schubert, Mendelssohn, Schumann, Brahms, Franck, Saint-Saëns, Tchaikowsky, Borodin, Taneyev, Glazunov, Smetana, Dvořák, Grieg, Gade, Sibelius, Kodály, Dohnányi, Bartók, Verdi, Hugo Wolf, Bruckner, Debussy, Ravel, Hindemith, Reger, Prokofieff, Martinù, Schönberg, Webern, Berg, Křenek, Milhaud and others, past and present.

The professional string quartet came into being through the enthusiasm of the aristocratic music-lovers. Many aristocrats who had learned to play an instrument supported professionals whose duties included composing chamber-works (with a good part for the master, to be sure) and attending to the music needs of the chapel and the ballroom. Haydn's employer, Prince Nicholas Esterházy, was known as a good baryton player — the baryton was a large viol with six or seven strings — and Haydn wrote one hundred twenty-five trios for baryton, viola and bass, in which he first tried out some of the experiments which he later brought off so gloriously in his string quartets. Frederick Wilhelm II, King of Prussia, was an able cello player who is now remembered for commis-

217

sioning both Carl Gotthard Langhans to build the Brandenburg Gate in Berlin and Wolfgang Amadeus Mozart to write six string quartets. Mozart completed three, K. 575, 589, and 590, and I daresay they will survive the Brandenburg Gate. Mozart succeeded in writing 'grateful' cello parts for the King, using the other instruments to compensate volume and achieve architectural balance. Haydn, also, dedicated several quartets to the cello-playing king. And when His Majesty didn't play works especially written for him, he could always fall back on compositions by Allegri, Scarlatti, Tartini, Pachelbel, Buxtehude and the Stamitzes.

After 1800, feudal patronage of chamber-music continued to thrive in Vienna, where the Habsburg Court, local aristocrats and princes of the church were all great enthusiasts. The names of Prince Schwarzenberg, Prince Lobkowitz and the afore-mentioned Prince Galitzin today live in the quartet dedications of Beethoven. In 1808, Count Andreas Rasumovsky, the Russian ambassador in Vienna and one of Beethoven's aristocratic friends — whose name became immortalized by Beethoven's dedication to him of the three quartets of Opus 59, forever known as the 'Rasumovsky quartets' — asked Ignaz Schuppanzigh, a local virtuoso, to form a regular quartet of professional musicians for the Count's musical *soirées*. (There is still a Palais Rasumovsky in Vienna.)

Schuppanzigh, an excellent fiddler, was also a musician of unusual foresight; at a time when famous musicians such as Weber and Spohr remained uninterested by Beethoven's later works, Schuppanzigh was fascinated by what he recognized as the music of genius and devoted himself with energy to its cause. It was for him and his colleagues that Beethoven wrote the later quartets. He could afford to write very difficult music, since Schuppanzigh was a virtuoso, but then he didn't make it easy for generations of ardent first fiddlers who came after Schuppanzigh and are baffled by the difficulties and hidden traps of the *quatuor concertant*. There is a cadenza-like passage between the slow movement and the last in Opus 59, No. 1, that has been the downfall of many first fiddlers.

Little did Count Rasumovsky know that he was making musical history when he hired the Schuppanzigh Quartet for his *soirées*. Chamber-music has never quite recovered from the shock. Until that time, chamber-music groups had been assembled casually, from the best amateur and professional talent at hand. Even Count Rasumovsky played for a while as Second Fiddle with Schuppanzigh — it would have been tactless to turn him down since he gave all these splendid *soirées* with plenty of food and drink — but after a while the Count must have felt rather out of place with three seasoned professionals. History doesn't relate whether he was politely asked to drop out or whether he left on his own. It must have been a delicate situation, but the Count had diplomatic training; perhaps he didn't have to be told. He knew. A first-rate second violinist came in and the Schuppanzigh Quartet was born.

At first they played in noble houses but word got around of their success and before long, to the horror of purists, they began 'going on tour' and performing in large auditoriums for the public. Anyone could get in who paid for his ticket. Chamber-music broke out of the chamber and into the concert hall. The present-day professional quartet was born.

Purists still feel that chamber-music belongs in the home; but though it has remained divided between small groups of highly-polished professional players performing in concert halls and large masses of well-meaning amateurs making music at home, the division has not been inimical. The best (though not always the most famous) professional quartets have something of the happy spontaneity and divine improvisation that is the heart of chamber-music, while ambitious amateurs get from the professionals an idea of how the works which they play at home ought to sound.

In western and central Europe chamber-music concerts are sponsored by municipalities and large groups. And in the United States, where the pursuit of happiness is efficiently organized from cradle to gave, it should surprise no one that a non-profit group, the *Amateur Chamber-Music Players*, exists for the sole purpose of bringing chamber-music players together. A serious magazine has called it 'private insanity of a most delightful kind'. The A.C.M.P.'s latest Directory lists over four thousand happy lunatics in America and several hundred in more than fifty other countries, by name, address, telephone number (very important), instrument and rating. Each member rates himself — A for excellent, B for good, C for fair, D for 'etc', which probably means not-so-fair, and Pro. for professional.

It is characteristic for chamber-music players' healthy sense of self-respect that there are relatively few D's in the Directory, I've played with some D's who should have rated themselves O for outrageous or Z for zero.

Players temporarily stranded in a place where a member is listed, will be assured, by simply making a 'phone call, of an evening of chamber-music hospitality, an endearing combination of music, food, drink and talk. Actually, only a small percentage of all chamber-music players are listed in the Directory; for each player in it there must be scores of unlisted ones. Many of us are anti-joiners who prefer the anonymity of our dimly-lighted music-rooms.

It is no accident that we chamber-music fans are completely un-interested in the private standing or professional activities of our fellow players. I have played music with people for months without knowing their first names or asking what they did for a living. We just don't care. Our post-musical conversation is always spirited and often controversial, mainly about missed rests, that trap after letter D, and didn't-we-play-that-adagio-too-fast, but it would never occur to us to discuss our emotional or professional problems. I have played with commercial travellers and unworldly artists, with Nobel Prize winners and housewives, with spin-sters and *divorcées*, with tax-collectors and tax-evaders, with general managers and file-clerks, with students and scholars, with millionaires and misogamists. I have not yet played with croupiers, truck-drivers or undertakers but I wouldn't be surprised if there were some chamber-music *aficionados* among them.

String quartet playing is not always pure and perfect bliss. It suffers from a delicate human-relations problem caused by the harsh fact that two members of the quartet play the same instrument. Which means that one of the two has to play second fiddle.

There are no Second Fiddles. There are only reluctant First Fiddles who agree to play second, exceptionally, unhappily, just tonight, to make a quartet possible. They approach their task with martyrdom and give the First Fiddler an acute feeling of guilt. Beware of people who are eager to play second: they often collapse in *vivace* and *presto* movements and sur-render to three flats or four sharps. A genuine second violinist — one who contributes dedication, a sense of rhythm, and enough technique to master his part — is an unmixed blessing. He always has the right 'A', like the symphony orchestra's oboe player. He radiates composure and exudes tranquillity. His steady bowing is the rope the first violinist holds on to while crossing atonal abysses filled with lightning runs and tricky chords. He does not get nervous when he has to play all by himself (as in the beginning of the Verdi), or is called upon to play difficult arabesques (as in Schubert's A minor), or a beautiful solo (as in the adagio of Beet-hoven's *Harp* quartet).

(You may have noticed that I mention some works by key, others by *opus* number, and some by name. Don't ask why it's just one of chamber-music's minor mysteries. For us 'the Verdi' means Verdi's only string quartet, an exciting piece with plenty of *Rigoletto*, *Otello* and *Falstaff* in it. 'The Debussy' and 'the Ravel' are the sole chamber-musical contri-butions of these composers to our literature and need no further indenti-fication. Both are uncontested masterpieces. When we talk of the *Bird*,

Joachim's quartet. The best professional quartets have something of the happy spontaneity and divine improvisation that is the heart of chamber-music

the *Lark*, the *Emperor*, we mean Haydn; the *Hunt* and the *Dissonant* are beloved Mozart jewels; 'fifty-nine, number one' is a Beethoven quartet that all cellists love and 'ninety-six' is the code number for Dvořák's '*American*'. For some unfathomable reason we talk of Schubert's 'A minor' but never of his 'D minor' which we call *Death and the Maiden*.)

In addition to the problem of the Second Fiddle there are the problems caused by the viola and the cello. Despite the celebrated examples of such noted viola players as Mozart, Dvořák, Hindemith and Primrose, many violists still suffer from an acute if unjustified inferiority complex which erupts sometimes after hours of placid co-operation. But a genuine violist – not an ex-fiddler hiding behind the thicker strings of the viola – is proud of his instrument with its beautiful sound. To appease your viola you can always play *the Smetana* with the finest viola part in the entire literature, which is a beautiful work anyway.

221

Cellists should be dealt with cautiously but firmly. I admit that they can play louder than anybody else in the quartet, but that doesn't entitle them to act like dictators. And even *their* parts contain passages marked *ppp*, though you would never think so when you listen to them. Their complaints should be patiently recorded and patiently ignored. When they accuse the first violin of 'having ruined that movement again', they should be asked to play the last movement of Beethoven's *Opus* 127, which is partly, and diabolically, written in the violin key. That will teach them a lesson.

Sheer modesty has kept me from discussing my own problems. Before arriving at the first violin, I served my apprenticeship playing Second Fiddle, and worked my way through puberty, voicebreak and Karl Ditters von Dittersdorf to become a First Fiddle. During a certain period in my life, which I care little to remember and less to discuss, I've played the viola and even the cello.

My formative years helped me to discover what the members of an amateur quartet have a right to expect from their first violinist. He should have enough personality, style, taste and technique to perform the works he has chosen to play. He should not consider himself a 'leader' — that's old-fashioned and went out with the previous generation — but, rather, *primus inter pares*. In many modern quartets the second violin part is almost as difficult as the first. The ideal amateur quartet should have no stars; no one should try to outshine the others. There should be a healthy balance of power; disagreements about programme, tempo, bowing, phrasing, rhythm and so on should be discussed and settled by majority decision.

Many disagreements are created by questions of speed. The violist wants to play the last movement as fast as he heard the Budapest do it, but the violist doesn't have to play many difficult runs. The violinist, who has plenty of difficult runs, is reluctant, and the fight is on. It will be quite an argument. Politeness is not customary among chamber-musicians.

In fact, a quartet evening is always something of a calculated risk. I don't subscribe to the theory that anybody should drop in next Thursday night and that anything will be played that happens to come to our mind. The evening should be lovingly planned and the programme carefully designed to please all the players. It should have its beginning, its climax and its aftersound, a faraway echo that leaves you with a sense of satisfaction and a feeling of accomplishment. Ideally, there should be no listeners (certain wives and girl-friends are not considered listeners, they just belong), for ideally chamber-music must never deteriorate into a 'performance'. It must remain music for the sake of making music.

English chamber-music in 1797

Some evenings start off badly. One of the players arrives late, out of breath, and his nervousness immediately affects the others. It is the habit among quartet players 'to play oneself in' with a Haydn, but some Haydns are much more than a sort of glorified warming-up exercise and the one chosen tonight bristles with difficulties. The first violinist is tired after a hectic day, unable to pull himself and his fellow-players out of the doldrums on his own bow-strings, in the style of the legendary Baron Münchhausen. Chamber-music players are a sensitive species of the human race. A sudden drop in the barometric pressure, a touch of *Föhn* may ruin their mood. I remember an evening in spring when we were sort of numb and nothing would come off, until we discovered that the room had been filled with fresh lilac. A wonderful scent but not good for making music.

On such evenings everything goes wrong. The first movement doesn't come off because the strings go down. The four players are not in tune — amateurs seldom are — since everybody carries his own A. Violinists love a high A and cellists prefer a low one, and since they have a harder time turning their pegs than we have, they usually win out though they are a majority of one. Just as the first violin starts to play his beautiful solo, the phone rings. The lights are too bright, the room is too hot (or too cold), one of the listeners, who shouldn't be there at all, makes a lot of noise. The evening seems to turn into an utter fiasco.

And then, abruptly, there is an inexplicable change. Somehow an invisible spark has been generated between the four players. All of a sudden they play all the notes in the score. Each player can hear his fellow-players as well as himself. They no longer perform the parts of a score but make music — which is a totally different matter.

A sense of elation grips the players. Using less force of bowing, they create more beautiful sound. Instead of just bringing off a movement, they penetrate beyond the surface into the very spirit of the music. Somewhere behind the notes there seems to be the face of the composer who has been dead for centuries, but now he is smiling. No wonder — the room is filled with harmony and happiness and with the subtle *rapport* achieved by four people who are emotionally and melodiously in tune.

It is in blissful moments like this that you understand why chamber-music has always been called 'the music of friends'.

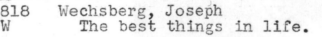